"Who, What Am I?"

"Who, What Am I?"

TOLSTOY STRUGGLES
TO NARRATE THE SELF

Irina Paperno

Cornell University Press
Ithaca and London

First published 2014 by Cornell University Press

Printed in the United States of America

Library of Congress Cataloging-in-Publication Data

Paperno, Irina, author.
  "Who, what am I?" : Tolstoy struggles to narrate the self / Irina
Paperno.
      pages cm
  Includes bibliographical references and index.
  ISBN 978-0-8014-5334-2 (cloth : alk. paper)
  1. Tolstoy, Leo, graf, 1828–1910—Criticism and interpretation.
2. Russian prose literature—19th century—History and criticism.
3. Autobiography—Authorship. 4. Identity (Psychology) in
literature. 5. Self in literature. I. Title.
  PG3410.P37   2014
  891.73'3—dc23   2014022379

Cornell University Press strives to use environmentally responsible
suppliers and materials to the fullest extent possible in the publishing
of its books. Such materials include vegetable-based, low-VOC inks
and acid-free papers that are recycled, totally chlorine-free, or partly
composed of nonwood fibers. For further information, visit our
website at www.cornellpress.cornell.edu.

Cloth printing   10 9 8 7 6 5 4 3 2 1

Contents

Acknowledgments   ix

Introduction   1

**Chapter 1. "So That I Could Easily Read Myself":
Tolstoy's Early Diaries   9**

Tolstoy Starts a Diary—The Moral Vision of Self and the Temporal Order
of Narrative—What Is Time? Cultural Precedents—"A History of Yesterday"—Time and Narrative—The Dream: The Hidden Recesses of Time—
What Am I? The Young Tolstoy Defines Himself—What Am I? Cultural
Precedents

Interlude: Between Personal Documents and Fiction   30

From Diaries to *Childhood*: Tolstoy Becomes a Writer (1852)—"I Think I
Will Never Write Again": Tolstoy Attempts to Renounce Literature (1859)—
"I . . . Don't Even Think about the Accursed Lit-t-terature and *Lit-t-terateurs*":
Tolstoy Renounces Literature Again (1870); and Again (1874–75)

**Chapter 2. "To Tell One's Faith Is Impossible. . . . How to Tell
That Which I Live By. I'll Tell You, All the Same. . . ." Tolstoy
in His Correspondence   39**

"What Is My Life? What Am I?": Tolstoy's Philosophical Dialogue
with Nikolai Strakhov—"I Wish that You, Instead of Reading *Anna*

Kar[*enina*], Would Finish It. . . ."—"In the Form of Catechism," "In the Form of a Dialogue"—To Tell One's Life—Rousseau and His Profession/ Confession—The Parting of Ways: Tolstoy Writes His *Confession,* and Strakhov Continues to Confess in His Letters to Tolstoy

Chapter 3. Tolstoy's *Confession*: ~~What Am I?~~   60

Tolstoy Publishes his Confession—The Conversion Narrative: Excursus on the Genre—Tolstoy's *Confession*: Step by Step—Tolstoy's *Confession* Related to Rousseau's and Augustine's—After *Confession*: "Presenting Christ's Teaching as Something New after 1,800 Years of Christianity"—Coda: Tolstoy's Influence

Chapter 4. "To Write *My Life*": Tolstoy Tries, and Fails, to Produce a Memoir or Autobiography   81

The Author Biography—"My Life": "On the Basis of My Own Memories"—"Reminiscences": "More Useful Than All That Artistic Prattle with Which the Twelve Volumes of My Works Are Filled"—"Reminiscences": "I Cannot Provide a Coherent Description of Events and States of Mind"— "The Green Stick": "Où Suis-Je? Pourquoi Suis-Je? Que Suis-Je?"—Tolstoy and the Autobiographical Tradition

Chapter 5. "What Should We Do Then?": Tolstoy on Self and Other   103

"Why Have You, a Man from a Different World, Stopped near Us? Who Are You?"—Master and Slave: Tolstoy Rewrites Hegel—Tolstoy and the Washerwoman—The Order of Things: The Church, the State, the Arts and Sciences—"Master and Man"—Coda: Nonparticipation in Evil

Chapter 6. "I Felt a Completely New Liberation from Personality": Tolstoy's Late Diaries   128

Tolstoy Resumes his Diary—The Temporal Order of Narrative: The Last Day—"On Life ~~and Death~~"—The Diary as a Spiritual Exercise—"I, the Body, Is Such a Disgusting Chamber Pot"—"I Am Conscious of Myself Being Conscious of Myself Being Conscious of Myself. . . ."—"I Have Lost the Memory of Everything, Almost Everything. . . . How Can One Not Rejoice at the Loss of Memory?"—Sleeping, Dreaming, and Awakening—Tolstoy's Dreams—Dreams: The World beyond Time and Representation—The

Book of life: "It Is Written on Time"—*The Circle of Reading*: "To Replace the Consciousness of Leo Tolstoy with the Consciousness of All Humankind"—"The Death of Socrates"—Tolstoy's Death

Appendix: Russian Quotations   159

Notes   201

Index   223

Acknowledgments

Major funding for this project was provided by the National Endowment for the Humanities (2012–2013). Financial support was also provided by the University of California, Berkeley, including a Research Assistantship in the Humanities Grant (2012–2013).

The staff at the Tolstoy Museum in Moscow and at Yasnaya Polyana provided invaluable assistance. I am especially grateful to G. V. Alekseeva, V. S. Bastrykina, T. T. Burlakova, N. A. Kalinina, T. G. Nikiforova, S. D. Novikova, and A. N. Polosina for their professional courtesy and expertise.

I am grateful to colleagues and friends who read (or heard) parts of this book over the years and offered suggestions and corrections. Caryl Emerson, Laura Engelstein, Hugh McLean, Carlos Montemayor, and Donna Orwin are among them. I owe a special debt to Robin Feuer Miller and Eric Naiman who read the entire manuscript. I thank Inessa Medzhibovskaya for her help and her opinion. I am grateful to Johanna Renate Döring for her interest and support.

I am grateful to John Ackerman of Cornell University Press for his generosity and judgment as editor and director.

Expert research and editorial assistance were provided over the years by Chloë Kitzinger and Alyson Tapp. Chloë Kitzinger edited the entire manuscript. I owe each a large debt of gratitude.

Parts of this book have earlier appeared as articles: "Tolstoy's Diaries: The Inaccessible Self," in *Self and Story in Russian History*, ed. Laura Engelstein and Stephanie Sandler (Ithaca, NY: Cornell University Press, 2000), 242–65;

"Leo Tolstoy's Correspondence with Nikolai Strakhov: The Dialogue on Faith," in *Anniversary Essays on Tolstoy*, ed. Donna Tussing Orwin (Cambridge, U.K.: Cambridge University Press, 2010), 96–119; "What, Then, Shall We Do: Tolstoy's Way," *Slavic and East European Journal* 56, no. 3 (Fall 2012): 333–46. This material has since been revised and amended.

A note on language: Throughout the main text of the book, the Russian text and Russian proper names are given in the Library of Congress transliteration system, except for names with an accepted English spelling (Tolstoy, Dostoevsky). In the notes, within references I use solely the Library of Congress transliteration.

Introduction

"God only knows how many diverse, captivating impressions and thoughts evoked by these impressions ... pass in a single day. If it were only possible to recount them all so that I could easily read myself and others could read me as I do, a most instructive and engaging book would result...." (1:279).[1] Such was the dream of the young Tolstoy (expressed in his first, unfinished work, "A History of Yesterday," 1851). Like Rousseau, he wanted to turn himself into an open book.

From his early years, Tolstoy realized that his narrative utopia would remain unfulfilled. For one thing, he knew that "there is not enough ink in the world to write such a story, or typesetters to put it into print" (1:279). And yet, until his death, he kept trying. Thus, Tolstoy engaged in the continuous narration of his daily history: He kept diaries. In the periods 1847–58 and 1884–1910, he wrote almost daily. The gigantic text of his diaries reflects Tolstoy's lifelong attempts to define, in writing, "Who, what am I?" (Tolstoy repeated this question incessantly.) Despair gripped the young diarist when he tried to describe a man or to capture his own feelings by "tracing characters on paper" (46:65). This despair remained with Tolstoy for life, growing especially acute in the diaries of his old age. The struggle that preoccupied Tolstoy the diarist also unfolded in his other personal writings, which were many and varied.[a] The achievements of Tolstoy the fiction writer brought no relief.

---

[a] To give the reader a rough idea of the scope of Tolstoy's nonfiction writings, fewer than one third of the volumes in the 90-volume edition of his works are occupied by fiction (including manuscript variants).

Scholars have shown that in his novels Tolstoy succeeded in describing states of the self that mostly remained beyond representation: stream of consciousness, subconscious processes, dreams. In this book I intend to show how in his nonfictional first-person writings—diaries, letters, reminiscences, autobiographical and confessional statements, essays (treatises)—Tolstoy attempted to describe and define his own self from the unmediated position of the speaking subject (I, Leo Tolstoy).

I argue that what was at stake was more than a literary task. He was involved in a struggle with the constraints that language and narrative impose on one's ability to know and represent the "I." Ultimately, Tolstoy refused to accept that the self—his self—was limited to what could be told. Inherent in the structure of any verbal narrative is a view of life that accords a predominant role to linear temporal order, which implies finitude. Tolstoy's lifelong attempt to describe his life (or self) was a project with philosophical, moral, and religious implications.

In his early diaries, this struggle unfolded on a daily basis, rooted in the mundane. The young Tolstoy worked on developing a method for capturing, in their entirety, his past, present, and future. In the evening of each day, he reviewed what he had done today in reference to the plan made yesterday, at the end of the previous entry (under tomorrow's date). Each day, he commented on the failure of today to meet the expectations of yesterday's tomorrow. The diary thus served as an instrument for keeping his wayward life under control. Striving to narrativize the very process of feeling and thinking, Tolstoy undertook an experiment: For one day, he would record all events, all impressions, and all thoughts evoked by these impressions. In the end, the narrative follows the narrator into sleep and ends with a dream that seems to have been recorded even as it was being experienced. This narrative, "A History of Yesterday," was, I will show, an attempt to create not a work of fiction but something like a book of life.

Soon (in the course of the 1850s), Tolstoy made a transition from diary-writing to professional authorship and to fiction. Before long, his diary came to an end; regular diaries do not exist for the years in which he worked on his major novels. It would seem that Tolstoy experienced conflicting impulses: to write diaries or to write fiction. At different points in his life, in 1859, 1869, and, most prominently in 1875, Tolstoy entertained the idea of giving up "literature." These were moments of acute crisis, and on such occasions he would turn to other forms of writing: personal, pedagogical, philosophical.

At about the age of fifty Tolstoy famously declared that he had made a decisive break with fiction-writing; this time he turned to religion. His conversion was prepared over the years 1875–79 in his correspondence with an intimate friend, the critic Nikolai Strakhov. For each correspondent, this was a self-conscious attempt to define "what I believe in": a philosophical dialogue on faith. This involved answering the question, "What is my life? What am I?" (Tolstoy's formulation).

What followed was a work that came to be known as *Tolstoy's Confession*, released in 1882 (initially under the title *What Am I?*). As I hope to show, the *Confession* is neither an autobiography nor a work of fiction: It is a conversion narrative (and, as such, it follows the logic of this genre). Like any conversion narrative, this text marks a rift in the continuity of self: By the end of the narrative, the "I" who wrote the story is not the same "I" whose life it describes (Leo Tolstoy the writer). What is more, toward the end the "I," now at one with God, moves toward its own dissolution as an individual self.

Still, Tolstoy continued to write. His *Confession* led him to a conviction that truth lies not in the self but in the Christian faith. But his was a conversion that required a revision of the Christian teaching. As Tolstoy put it, he found himself in the strange situation of "presenting Christ's teaching as something new after 1,800 years of Christianity" (23:335). Remarkably, the majority of Tolstoy's influential religious works—such as the treatise *What I Believe?* (1883–84) and even his revisions of the Gospels, *The Four Gospels Harmonized and Translated* and *The Gospel in Brief*—were written from a personal perspective.

In all of Tolstoy's self-narratives, from his first diaries to his religious treatises, there is an essential moral and social dimension to the question of the self. He knew that to know and to say who you are is to be oriented in moral space, deciding, "What ought I to do?" (Tolstoy borrowed Kant's phrase). He addressed this question in a number of writings, from early pedagogical essays (some in diary form) that describe his efforts to teach peasant children to read and write to the intensely personal treatise that deals with his later attempts to help the urban poor, *What Should We Do Then?* (1882–89). In this essay, Tolstoy defined himself in terms of his position vis-à-vis the other: "Who am I who wishes to help people?" (25:245). As I will show, Tolstoy did this by rewriting, in a religious key, Hegel's master-and-slave dialectic.

On two occasions, Tolstoy made abortive attempts to write a memoir or autobiography, producing "My Life" (1878) and "Reminiscences" (1903–06). At first, Tolstoy decided that he would tell the story of his life solely on the basis of his actual memories. Was this possible? In this book I show how, proceeding by way of a narrative experiment, Tolstoy came up with what Freud would later call "screen memories." His second attempt, "Reminiscences," had a predominantly moral goal: to write "a history of my life" that "would

be more useful to people than all the twelve volumes of my collected fiction." He would give an "absolutely truthful" account of everything in his
life, "even more truthful than that of Rousseau" (73:279). Unlike Rousseau's
book, its main use would be to inspire disgust for the author in his readers
(34:248). But this was not all. In both cases, there was also a metaphysical
dimension. He was aware that memoirists mostly confined themselves to the
limits of biological life, and yet, like Augustine in his *Confessions*, Tolstoy
asked: "When did I begin to live? . . . Why is it a joy to me to imagine myself
back then . . . when I will again enter that state of death of which there will
be no memories that can be expressed in words?" (23:470). No wonder that
his autobiographical projects remained unfulfilled. I will try to explain why
the author of *Childhood*, *War and Peace*, and *Anna Karenina* found himself
unable to write his own life.

Soon after the release of his *Confession*, Tolstoy resumed, after a long interruption, his diaries. The diaries of Tolstoy's late years were written in the
face of approaching death. For almost twenty years he expected death daily.
This called for a special time scheme: The diary entry ended not with a plan
for tomorrow, but with the phrase "if I live" (*esli budu zhiv*, abbreviated *e. b.
zh.*) placed under tomorrow's date. The next day's entry often started with the
affirmation "alive." As his late diaries show, the older Tolstoy got, the more he
longed to stop being not only a writer but also an individual: to give up both
authorship and self. He now believed that "[i]t's precisely what is not 'I' that
is immortal" (49:129). Tolstoy joyfully recorded evidence of the deterioration
of his body and the weakening of his memory: welcome signs of a "completely
new liberation from personality" (56:98). And yet he continued to write his
diary. His lifelong search for the true self turned into an impossible mission:
to define the non-self of the true being that lay outside language and time.
Tolstoy was tormented with the paradoxical desire to write himself into a
state of silence. As he put it in a letter from 1909, "If this were not a contradiction, to write about the necessity to be silent, I would have written: *I can be
silent. I cannot be silent*. I wish I could live by God alone. . . ." (57:6). He longed
to read, rather than write, the book of life. The old Tolstoy dedicated himself
to compiling almanacs (commonplace books) that offered readings, drawn
from his own thoughts and the thoughts of others, for every day of the year
(*The Circle of Reading*). In this way, he felt, the consciousness of "Leo Tolstoy"
would be replaced with "the consciousness of all humankind" (56:123). In his
last years Tolstoy read his almanacs—pre-printed diaries that made a complete calendar circle that did not depend on the proviso "if I live"—on a daily
basis. As Andrey Bely put it, "*The Circle of Reading* is Tolstoy's silence."[2] His
last hope was death: It was in death that the author might finally experience

the truth of a selfless being. It would seem that, against all reason, he hoped to leave a record of this experience. In his late diaries, Tolstoy tried to envision "a book of life" that would not be written "with characters and lines" and, most important, would not be written "on time" (57:19). He suggested that such a book could only be read "abroad, in a foreign language," but he still believed that "one would certainly read it" (50:4).

In the end, while "a history of my life" remained unwritten, Tolstoy's ideas about the self did reach the reader. Even his diaries, letters, and scrapbooks were eventually published (mostly posthumously).[3] His personal struggles with a sense of self left their mark: For many of his readers, in Russia and beyond, Tolstoy has been an example by which they seek to orient their own lives.

In his turn, Tolstoy was of course aware that he was following in a long line of authors. In asking "Who, what am I?" he self-consciously echoed Socrates, Marcus Aurelius, Augustine, Descartes, Pascal, Kant, Rousseau. But he believed that ordinary peasants asked it as well. Tolstoy particularly loved a story about his old nanny. She would lie alone listening to the clock ticking on the wall; the clock asked: "Who are you—what are you? Who are you—what are you?" (*Kto ty—chto ty? Kto ty—chto ty?*). Tolstoy echoed: "This is the entire essence of life: Who are you? What are you?"[4]

This book, then, addresses Tolstoy's experimentation with the narration and exploration of "self" in his nonfiction: in the various writings in which he says "I" in relation to his own self, Leo Tolstoy.

Many scholars have discussed the idea of the self, its cultural sources, and ways of expressing a sense of self in the first-person narrative. In recent years, arguments about the uses and abuses of the concept of self have been mounted on the basis of intellectual history, philosophical approaches, psychoanalysis, narrative theories, and genre studies.[5] This description of Tolstoy's paradoxical efforts to create a narrative representation of both the self and the selfless being (informed by my training in literature, intellectual history, and psychology) may contribute to these discussions. But my intention is to address not only academic audiences but also general readers who read Tolstoy.

I tell the story of Tolstoy's quest several times, each time following a specific thread—a line of thought as well as a set of texts. Chapter 1 is devoted to his early diaries, focusing on the creation of the narrative of self within a temporal scheme. The "Interlude" describes the transition from the diary to fiction writing and marks subsequent moments at which Tolstoy attempted to abandon *belles lettres* for another kind of writing. Chapter 2, which looks at Tolstoy's correspondence with Strakhov, is devoted to Tolstoy's dialogic elaborations of his personal faith in the years of the decisive transition to nonfiction. Chapter 3 deals with his *Confession* and, in brief, his subsequent religious treatises. Chapter 4 describes Tolstoy's unfinished attempts to write a memoir or autobiography ("My Life" and "Reminiscences"), with emphasis on how and why he failed. Chapter 5 deals mainly with *What Should We Do Then?* and addresses the issue of the self's duty to the other (moral selfhood). Chapter 6 deals with Tolstoy's late diaries and his almanacs for daily reading, focusing on the dialectics of self and selflessness.

In all chapters, I pay close attention to Tolstoy's dreams, which he carefully recorded throughout his life; he hoped that these alternative narratives, with their nonlinear temporality, might open a window, albeit momentarily, onto some other form of consciousness.

Inevitably, these discussions engage with a number of thinkers who struggled with the problems of self, time, consciousness and the unconscious, memory, narrative. I attempt to situate Tolstoy amidst a wide range of authors: those whom he followed or echoed (Plato, Augustine, Descartes, Locke, Sterne, Rousseau, Kant, Fichte, Schopenhauer, Marx), ostensibly rejected (Hegel, Nietzsche), ignored (Freud), or prefigured (Wittgenstein).

A brief comment is due on the position of Tolstoy's idea of self in the history of ideas. In his personal quest, Tolstoy retraced the steps of subject-centered thinkers (from Descartes to Kant to Fichte), and he repeatedly came to the impasse of the *Ich-an-sich*: the autonomous, inaccessible self. In his diary, he described this move as a matter of immediate experience: "I will ask myself: what, who am I?—And I will answer: I am I"; yet he longed for "an I that is beyond space, beyond time" (58:42). Over the years, he considered various alternatives: turning back to the Platonic concept of "universal reason" (rather than the individual self); embracing Schopenhauer's idea of death as shedding the self and merging with the divine; trying out the mystical practices of Eastern Orthodox Christianity.[6] He also considered (in the footsteps of Schopenhauer) the alternatives to self provided by Hindu and Buddhist thought, and he was interested in Confucius and Lao Tzu.[7] And yet he stubbornly aspired to come up with a solution of his own, one that lay beyond philosophy.

Tolstoy's main difficulty, I would argue, was in accepting the progress of secularization. When he started, in the 1850s, he entered an intellectual context that gave increasing attention to secular conceptions of the self. In many ways his reference point was Rousseau. Intellectual historians link Rousseau and Augustine to pose a trajectory in the development of the conception of self and narrative: Rousseau (in his *Confessions* and in "Profession de foi du Vicaire Savoyard") created secular forms of writing about the self, but in a way that cannot be understood without reference to earlier religious narratives. In this book, I attempt to place Tolstoy's self-writings in this tradition. As I hope to show, in his late years—with his *Confession*, his religious treatises, his memoiristic pieces, and, finally, his late diaries—Tolstoy made consistent attempts to reverse singlehandedly the progress of Western thought: its course toward individualism and secularization. At the threshold of the twentieth century, Tolstoy attempted to resacralize the narrative of self through a retrogressive move: going backward but, of course, with the full benefit of hindsight. He tried to serve the needs of a modern man: a secular man equipped with elaborate literary forms—to which Tolstoy as a fiction writer had himself made a major contribution—but who faced death without the protection of faith.

Needless to say, Tolstoy's self-writings, both private (diaries and letters) and public (essays and treatises), derive much of their significance from his reputation as a writer, the celebrated author of *War and Peace* and *Anna Karenina* who renounced literature.

Many people (from contemporaries to present-day scholars) have spoken of two Tolstoys, the (good) writer and the (bad) philosopher and moralist. Others have tried to make Tolstoy whole, arguing that most of the ideas and beliefs expounded by the late Tolstoy appeared in his earliest writings, including the early diaries.[8] Some want to have it both ways. Vladimir Nabokov, speaking as a professor of Russian literature, tried to put two incompatible approaches together in a memorable image: "What one would like to do, would be to kick the glorified soapbox from under his sandaled feet and then lock him up in a stone house on a desert island with gallons of ink and reams of paper—far away from the things, ethical and pedagogical, that diverted his attention from observing the way the dark hair curled above Anna's white neck." But Nabokov knew that "the thing cannot be done": "Tolstoy is homogenous, is one." Even Nabokov (much as he preferred Tolstoy the artist) understood that Tolstoy is all about the self: "Whether painting or preaching, Tolstoy was striving, in spite of all obstacles, to get at the truth . . . this truth was he. . . ."[9]

My goal in this book is to show that, locked in a house with gallons of ink and reams of paper, Tolstoy would have written a diary. Having completed this investigation of Tolstoy's attempts to articulate a sense of self by saying "I," I believe that it is a fundamentally different act from representing the notion of self in fiction, the self embedded within the structure of a novel, with its array of characters and layered narrative. Of course, as scholars remind readers, "we should never confuse the novelist with his character, especially if he has drawn the character from himself."[10] Mikhail Bakhtin posed the problem of the relationship between author and hero as an issue in philosophical anthropology: a key to "aesthetic activity."[11] But it remains far from easy to unravel this involved relationship. Students of narrative have advanced still other arguments separating the novelist from his or her fiction. For one thing, the novel as a genre relies on narration with multiple, shifting point of views in which the speaking "I" is never alone and seldom, if ever, speaks for him- or herself. Furthermore, the novel attempts to represent the nonspeaking, extralinguistic self.[12] Representing the inner self is one of the major tasks of the modern novel, and it may not be an accident that one of the greatest novelists who worked on this literary task also attempted to resolve it in private: as a speaking subject.

CHAPTER ONE

"So That I Could Easily Read Myself": Tolstoy's Early Diaries

Tolstoy Starts a Diary

Tolstoy's first diary, started on March 17, 1847, at the age of eighteen, began as a clinical investigation launched under laboratory conditions: in the isolation of a hospital ward, where he was being treated for a venereal disease. A student at Kazan University, he was about to drop out due to lack of academic progress. In the clinic, freed from external influences, the young man planned to "enter into himself" for intense self-exploration (*vzoiti sam v sebia*; 46:3). On the first page, he wrote (then crossed out) that he was in complete agreement with Rousseau on the advantages of solitude. This act of introspection had a moral goal: to exert control over his runaway life. Following a well-established practice, the young Tolstoy approached the diary as an instrument of self-perfection.

But this was not all. For the young Tolstoy, keeping a diary (as I hope to show) was also an experimental project aimed at exploring the nature of self: the links connecting a sense of self, a moral ideal, and the temporal order of narrative.

From the very beginning there were problems. For one, the diarist obviously found it difficult to sustain the flow of narrative. To fill the pages of his first diary, beginning on day two, Tolstoy gives an account of his reading, assigned by a professor of history: Catherine the Great's famous *Instruction* (*Nakaz*), as compared with Montesquieu's *L'Esprit de lois*. This manifesto aimed at regulating the future social order, and its philosophical principles, rooted in the French Enlightenment (happy is a man in whom will rules over passions, and happy is a state in which laws serve as an instrument of such control), appealed to the young Tolstoy. But with the account of Catherine's utopia (on March 26), Tolstoy's first diary came to an end.

When he started again (and again), Tolstoy commented on the diary itself, its purpose and uses. In his diary, he will evaluate the course of self-improvement (46:29). He will also reflect on the purpose of human life (46:30). The diary will contain rules pertaining to his behavior in specific times and places; he will then analyze his failures to follow these rules (46:34). The diary's other purpose is to describe himself and the world (46:35). But how? He looked in the mirror. He looked at the moon and the starry sky. "But how can one write this?" he asked. "One has to go, sit at an ink-stained desk, take coarse paper, ink . . . and trace letters on paper. Letters will make words, words—phrases, but is it possible to convey one's feeling?" (46:65). The young diarist was in despair.

Apart from the diaries, the young Tolstoy kept separate notebooks for rules: "Rules for Developing Will" (1847), "Rules of Life" (1847), "Rules" (1847 and 1853), and "Rules in General" (1850) (46:262–76). "Rules for playing music" (46:36) and "Rules for playing cards in Moscow until January 1" (46: 39). There are also rules for determining "(a) what is God, (b) what is man, and (c) what are the relations between God and man" (46:263). It would seem that in these early journals, Tolstoy was actually working not on a history but on a utopia of himself: his own personal *Instruction*.

Yet another notebook from the early 1850s, "Journal for Weaknesses" (*Zhurnal dlia slabostei*)—or, as he called it, the "Franklin journal"—listed, in columns, potential weaknesses, such as laziness, mendacity, indecision, sensuality, and vanity, and Tolstoy marked (with small crosses) the qualities that he exhibited on a particular day. Here, Tolstoy was consciously following the method that Benjamin Franklin had laid out in his famous autobiography.

There was also an account book devoted to financial expenditures. On the whole, on the basis of these documents, it appears that the condition of Tolstoy's moral and monetary economy was deplorable. But another expenditure presented still graver problems: that of time.[1]

Along with the first, hesitant diaries, for almost six months in 1847 Tolstoy kept a "Journal of Daily Occupations" (*Zhurnal ezhednevnykh zaniatii*; 46:245–61), the main function of which was to account for the actual expenditure of time. In the journal, each page was divided into two vertical columns: the first one, marked "The Future," listed things he planned to do the next day; a parallel column, marked "The Past," contained comments (made a day later) on the fulfillment of the plan. The most frequent entry was "not quite" (*nesovsem*). One thing catches the eye: there was no present.

The Moral Vision of Self and the Temporal Order of Narrative

Beginning in 1850, the time scheme of Tolstoy's "Journal of Daily Occupations" and the moral accounting of the Franklin journal were incorporated
into a single narrative. Each day's entry was written from the reference point
of yesterday's entry, which ended with a detailed schedule for the next day—
under tomorrow's date. In the evening of the next day, Tolstoy reviewed what
he had actually done, comparing his use of time to the plan made the previous day. He also commented on his actions, evaluating his conduct on a
general scale of moral values. The entry concluded with a plan of action and
a schedule for yet another day. The following entry (from March 1851) is typical for the early to mid-1850s:

24. Arose somewhat late and read, but did not have time to write. Poiret
came, I fenced, and did not send him away (*sloth and cowardice*). Ivanov
came, I spoke with him for too long (*cowardice*). Koloshin (Sergei) came
to drink vodka, I did not escort him out (*cowardice*). At Ozerov's argued
about nothing (*habit of arguing*) and did not talk about what I should
have talked about (*cowardice*). Did not go to Beklemishev's (*weakness
of energy*). During gymnastics did not walk the rope (*cowardice*), and
did not do one thing because it hurt (*sissiness*).—At Gorchakov's lied
(*lying*). Went to the Novotroitsk tavern (*lack of fierté*). At home did not
study English (*insufficient firmness*). At the Volkonskys' was unnatural
and distracted, and stayed until one in the morning (*distractedness, desire to show off, and weakness of character*). 25. [This is a plan for the
next day, the 25th, written on the 24th—I.P.] From 10 to 11 yesterday's
diary and to read. From 11 to 12—gymnastics. From 12 to 1—English.
Beklemishev and Beyer from 1 to 2. From 2 to 4—on horseback. From 4
to 6—dinner. From 6 to 8—to read. From 8 to 10—to write.—To translate something from a foreign language into Russian to develop memory and style.—To write today with all the impressions and thoughts it
gives rise to.—
    25. Awoke late out of *sloth*. Wrote my diary and did gymnastics,
hurrying. Did not study English out of *sloth*. With Begichev and with
Islavin was *vain*. At Beklemishev's was *cowardly* and *lack of fierté*. On
Tver Boulevard *wanted to show off*. I did not walk on foot to the Kalymazhnyi Dvor (*sissiness*). Rode with *a desire to show off*. For the same
reason rode to Ozerov's.—Did not return to Kalymazhnyi, *thought-
lessness*. At the Gorchakovs' dissembled and did not call things by their
names, *fooling myself*. Went to L'vov's out of *insufficient energy* and

the habit of doing nothing. Sat around at home out of *absentmindedness* and read Werther inattentively, *hurrying.* 26 [This is a plan for the next day, the 26th, written on the 25th—I.P.] To get up at 5. Until 10—to write the history of this day. From 10 to 12—fencing and to read. From 12 to 1—English, and if something interferes, then in the evening. From 1 to 3—walking, until 4—gymnastics. From 4 to 6, dinner—to read and write.— (46:55).

An account of the present as much as a plan for the future, this diary combines the prescriptive and the descriptive. In the evening of each day, the young Tolstoy reads the present as a failure to live up to the expectations of the past, and he anticipates a future that will embody his vision of a perfect self. The next day, he again records what went wrong today with yesterday's tomorrow.[2] Wanting reality to live up to his moral ideal, he forces the past to meet the future.

In his attempt to create an ordered account of time, and thus a moral order, Tolstoy's greatest difficulty remains capturing the present. Indeed, today makes its first appearance in the diary as tomorrow, embedded in the previous day and usually expressed in infinitive verb forms ("to read," "to write," "to translate"). On the evening of today, when Tolstoy writes his diary, today is already the past, told in the past tense. His daily account ends with a vision of another tomorrow. Since it appears under tomorrow's date, it masquerades as today, but the infinitive forms of the verbs suggest timelessness.

In the diaries, unlike in the "Journal of Daily Occupations," the present is accorded a place, but it is deprived of even a semblance of autonomy: The present is a space where the past and the future overlap. It appears that the narrative order of the diary simply does not allow one to account for the present.

The adolescent Tolstoy's papers contain the following excerpt, identified by the commentators of Tolstoy's complete works as a "language exercise": "Le passé est ce qui fut, le futur est ce qui sera et le présent est ce qui n'est pas.—C'est pour cela que la vie de l'homme ne consiste que dans le futur et le passé et c'est pour la même raison que le bonheur que nous voulons posséder n'est qu'une chimère de même que le présent" (1:217).[a] Whether he knew it or not, the problem that troubled the young Tolstoy, as expressed in this language exercise, was a common one, and it had a long history.

---

[a] The past is that which was, the future is that which will be, and the present is that which is not. That is why the life of man consists in nothing but the future and the past, and it is for the same reason that the happiness we want to possess is nothing but a chimera, just as the present is.

What Is Time? Cultural Precedents

It was Augustine, in the celebrated Book 11 of the *Confessions*, who first expressed his bewilderment: "What is time?" He argued as follows: The future is not yet here, the past is no longer here, and the present does not remain. Does time, then, have a real being? What is the present? The day? But "not even one day is entirely present." Some hours of the day are in the future, some in the past. The hour? But "one hour is itself constituted of fugitive moments." Time flies quickly from future into past. In Augustine's words, "the present occupies no space." Thus, "time" both exists (the language speaks of it and the mind experiences it) and does not exist. The passage of time is both real and unreal (11.14.17–11.17.22). Augustine's solution was to turn inward, placing the past and the future within the human soul (or mind), as memory and expectation. Taking his investigation further, he argues that these qualities of mind are observed in storytelling and fixed in narrative: "When I am recollecting and telling my story, I am looking on its image in present time, since it is still in my memory" (11.18.23). As images fixed in a story, both the past and the future lie within the present, which thus acquires a semblance of being. In the mind, or in the telling of one's personal story, times exist all at once as traces of what has passed and will pass through the soul. Augustine thus linked the issue of time and the notion of self. In the end, the question "What is time?" was an extension of the fundamental question of the *Confessions*: "What am I, my God? What is my Nature?" (10.17.26).[3]

For centuries philosophers continued to refine and transform these arguments. Rousseau reinterpreted Augustine's idea in a secular perspective, focusing on the temporality of human feelings. Being attached to things outside us, "our affections" necessarily change: "they recall a past that is gone" or "anticipate a future that may never come into being." From his own experience, Rousseau knew that the happiness for which his soul longed was not one "composed of fugitive moments" (*"le bonheur que mon cœur regrette n'est point composé d'instants fugitives"*) but a single and lasting state of the soul. But is there a state in which the soul can concentrate its entire being, with no need to remember the past or reach into the future? Such were Rousseau's famous meditations on time in the fifth of his *Reveries of the Solitary Walker* (*Rêveries du promeneur solitaire*), a sequel to the *Confessions*. In both texts Rousseau practiced the habit of "reentering into himself," with the express purpose of inquiring "What am I?" (*"Que suis je moi-même?"*).[4]

Since the mid-eighteenth century, after Rousseau and Laurence Sterne, time, as known through the mind of the perceiving individual, had also been the subject of narrative experiments undertaken in novels and memoirs. By the 1850s, the theme of the being and nonbeing of time in relation to human consciousness, inaugurated by Augustine and secularized by Rousseau, could serve as the topic of an adolescent's language exercise.

In his later years, as a novelist, Tolstoy would play a decisive role in the never-ending endeavor to catch time in the act. In the 1850s, in his personal diary, the young Tolstoy was designing his first, homemade methods of managing the flow of personal time by narrative means. As we have seen, this dropout student was not without cultural resources. The young Tolstoy could hardly have known Augustine, but he did know Rousseau, whose presence in the early diaries is palpable.[5] (In later years, when he does read Augustine, he will focus on the problem of narrating time and fully appreciate its theological meaning.)[6] But mostly he proceeded by way of his own narrative efforts: his diary. Fixed in the diary, the past would remain with him; planned in writing, the future was already there. Creating a future past and a present future, the diarist relieved some of the anxieties of watching life pass. But in one domain his efforts fell short of the ideal: not even one day was entirely present.

"A History of Yesterday"

In March 1851, the twenty-two-year-old Tolstoy embarked on another long-planned project: to write a complete account of a single day—a history of yesterday. His choice fell on March 24: "not because yesterday was extraordinary in any way . . . but because I have long wished to tell the innermost [zadushevnuiu] side of life in one day. God only knows how many diverse . . . impressions and thoughts . . . pass in a single day. If it were only possible to recount them all so that I could easily read myself and others could read me as I do. . . . " (1:279).

An outgrowth of the diary, "A History of Yesterday" (Istoriia vcherashnego dnia) was conceived as an experiment: Where would the process of writing take him?[7] (Tolstoy was writing for himself alone; indeed, in his lifetime, "A History of Yesterday" remained unpublished.)

The metaphor of self, or life, as a book, an image to which Tolstoy would return throughout his life, makes its first appearance here.[8] Rousseau, in whose footsteps Tolstoy followed in wanting to make himself into an open book, believed that self-knowledge was based on feeling and that all he had to do was "to make my soul transparent to the reader." The young Benjamin Franklin, who was a printer, used the image in his own epitaph: He imagined a typeset book of his life and expressed his belief that it would appear once more in a new edition, "revised and corrected by the author."

Tolstoy, in 1851, seems to have suspected that the problem lay in the narrative itself. Knowing that "there is not enough ink in the world to write such a story, or typesetters to put it into print" (1:279), he nevertheless embarked upon this project.

In the end it turned out that after about twenty-four hours of writing (spread over a three-week period), Tolstoy was still at the start of the day. Having filled what amounts to twenty-six pages of printed text, he abandoned his "History." By that time Tolstoy was in a position to know that the enterprise was doomed, and not only because of empirical difficulties ("there would not be enough ink in the world to write it, or typesetters to put it in print"), but also because of major philosophical problems (such as the constraints inherent in the nature of narrative).

"A History of Yesterday" starts in the morning: "I arose late yesterday—at a quarter to 10." What follows is a causal explanation that relates the given event to an earlier event, which happened on the day before yesterday: "—because I had gone to bed after midnight." At this point, the account is interrupted by a parenthetical remark that places the second event within a system of general rules of conduct: "(It has long been my rule never to retire after midnight, yet this happens to me about 3 times a week)." The story resumes with a detailed description of those circumstances which had led to the second event and a minor moral transgression (going to bed after midnight): "I was playing cards. . . ." (1:279). The account of the action is then interrupted by another digression—the narrator's reflections on the nature of society games.

After a page and a half, Tolstoy returns to the game of cards. The narrative proceeds, slowly and painfully, tracing not so much external actions as the webs of the protagonist/narrator's mental activity, fusing two levels of reflections: those that accompanied the action and those that accompany the act of narration. After many digressions, the narrative follows the protagonist home, puts him to bed, and ends with an elaborate description of his dream, leaving the hero at the threshold of "yesterday."

What, then, is time? In Tolstoy's "History," the day (a natural unit of time) starts in the morning, moves rapidly to the previous evening, and then slowly makes its way back towards the initial morning. Time flows backward, making a circle. In the end, Tolstoy wrote not a history of yesterday but a history of the day before yesterday.

This pattern would play itself out once again in Tolstoy's work when, in 1856, he started working on a historical novel, the future *War and Peace*. As he later described it (in an explanatory note on *War and Peace*), Tolstoy's original plan was to write a novel about the Decembrists. He set the action in the present, in 1856: An elderly Decembrist returns to Moscow from Siberian exile. But before Tolstoy could move any further, he felt compelled to interrupt the narrative progression: "involuntarily I passed from today to 1825" (that is, to the Decembrist uprising). In order to understand his hero in 1825, he then turned to the formative events of the war with Napoleon: "I once again discarded what I had begun and started to write from the time of 1812." "But then for a third time I put aside what I had begun"—Tolstoy now turned to 1805 (the dawn of the Napoleonic age in Russia; 13:54).[9] The narrative did not progress in time; it regressed. In both an early piece of personal history, "A History of Yesterday," and the mature historical novel, *War and Peace*, Tolstoy saw the initial event as the end of a chain of preceding events, locked into causal dependency by the implications of the narrative order. At the time he made this comment on the writing of his novel, Tolstoy seemed to hold this principle as the inescapable logic of historical narrative.

In "A History of Yesterday," temporal refraction does not end with a shift from the target day to the preceding day. In the description of "the day before yesterday" itself, time also does not progress: It is pulled apart to fit an array of simultaneous processes. The game of cards has come to an end. The narrator is standing by the card table involved in a (mostly silent) conversation with the hostess. It is time to leave, but taking leave does not come easily to the young man; nor is it easy to tell the story of leaving:

> I looked at my watch and got up. . . . Whether she wished to end this conversation which I found so sweet, or to see how I would refuse, or whether she simply wished to continue playing, she looked at the figures which were written on the table, drew the chalk across the table— making a figure that could be classified neither as mathematical nor as pictorial—looked at her husband, then between him and me, and said: "Let's play three more rubbers." I was so absorbed in the contemplation not of her movements alone, but of everything that is called *charme*, which it is impossible to describe, that my imagination was very far away, and I did not have time to clothe my words in a felicitous form; I simply said: "No, I can't." Before I had finished saying this I began to regret it,—that is, not all of me, but a certain part of me. . . .
>
> —I suppose this part spoke very eloquently and persuasively (although I cannot convey this), for I became alarmed and began to cast about for arguments.—In the first place, I said to myself, there is no great pleasure in it, you do not really like her, and you're in an awkward position; besides, you've already said that you can't stay, and you have fallen in her estimation. . . .

"*Comme il est aimable, ce jeune homme.*" [How pleasant he is, this young man.]

This sentence, which followed immediately after mine, interrupted my reflections. I began to make excuses, to say I couldn't stay, but since one does not have to think to make excuses, I continued reasoning with myself: How I love to have her speak of me in the third person. In German this is rude, but I would love it even in German. . . . "Stay for supper," said her husband.—As I was busy with my reflections on the formula of the third person, I did not notice that my body, while very properly excusing itself for not being able to stay, was putting down the hat again and sitting down quite coolly in an easy chair. It was clear that my mind was taking no part in this absurdity. (1:282–83)

Written from memory, in the past tense, this narrative nevertheless strives to imitate a notation of immediate experience—something like a stenographic transcription of a human consciousness involved in the act of apprehending itself.

Some critics see this as an early instance of what would later be called the "stream of consciousness" or even read Tolstoy's desire to describe what lies "behind the soul" as an attempt to reach "what we now call the subconscious."[10] But this is a special case: a stream of consciousness with an observer.

As an external observer, the narrator can only guess at what is going on in the other's mind. As a self-narrator who describes the *zadushevnuiu*—"innermost," or, translating literally, the "behind-the-soul"—side of one day's life, he faces other difficulties.

Indeed, the narrator deals with internal multiplicity, with speech, thought, and bodily movement divided, with ambivalent desires, with the dialectical drama that stands behind a motive. There is yet another layer: the splitting of the self into a protagonist and a narrator, who operate in two different timeframes. Moreover, the narrator (even when he is lost in reverie) is involved in reflections not only on the process of narrating but also on general (meta-) problems in the "historiography" of the self. Finally, he keeps referring to the residue of that which cannot be expressed and explained. How could such multiplicity be represented in the linear order of a narrative?

Time and Narrative

Unbeknownst to the young Tolstoy, Kant had long since deplored the limitations of narrative in *The Critique of Pure Reason*. In narrative representation, one event as a matter of convention follows upon another. In Kant's words, "the apprehension of the manifold of appearance is always successive"; "the representations of the parts" succeed one another. It does not follow, however, that what we represent is also in itself successive; it is just that we "cannot arrange the apprehension otherwise than in this very succession." This is the way "in which we are first led to construct for ourselves the concept of cause": succession suggests causality.[11]

As yet unfamiliar with Kant's deductions, Tolstoy attempted to break the rule of succession—to stretch the temporality of his narrative in order to account for actions and processes that occur as if simultaneously.[12] As a result, he extended time beyond the endurance of the narrative form: the story breaks off. The narrator who describes his own being from within knows (if only subconsciously) more than he can possibly tell. Is it humanly possible to give an account of even one day in one's own life?

There were, of course, cultural precedents. Tolstoy's narrative strategies were largely borrowed from Laurence Sterne, who, along with Rousseau, was among his first self-chosen mentors.[13] In 1851, in his diary, Tolstoy called Sterne his "favorite writer" (49:82). In 1851–52, he translated *A Sentimental Journey* from English into Russian as an exercise.

Informed by Locke's philosophy, Sterne's narrative strategy was to make the consciousness of the protagonist/narrator into a locus of action. Locke, unlike Augustine, hoped that time itself could be captured: He derived the idea of time (duration) from the way in which we experience a train of ideas that constantly succeed one another in our minds.[14] It followed that the sense of self derives from the continuity of consciousness from past to future.

Sterne followed suit by laying bare the flow of free associations in the mind of the narrator.[15] One of his discoveries concerned time and narrative: Turning the narration inward, Sterne discovered that there is a psychic time that diverges from clock time. The splitting of time results in living, and writing, simultaneously on several levels. To be true to life, Sterne's narrator digresses. The author confronted the necessity for interweaving movements forward and backward, which alone promised to move beyond the confines of time. The combination of progression and digression, including retrospective digression, created a narrative marked by experimentation, with the narrator openly commenting on his procedures.[16] In the end, Sterne's experimentation—his "realistic" representation—revealed flaws in Locke's argument: Successive representation could not catch up with the manifold perceptions of the human mind. In brief, the narrative that attempted to represent human consciousness did not progress.

By mimicking Sterne's narrative strategy, Tolstoy learned his first lessons in epistemology: the Cartesian shift to the point of view of the perceiving individual, the modern view on the train and succession of inner thoughts, the dependence of personal identity on the ability to extend consciousness backward to a past action, and so on. Tolstoy also confronted the restrictions that govern our apprehension and representation of time—limitations that he would continue to probe and challenge throughout his life and work, even after he had read, and fully appreciated, Kant's *Critique of Pure Reason* (in 1869, as he was finishing *War and Peace*).[17]

In his first diaries and in "A History of Yesterday," proceeding by way of narrative experiments, the young Tolstoy discovered a number of things. He discovered that there was no history of today. Even in a record almost concurrent with experience, there was no present. A history was a history of yesterday. Moreover, writing a history of the individual and a self-history, he was confronted with the need to account not only for the order of events but also for a whole other domain: the inner life. Uncovering the inner life led to further temporal refraction: From an inside point of view, it appeared that behind an event or action there stood a whole array of simultaneous processes. This led to another discovery.

The Dream: The Hidden Recesses of Time

Let us return to the scene by the card table. Tolstoy indicates that the woman's remark, "*Comme il est aimable, ce jeune homme*," immediately followed his statement, "No, I can't," interrupting his reverie. A question arises: when (or, in spatial terms, where) did his lengthy reflections take place? The present seems to have an extension behind the scene. Since Augustine, many have thought that the present has no duration or length. In the intimacy of his diary, the young Tolstoy seems to have discovered this on his own. Under the laboratory conditions of his "History of Yesterday," he also found out (or so it seems) that the present had depth: Life had hidden recesses outside time and space. One such recess, he discovered, was the domain of dreams.

"A History of Yesterday" follows the protagonist/narrator to bed and into his dreams. With its dreams, sleep provides a transitional space between days, and it is essential to represent this boundary space. What is more, dreaming is traditionally regarded as a transitional realm between man's inward and outward self. In the representation of the dream, Tolstoy continues his investigation into the nature of time and consciousness; he also investigates the relationship between external stimuli and internal sensations. The protagonist/narrator observes and records the very process of the dissolution of his consciousness: the "I" abandons himself to sleep, writing as if from dictation; at the same time, the "I" makes self-observations and meta-remarks. Such a narrative would seem to be impossible, and yet Tolstoy writes it. (If this is possible, it would also seem possible to leave an account of one's own death—a possibility that the old Tolstoy in his late diaries will entertain.) Here is the text of the dream:

> "Morpheus, enfold me in your embrace." This Divinity whose priest I would willingly become. And do you remember how the lady was offended when they said to her: "Quand je suis passé chez vous, vous étiez encore dans les bras de Morphée." [When I stopped by, you were still in the arms of Morpheus.] She thought Morphée was a name like André or Malapheé. What a comical name! . . . A splendid expression, *dans les bras*; I picture to myself so clearly and elegantly the condition *dans les bras,*—and especially clearly the *bras* themselves—arms bare to the shoulder, with little dimples and creases, and a white chemise indiscreetly open.—How wonderful arms are in general, especially that one little dimple!—I stretched. Do you remember, St. Thomas forbade stretching. He looks like Diedrichs. We rode with him on horseback. What fine hunting it was, how Gelke, riding beside the policeman, hallooed, and Nalyot was doing his best, even on the frozen mud. How vexed Seryozha was! He is at sister's.—What a treasure Masha is—if only I could find such a wife! Morpheus would be good on a hunt, only he would have to ride naked, or else you might find a wife.—Oh, how St. Thomas is tearing along—and the lady has already set off to overtake them all; only she shouldn't have stretched out, but then that wonderful *dans les bras.*—Here I suppose I went to sleep completely.—I dreamt that I wanted to overtake the lady, suddenly there was a mountain, I pushed it with my hands, pushed it again—it collapsed (I threw down the pillow) and I came home for dinner. Not ready yet. Why not?—Vasily was swaggering loudly (it was the landlady behind the partition asking what the noise was, and the chambermaid answering her; I heard this, that is why I dreamt it). Vasily came in just as everyone wanted to ask him why it wasn't ready. They saw that Vasily was in a frock coat and a ribbon across his chest; I became frightened, I fell on my knees, cried and kissed his hands; it was as pleasant to me as though I were kissing her hands—even more so. (1:291–92)

For Tolstoy, representing a dream is an opportunity to free the narrative from the rule of succession and implied causality: Instead, the principle of association of words, memories, and bodily sensations rules the text. The starting point is a verbal formula related to the theme of dreaming: "Morpheus, enfold me in your embrace." The narrative unfolds through a series of associations with the initial idiom, *dans les bras*. The body then takes over the verbal consciousness: The next step is physical—an involuntary movement ("I stretched").

This evokes a memory of childhood: Tolstoy's French tutor ("governor"), St. Thomas, admonishing the boy ("St. Thomas forbade stretching"). It should be noted that, in addition to the obvious associative connections, there is a subliminal layer with emotional potential: St. Thomas, a Frenchman living in Russia, wanted to marry a rich Russian lady; he oppressed and humiliated the boy.[b]

The theme of horseback riding, with its obvious physicality, enters at this point and expands into a hunting theme, replete with erotic imagery. Tolstoy's beloved sister Masha appears in this context. The image of the servant Vasily in a frock coat with a ribbon across his chest ("I became frightened, I fell on my knees, cried and kissed his hands; it was as pleasant to me. . . .") has a literary subtext familiar to many a Russian in Pushkin's *The Captain's Daughter*: The young hero proudly refuses to kiss the hand of the impostor, the peasant masquerading as the tsar. By contrast, the dream's protagonist surrenders to the illegitimate authority of the peasant with erotic passion.[18]

(The workings of the unconscious—the linking of bodily sensations, erotic impulses, and childhood memories with the theme of power and oppression, introduced through a cultural reference—are elaborated in a way that might have intrigued twentieth-century psychoanalysts. This is not a surprise: There is hardly a concept of psychoanalysis that was not anticipated by Romantic philosophy or literature.[19] But the young Tolstoy seems to be more interested in the workings of narrative and temporality.)

When the dream has made a circle, returning to the initial formula, *dans les bras*, the process of losing consciousness is complete: "Here I suppose I went to sleep completely." However, the narrative continues. The logic that

---

[b] Throughout his life Tolstoy kept returning to the episode in which his governor, St. Thomas, confined him in a room and threatened him with corporal punishment. In his old age Tolstoy recalled this punishment in his diary on July 31, 1896 (53:105) and in the draft for his pamphlet against corporal punishment, "Shame" (*Stydno*, 1895; 31:245). In the notes for his unfinished *Reminiscences* (*Vospominaniia*, 1902–06), Tolstoy suggested that this episode might have been the cause of his "lifelong horror of and disgust for violence" or for the exercise of power over another (34:396).

governs this narrative, akin to that described in Locke's *Essay* and enacted in Sterne's prose, is radically different from the logic of strict temporal succession, allied with reason and used in traditional narratives.

In the second part of his dream narrative, Tolstoy goes beyond the epistemology of Locke and Hume, beyond Sterne. Showing the ways in which the sleeping self deals with external impressions or physical stimuli ("I threw down the pillow," "the landlady behind the partition"), he suggests that the temporal/causal order known to us from logical narratives might be limited. In sleep, freed from the constraints of common sense, consciousness mixes external impressions and internal creations of the sleeping mind, arranging them into plots propelled by something other than reason. On several occasions, dream narrative reconfigures physical time and causal order. Further on in his "History," Tolstoy reflects on this type of dream: "You have a long dream which ends with the circumstance that awakened you: you dream that you are going hunting, you load your gun, flush the game, take aim, fire—and the noise which you take for the shot is the carafe which you knocked onto the floor in your sleep" (1:293). In physical time, the gunshot (an external occurrence) is an impulse that initiates narrative consciousness; in dream time, the gunshot concludes a whole sequence of events. Thus, the narrative is constructed retroactively. Like the time flow in "A History of Yesterday" as a whole, dream time moves from the present (the initial external event) to the past and then makes its way back to the initial event, catching up with the present at the moment of awakening. The effect comes before the cause. Most importantly, since the moment of awakening is simultaneous with the initial impulse, in the dream (as in the conversation with the woman at the card table), the action occurs as if in some hidden recess of time. To reiterate, making a faithful record of his day and night, complete with a dream, Tolstoy discovered that life had hidden recesses outside time and space. Inaccessible to standard narrative, such recesses—the "behind-the-soul" side of the day—were penetrated by another kind of consciousness and another kind of narrative: the dream.[20]

There were cultural precedents and parallels. Carl Gustav Carus in his famous *Psyche* (1846) maintained that the key to the knowledge of the nature of "the soul's conscious life" lies "in the realm of the unconscious," manifest in dreams and in states between sleep and waking.[21] Later in the nineteenth century, students of dreams tried to develop techniques that would allow them to test links between sensory stimuli and dreams and to conduct observations on one's dreams while falling asleep. What is more, "retrospective dreams" were known to students of dreams in Tolstoy's time. Perhaps the most famous of such dreams was Alfred Maury's vision of the

French Revolution, reported in his *Sleep and Dreams* (*Le sommeil et les rêves*, 1861). In his dream Maury witnessed scenes of the Revolution, met Robespierre and Marat, and himself fell victim to the Terror: Condemned to death, he mounted the scaffold, put his head under the guillotine, and sensed it separating from his body. At this moment he awoke—to discover that the headboard of his bed had fallen and struck him on the back of his neck. Also widely known was Napoleon's dream, as retold in Adolphe Garnier's book on the capacities of the human soul, *Traité des facultés de l'âme* (1852). Asleep in his carriage, Napoleon dreamed that he was crossing the Tagliamento; at the moment when, in his dream, the Austrians started bombarding, he was awakened by a bomb explosion nearby. Remarkably, it was history—and recent history, such as the French Revolution and the Napoleonic wars—that provided the material for these much-cited retrospective dreams. From such dream experiences, these mid-nineteenth-century philosopher-psychologists drew far-reaching conclusions about the peculiar power of the dream consciousness to weave impressions from the world into structures that were not governed by cause-and-effect logic or linear narrative.[22] Yet such dreams remained an enigma.

It seems unlikely that Tolstoy knew of such psychological studies in 1851. Most likely, he discovered the reverse temporality and inverted logic of dream narratives through personal experience while making faithful records of his reveries and dreams. The discovery held enormous potential.

In the 1850s, the young Tolstoy interpreted his discovery as a psychological phenomenon that had immediate implications for the task of representing human consciousness and semiconscious or unconscious being. In a word, the dream experience offered one way to represent time; standard narratives, another. In "A History of Yesterday" Tolstoy suggests that, while relating such a dream, many people, including himself, would be inclined to translate this peculiar experience into a logically coherent structure with a linear temporal development. The reason lies in the fact that we are accustomed to "continuity and to the form of time in which life manifests itself" (1:293). (Here, the young Tolstoy seems to speak in a distinctly Kantian way.) While in the so-called retrospective dream the mind seems instantly to invent—in retrospect—a whole sequence of events to explain the initial impression, in the act of remembering and narrating this dream, the occurrences are reordered in favor of sequential linearity.

A decade later, in the 1860s, working on *War and Peace*, Tolstoy drew further conclusions from observation of the type described in his "History of Yesterday." These later conclusions concerned not only psychology and narrative but also historiography. Tolstoy describes his discovery in one of his explanatory comments on the novel: Intrigued by the ways in which we represent historical events, he decided that lying was inherent in the very act of verbal description. In an explanatory note entitled "A Few Words about the Book *War and Peace*" (1867–68), Tolstoy writes of "the necessity to lie, stemming from the need to describe in only a few words the actions of thousands of people, spread over several miles." A person who wants to find out "how things are" exchanges the "infinitely diverse and vague impressions" that have formed inside him for "a deceitful but clear . . . representation" (16:10–11). Some translate "infinitely diverse" impressions into logical, linear narratives. Others provide retroactive justifications of events (Tolstoy's description of this strategy suggests the inverted logic of dreams). Thus, after *War and Peace*, working from "observations on human psychology" (his phrase), Tolstoy concluded that what obstructs access to things "as they really are" is "the ability of man to retroactively and instantaneously fabricate an entire array of seemingly free deductions for every occurred fact" (16:15).[23] As Viktor Shklovsky put it, in *War and Peace* Tolstoy returned "to a psychology of dreams, which 'fabricate causes.' "[24]

It seems that after *War and Peace,* Tolstoy treated all available forms of representation, invented by men to express their "infinitely diverse and vague impressions," with equal suspicion. On the one hand, he distrusted the Kantian way: the rule of linear succession that leads us to construct causality. On the other, he was suspicious of the ability of men to follow the nonlinear, retroactive logic of spontaneous dream narratives. In *War and Peace*, Tolstoy made a special effort to show various forms of "false stories," narratives misrepresenting actual events.[25] He seemed to think that histories—of individuals as well as of nations—were either clear but deceitful linear narratives or, like retroactive dreams, instant reinventions of the past aimed at explaining the present.

Thus, in *War and Peace*—or, rather, in his reflections on *War and Peace*—Tolstoy turned the self-analysis performed in the narrative experiment of his early diaries and his "History of Yesterday" into a philosophy of historical representation.

Jumping ahead, I will mention that in the diaries of his late years, Tolstoy (who faithfully recorded his dreams in his diary) would return to the inverted temporality of retroactive dreams. The old Tolstoy would fully appreciate the transcendental potential of dreams, which open a hidden recess of linear time, and he would mobilize this natural resource in his struggle with the metaphysics of finitude (these later developments will be discussed in chapter 6). But in the 1850s and 1860s, his main concerns lay elsewhere.

What Am I? The Young Tolstoy Defines Himself

Throughout the 1850s, in his diary, Tolstoy diligently engaged in daily exercises of self-examination and moral accounting. In fact, his investigations of temporality in narrative may have been a by-product of the diary's explicit purpose: self-improvement.

In July 1854, he decided to make an overview of his current condition. He started by asking a classic question: "What am I?" (*Chto ia takoe?*). At this point, this question referred to the moral value of his innate and acquired character traits as they related to his family, social, and biographical situation.

> 7 July [1854]. . . .
>
> What am I? I am one of the four sons of a retired Lieutenant Colonel, left at the age of seven without parents, under the care of women and strangers, a man without social or academic education, independent from the age of seventeen; a man without much capital, without social standing and, most important, without any rules in life; a man who has damaged his financial affairs to the utmost, who has spent the best years of his life without purpose or pleasure; a man who, in the end, has exiled himself to the Caucasus so as to escape his debts and, most importantly, his habits, and who has used some kind of connection between his father and the army commander to join the Danube Army at the age of twenty-six as an Ensign, almost without means, except his salary (because the money he has must be used to pay his remaining debts), without patrons, without the knack of living in high society, without any knowledge of military service, without practical skills, but with enormous *amour-propre*! This is my social situation.
>
> Let us see what my personality is like.
>
> I am ugly, awkward, uncouth, untidy, and socially unskilled.—I am irritable, boring, immodest, intolerant, and bashful as a child. I am almost an ignoramus. What I do know, I have learned haphazardly, on my own, in fits and starts, without a system, without meaning— and not much even of that.—I am unreserved, indecisive, unstable, stupidly, vain, and fiery, like all people who lack character. I am not courageous. I am unscrupulous in daily life and so lazy that sloth has become an almost insurmountable habit.—I am intelligent, but my intelligence has never been seriously tested. I have neither practical intelligence, nor social intelligence, nor business intelligence.—I am honest, that is, I love virtue, have made a habit of loving virtue, and

I am unhappy with myself when I stray from virtue and return to it
with joy; but there are things I love more than virtue—glory. I am so
ambitious, and this feeling has been so little satisfied, that I am afraid
that I could choose glory over virtue, if I had a chance to choose between them.

—Yes, I am not modest; that is why I am proud within myself, but
bashful and shy in high society.—(47:8)

In this summary, as in his daily entries (focused as they are on the ways in
which his life has fallen short of expectations), Tolstoy evaluates himself neg-
atively. His main problem, he thinks, is vanity. On another occasion, he wrote
of vanity as a "moral disease": "[I]t penetrates gradually and imperceptibly
and then it spreads through the whole organism . . . like a venereal disease"
(46:94).

Acute consciousness of his vanity was to torment Tolstoy for life. All his
life, he would morally abhor his (strong) sexual urges.

At the time, Tolstoy was serving in the army in the south of Russia (in
several months, he would be sent into the heart of the Crimean War, Sevastopol). He was again treated for venereal diseases; he still played cards, still lost,
and still tried to control his behavior by writing rules. He continued to follow
Franklin's method of accounting for his moral weaknesses.

Tolstoy also prayed (like Rousseau, he made up his own prayers), asking
God to help him rid himself of his vices and to deliver him from illnesses,
suffering, quarrels, debts, and humiliations (in this order) (47:12). About a
year later, Tolstoy, like Rousseau before him, conceived the idea of "founding a new religion befitting the development of humankind, the religion of
Christ, but the one purged from faith and mystery, a practical religion. . . ."
(March 4, 1855; 47:37).

What Am I? Cultural Precedents

In these struggles the young Tolstoy, of course, was following in the footsteps
of a long tradition. He followed Rousseau, among other things, in his emphasis on introspection and in his desire for self-revelation. (He also followed
Rousseau in his lifelong rebellion against the idea of progress.) Throughout his life, Tolstoy was eager not only to acknowledge Rousseau (whom he
claimed to have first read, and revered, at age fifteen) as his teacher but also to
appropriate Rousseau's ideas as his own. As the old Tolstoy put it, "I read all of
Rousseau, all twenty volumes. . . . I more than admired him—I deified him.

At age fifteen, I wore a medallion with his portrait around my neck like a holy image. Many pages by him are so near to me that it seems as though I wrote them myself."[26]

As for Laurence Sterne, from whom Tolstoy borrowed the technique of associative narrative that follows the vagaries of the Lockean perceiving consciousness, Tolstoy actually had written many pages by Sterne himself: he had translated him into Russian.

From Benjamin Franklin, Tolstoy borrowed his famous "method" of rational self-formation aimed at bringing one's life into a moral order in accordance with a strict pattern.[27]

Tolstoy's immediate sources were secular, but they were informed by religious traditions. Thus, Benjamin Franklin's method had theological underpinnings in the Puritan imperative to follow the workings of God within one's soul (which gave rise to a whole culture of diary writing in seventeenth- and eighteenth-century England and America). Arguably, the theological background was transparently present, even though for Franklin, a self-classified deist, the need for self-examination in the service of salvation was superseded by a secular urge toward self-perfection. In his emphasis on self-examination, Rousseau (also a deist) secularized Augustinian inwardness in the spirit of the Enlightenment idea of human perfectibility.[28]

There were, of course, yet other sources; not only classics but also common books. I will describe one such source: John Mason's didactic treatise *Self-Knowledge*; written by a nonconformist British clergyman (in 1745), this book was widely used across Europe and in America. There is a copy of the 1818 English-language edition in Tolstoy's library.[29] In Russia, in the late eighteenth and early nineteenth centuries, the book was adopted in Masonic circles, and it influenced the domestic culture of self-reflection fostered by the Russian Sentimentalists. The results (such as the diaries of the young Vasily Zhukovsky from 1804–06) are strikingly similar to Tolstoy's diaries, written half a century later.[30] Indeed, Tolstoy seems to have looked to the past, rather than to his contemporaries, for his models.[31]

A practical manual for young people, *Self-Knowledge* teaches principles, methods, and practical means of self-examination drawn from diverse sources, from Socrates and the Stoics (Plutarch, Epictetus, Seneca), to the New Testament and Augustine, to Locke (his reflections on memory and the connection of ideas), to Richard Baxter and Edward Young (his *Night Thoughts*). Mason's book allows its reader to view the practical pursuit of self-knowledge as part of an uninterrupted tradition that extends from the Greeks through the early Christians to modern times (to the Puritans and Sentimentalists). In fact, Mason made special efforts to translate the "Know thyself" precepts of the "ancient sages" into the language of the Old and New Testament and to relate this language to the contemporary poetic idiom. Self-examination, as taught by Mason, involves practical techniques for exploring one's natural temper, constitutional inclinations, favorite passions, and the true motives and secret springs of one's actions as well as one's appetite for fame and the applause of others. But theology supersedes psychology: The goal is to examine oneself in one's relations "to Him who gave us our being." Thus, the Socratic maxim "Know thyself" is superseded by the Pauline commandment "Let a man examine himself . . . " (1 Corinthians 11:28), which stems from Old Testament dispensation "Examine me, O Lord, and prove me. . . ." (Psalm 26:2). It is in this spirit that Mason provides immediate guidelines: "Reader! Try the experiment; retire now into thyself . . . by closely urging such questions as these: What am I? For what was I made? . . . What have I been doing since I came into the world? . . . Am I now in that state I wish to die in?"[32] This scrutiny, Mason instructs, must be made every morning and every evening.

As we have seen, when Tolstoy asked "What am I?" in his diary in 1854, he looked for answers mostly in the mundane. At age twenty-five, he was not yet thinking of death on a daily basis (that was to come when he turned fifty). And yet, perusing these books, Tolstoy was exposed to the theological meanings of inwardness even as he indulged in Rousseau's sentimental introspection and followed Franklin's rational impulse toward self-perfection. The secular practices of self-examination that were at the young Tolstoy's disposal carried barely submerged religious and theological potential. They held a potential for another turn: the resacralization of the self.

So, what do we learn from the personal writings of the young Tolstoy?

In their classic studies, Boris Eikhenbaum and Viktor Shklovsky, who have left a permanent stamp on our reading of Tolstoy, view his early diaries and his "History of Yesterday" as, first and foremost, a "preparatory step for authorship"—laboratories for developing the "method" and "devices" for his future works of literature.[33] The diaries, Eikhenbaum claims, helped to produce "Tolstoy's unique method of representing psychic life," the method of capturing the very process of thinking and feeling, the "dialectics of the soul," that would become a trademark of his fiction.[34] Other scholars have productively treated Tolstoy's early diaries as a literary text.[35]

In this book, I have chosen to approach Tolstoy's early diaries and "A History of Yesterday" differently: as an attempt to create not works of literature but "a book of life" (as Tolstoy would later call his diaries), a narrative representation of his own self written with a moral and metaphysical purpose in mind.

From this perspective, the diaries of Tolstoy's late years, written after he had decided to abandon *belles lettres*, are part of the same lifelong project. As an attempt at the complete textualization of the self, this project was doomed, but the process proved fruitful, even at the early stages.

In his early years, Tolstoy found himself pursuing two strategies, which alternate and compete with each other. In diaries and notebooks (especially, but not exclusively, in 1847–51), the young Tolstoy subjects his life to a narrative, temporal, and moral grid. He aims both at bringing moral order to his life and at capturing, on a daily basis, the ever-elusive essence of experience in writing. In the experimental "A History of Yesterday," he attempts to represent life "as it is," transcending the limitations of narrative, such as the forms of sequential time and causal logic, the need for coherent meaning and closure, and the division between subject and object (he even attempted to penetrate "behind the soul," into what we may call the unconscious). But in the end, the ever-expanding flow of consciousness erodes the narrative. Indeed, what Tolstoy cannot transcend is consciousness itself: Self-consciousness pursues the writer even into sleep, weaving a text. And yet the text of his early diaries seems more adequate to life and to the self as we know them in daily experience: fragmented, inconsistent, and inevitably incomplete.[36] This text holds the potential for an alternative metaphysics of daily life and an alternative vision of the self.

Interlude: Between Personal
Documents and Fiction

Several times in his life, Tolstoy found himself caught between different kind of writings: the kind with immediate reference to his own "I" (diary, letter, or essay) and fiction. This interlude will briefly outline these transitions, from available biographical information about Tolstoy.[1]

From Diaries to *Childhood*: Tolstoy Becomes a Writer (1852)

As scholars tend to agree, in 1851–52, Tolstoy, aged twenty-four, made a transition from intense reading and diary-writing to fiction and professional authorship, and this transition occurred in the writing of *Childhood*.[2] He recorded his progress in his diary: "Read Hume, wrote Ch[ildhood], read Rousseau" (June 27, 1852; 46:127).

Judging by his diary and letters, the transition was easy, almost casual. In November 1851, Tolstoy wrote to his aunt (in French): "Do you remember, dear Auntie, that you once advised me to make novels [*faire des romans*]?" At the time, he was living in the Caucasus, hoping to enlist in the army; waiting for the arrival of the necessary documents, he was idle. Following his aunt's advice, he tried a new occupation. He added that he did not yet know whether what he was writing would ever appear in print and that he had gone too far in this work to abandon it (59:117).[3] The result was *Childhood*, and it would launch Tolstoy's literary career.

It has been suggested that, in its form and method, "A History of Yesterday" (written in March 1851) served as a "bridge" between the diary and *Childhood* (written mostly during the summer of 1851). Scholars who view *Childhood* side by side with "A History of Yesterday" (Tolstoy's experimental attempt to describe "all of the diverse impressions and thoughts that pass through consciousness in a single day") see *Childhood* as a partial surrender to the conventions of fiction. An extension of the diary, "A History of Yesterday" (I claim) was written without the intention of producing literature. *Childhood,* on the other hand, was literature.[4]

Tolstoy seems to have thought of *Childhood* not as a personal history but as a picture of a distinct stage in human life. He was incensed when, in its first publication, the editor changed his title from "Childhood" to "My Childhood": "Who cares about the history of *my* childhood?" (59:214).[5] He had originally planned a larger novel, entitled *The Four Epochs of Life* (*Chetyre epokhi zhizni*), that would cover the span of human development from childhood to early adulthood. But he felt constrained by "the autobiographical form and the obligatory link between preceding and succeeding parts" (59:202).[6] Tolstoy even contemplated leaving the first part without a continuation. He was also constrained by his intimate relationship to the hero. A few months later, he tried again, cultivating a sense of distance from his hero: "I can write about him because he is distant from me" (46:150–51).[7] In the end, Tolstoy produced three parts, *Childhood, Boyhood,* and *Youth,* abandoning his plan to take his hero to maturity, to the moment of writing.[8] And after the publication of his trilogy, Tolstoy abandoned the autobiographical form for good.

Tolstoy's first literary work (some scholars maintain) carries the residue of personal writing. Indeed, told in the first person, *Childhood* seems to resemble the diary: Almost the entire action of the first part comprises one day in the life of the narrator, described circumstantially, step by step. The characters and plot remain underdeveloped. What is more, this work uses some autobiographical material from Tolstoy's life. And yet, *Childhood* is definitely fiction. Thus, in contrast to the diary and "A History of Yesterday," the narrator and the author of *Childhood* are clearly not the same person.[9] As Tolstoy himself continually insisted, *Childhood* is not an autobiography but a fictional autobiography. Tolstoy had separated the speaking "I" from the personality of the author. This may have not been clear to a naive reader (especially since this was the first work by an unknown author, and it was signed not with his name but with his initials). But for Tolstoy himself, the separation clearly took place. On a psychological level (as his diary indicated), this made Tolstoy feel that he could write not for the diary but for the public. As one critic has put it, "[T]he conventions of the novel do at least offer an escape route for the author from his art, a ladder by which he can enter and leave his creations at will."[10] One could say that *Childhood* catches the young author in the process of escaping from his work. In this sense, *Childhood* is a kind of compromise: a "threshold genre."[11] With this threshold work, Tolstoy stepped into a career in literature.

Childhood was published in the September 1852 issue of Russia's leading journal, *The Contemporary* (Sovremennik), to instant acclaim. In the meantime Tolstoy succeeded in enlisting in the army and requested a transfer to the theater of military action. Nevertheless, he worked on the sequel to *Childhood* and on other literary projects. (*Boyhood* appeared in 1854.) With the beginning of the Crimean War, he found himself in battle. In 1855, "Sevastopol in May" (Sevastopol' v mae) "Sevastopol in December"(Sevastopol' dekabre), and other powerful dispatches from the front lines started to appear in print, attracting intense attention. These stories, or sketches, "exist on the liminal boundary between reportage and fiction": The characters are fictional, but the reader knows that "Tolstoy was there." What is more, the stories are framed as month-by-month chronicles, and they experiment with first-person, third-person, and even second-person narration.[12] When in late 1855, after Russia's defeat in the Crimean War, Tolstoy arrived in St. Petersburg, he was welcomed into the tight-knit circle of Russian writers as an established author. In Petersburg he continued writing. (The third part of his fictional autobiography, *Youth*, appeared in 1857.)

In 1857, Tolstoy set off on what was an essential experience in the *Bildung* of a Russian writer: a journey through Europe. He witnessed a public execution in Paris, and the memory of the guillotine long haunted his dreams; on that day he wrote that he had renounced politics for "morality and art" (47:121–22). He wandered in Rousseau's footsteps through France and Switzerland. He worked intermittently on a number of literary projects. After 1857, Tolstoy's diary becomes increasingly sketchy.

"I Think I Will Never Write Again": Tolstoy Attempts to Renounce Literature (1859)

Not long after his return, in spring 1859, Tolstoy made a sudden decision to "renounce literature." He left Petersburg to settle on his country estate, Yasnaya Polyana. He was experiencing the first in a series of crises that would punctuate his life and work.[13]

Tolstoy described his situation—an acute sense of religious and moral impasse—in a letter to his cousin Alexandra Tolstaya (who would serve as an addressee of his confessions for much of his life). He starts with his *profession de foi*: "A person's convictions—not the ones he relates to others but the ones that he's lived out of his whole life—are difficult for another to grasp, and you do not know mine. . . . Still, I will try to make my *profession de foi*." He writes about his falling away from faith (at the age of fourteen) and his later discovery, in the Caucasus (where he lived in 1851–54), "that there is immortality, that there is love, and that one should live for the sake of another" (60:293).[14] (Back then, as we know from his diary, Tolstoy read Rousseau's "Profession de foi du Vicaire Savoyard" constantly, even at the dinner table.)[15]

In his confessional letter to his devout cousin, Tolstoy speaks about his present despair: "There is nothing to live for. This occurred to me yesterday, with such force. . . . To whom do I do any good? Whom do I love? Nobody! . . ." But he hastens to add: "I'm not asking you to tell me . . . what to do." From the subject of existential despair, he passes to a painful reversal in his literary work: "I have another grief. My Anna, when I came to the country and reread it, turned out to be such a contemptible and revolting thing that I cannot recover from the shame, and I think I will never write again. And it has already been published" (60:293–95). Tolstoy is referring here to his recently published novella, *Family Happiness* (*Semeinoe schast'e*).

In a letter to the critic Vasily Botkin, written on the same day, Tolstoy speaks of his novella with the same sense of shame and regret (but he uses diction befitting a male-to-male communication): "Vasily Petrovich! Vasily Petrovich! What have I done with my 'Family Happiness.' Only now, here in the open country . . . having read the proofs . . . have I seen what a piece of shit, what a blemish, not only artistic but also human, is this disgusting composition" (60:296). He describes experiencing a stylistic failure as a moral transgression (and links the recovery of clear vision to liberation from the urban environment). It remains unclear why, on more than one occasion, Tolstoy called his book "My Anna." In the published version, the first-person narrator and heroine of *Family Happiness* is called Maria, or Masha.[16]

In many ways, *Family Happiness* (1859) is a conventional novel (albeit a short one), with a set of fully developed characters and a standard plot. Focused on courtship, marriage, and married life, the plot follows the dynamics of disillusionment in romantic ideals and reconciliation with real life. *Family Happiness*, like Tolstoy's *Childhood*, *Boyhood*, and *Youth*, was written in the first person, but this time nobody could doubt that it was an assumed, literary "I": the narrative "I" is a young woman. This radical move may have helped Tolstoy to rob the reader of any illusion of identity between the narrator's "I" and the author's (Leo Tolstoy's) and to mark his work as fiction. But this came at a price. When he read the proofs, Tolstoy became aware of the artificial form and stilted language. In his late years, he would describe such a feeling as "a sense of aesthetic shame": a genuine shame (he claimed) that he experienced, throughout his life, when he read something "artificial and false."[17]

Soon afterward, Tolstoy told everybody that he would write no more. First and foremost, he wanted to escape from the ranks of professional authorship. Thus, he asked that his name be removed from the list of Russian writers prepared for a newly established institution, the Literary Fund. He told a fellow author (who asked for his support for the Fund) that he did not want to be considered a member of "the literary circle."[18] He wrote to a friend that his "renunciation of literature" (*otrechenie ot literatury*) was very hard for him, but that, nevertheless, he would rather work the land and teach peasants than share in the self-delusions and vanity of artists and spend his life "exploiting the labor of others" (60:316, 327).[19]

Tolstoy made an alternative life plan: cultivation of his estate and pedagogical work with peasant children. He linked his decision to the current social situation: the preparations for the liberation of the serfs. "Literature, or belles lettres," he claimed in another letter, addressed to the critic Vasily Botkin, "has absolutely no place now in society" (60:247).[20] In the same letter Tolstoy sent a piece of fiction: written in the form of a dream record, it depicted him speaking to millions of people who are listened with rapt attention. But in the end this piece, based on a real dream (not the author's own, but his brother's), remained unpublished.[21]

Soon after, in a letter to another friend, Egor Kovalevsky (whose brother was a minister of education), Tolstoy explained his decision to abandon literature for public education as a matter of moral and social responsibility to the other: "This is what it's all about. Practical wisdom . . . lies not in knowing what should be done but in knowing what to do first and what next. I believe that in the matter of progress in Russia, however useful may be telegraphs, roads, steam ships . . . literature (with its own fund and all), theaters, the Academy of Arts, etc., all of this is premature and all in vain while in Russia only one percent of the population is being educated. . . ." (March 12, 1860; 60:328–29). Tolstoy then outlined his proposal for the establishment of a Society for Public Education, of which he was the sole representative.

The death of Tolstoy's beloved brother Nikolai from consumption (during Tolstoy's second trip to Europe) exacerbated his prolonged crisis: A confrontation with death rendered life entirely meaningless. To accept life "as is," he wrote in a letter to his intimate friend Afanasy Fet on October 17, 1860, is a "banal, revolting, and false condition." This was his heartfelt moral conviction, and he would practice this conviction but not in the form of art: "Art is a lie, and I can no longer love a beautiful lie" (60:358).

To highlight the key elements of Tolstoy's first crisis, there is a confrontation with death, a sense of existential despair, an acute sense of the surrounding social evil and his own privileged condition, the distrust of literary form as artificial and false, the turn to religion and religious discourse ("*profession de foi*"), the rejection of literature (specifically, "belles lettres") as socially irrelevant, the renunciation of the profession of a writer, and the announcement, "I will never write again."

In the course of his life, Tolstoy was to experience other critical periods in which he questioned the meaning and purpose of his life and work, and, as we shall see, his crises followed a similar pattern. Each time, Tolstoy experienced failures of literary form and style with the intensity of a moral feeling. Each time, he turned to religion. In each case, he attempted to abandon fiction as a mode of writing and literary authorship as a profession, but, in one form or another, he continued to write.

In 1859–60, it seemed clear what was to be done as an alternative to literary authorship: the underprivileged (peasants) must be taught how to read and write. Yet, in the same letter to Kovalevsky, Tolstoy asserts that "literacy, the process of reading and writing, is harmful" (60:329). He qualifies this shocking statement by adding that there is no "good literature for the people," but his comment still poses a paradox. Tolstoy placed himself in an untenable position, and yet he embarked on a program of practical action.

The results were a school for peasant children on his estate, in which Tolstoy himself was the main teacher, and a pedagogical journal, entitled *Yasnaya Polyana*. The journal published day-by-day chronicles (diaries) of the school ("The Yasnaya Polyana School in November," "The Yasnaya Polyana School in December," 1861) as well as Tolstoy's own pedagogical articles, including two that would become famous, "On Public Education" (*O narodnom obrazovanii*, 1862) and "Who Should Learn to Write from Whom, the Peasant Children from Us or We from the Peasant Children?" (*Komu u kogo uchit'sia pisat', krest'ianskim rebiatam u nas, ili nam u krest'ianskikh rebiat?* 1862).

In the latter article, Tolstoy advocates a sort of reciprocal anarchy in peda-gogy: the student and the teacher learn writing from each other. He describes, step by step, how two peasant children in his school went about composing a piece of fiction. (Their story resembled in form and style the so-called "people's stories" [*narodnye rasskazy*] that Tolstoy himself, after the 1880s, would pro-duce in great numbers for the peasant reader.) Tolstoy felt quite helpless. On the one hand, it seemed "strange and humiliating" that "I, the author of *Child-hood*," could hardly help an eleven-year-old to write. On the other, he felt that asking peasant children to write fiction was tantamount to sexual corruption of the young. (In this context, Tolstoy affirms Rousseau's thesis that man was born innocent and perfect; 8:322.) This is how Tolstoy describes the feelings— excitement and self-disgust—he experienced as he watched the peasant chil-dren create literature under his tutelage: "It seemed to me that I had corrupted the pure, primordial soul of a peasant child. I had a vague feeling of repentance from an act of sacrilege. I recalled the children whom idle and depraved old men force to take on obscene postures so as to fire their tired, played-out imag-inations. . . ." (8:307). As we see, even as he diligently immersed himself in the education of the ninety-nine percent, Tolstoy was busy raising moral objections against such education and, still more, against fiction-writing. And he describes his activities (which he associates with illicit eroticism) as a sin that calls for repentance.

Soon Tolstoy's first engagement with the "other" came to an end: in 1862, shortly after publishing his pedagogical articles, Tolstoy married, and he stopped working at the Yasnaya Polyana school. What followed was the writ-ing of *War and Peace* (1863–69). (For several months in 1862 and 1863, he wrote in his diary to record the progress of his courtship and the first months of his married life; there is not a single entry between 1866 and 1872.)

To turn from biographical events to the uses of literary form, there is a "gap" (critics have noted) between the "personality of the author" as it appears in *Childhood*, with its autobiographical residue, and in *War and Peace*, which features scores of fully embodied characters and intricate plots. This gap is bridged by a number of transitional texts, some of which continue to play with autobiographical reference and first-person narrative. One of them is *The Cossacks* (Kazaki, started in 1852–53 in the Caucasus, resumed in 1857–58, but published only in 1863, when Tolstoy urgently needed money to cover a large gambling debt). This is a third-person narrative, but one that features a vaguely autobiographical hero (Olenin) and, what is more, this hero does not reach (as one critic has put it) the "objectively plotted status" of Andrei and Pierre from *War and Peace*.[22] Another is *Kholstomer*, the story of a horse, written in the first person from the horse's point of view (completed in 1863, it was published only in 1885).

"I . . . Don't Even Think about the Accursed Lit-t-terature and *Lit-t-terateurs*": Tolstoy Renounces Literature Again (1870); and Again (1874–75)

In 1869 or 1870, soon after *War and Peace,* Tolstoy decided to abandon literature yet again.[23] As he wrote to Afanasy Fet, on June 14, 1870, "Thank God, this summer I feel stupid as a horse. I work, fell the wood, dig, dig, mow, and, thank God, don't even think about the accursed lit-t-terature and lit-t-terateurs" (61:236–37). At the very least, he would not write the way he used to: "I do not write and would never again write such verbose nonsense as *War [and Peace]*" (January 1871; 61:247). Again, Tolstoy turned to the "people": he worked on an ABC book for peasant children, *Azbuka* (published in 1872), entered debates on public education, and resumed his work in the Yasnaya Polyana school. But he was soon diverted by another novel, *Anna Karenina,* started in 1873. (In 1873 Tolstoy made several entries in his diary, but the project soon came to nothing.)

The next, decisive crisis in Tolstoy's life—and another attempt to abandon literature—came in the midst of his work on *Anna Karenina.*

In May 1874, Tolstoy confessed to his friend, the critic Nikolai Strakhov, that he was in deep despair and felt an urge to abandon *belles lettres* for a worthier cause. He admitted that he had neglected *Anna Karenina* to work on an article "in the form of my pedagogical *profession de foi.*"[24] The result was another "On Public Education" (*O narodnom obrazovanii,* 1874), featuring some of the same arguments as the 1862 article of the same name. But an unfinished project stood in the way of his new aspirations: "I'm at work at the moment on that dreary, vulgar A[nna] Karen[ina] and all I ask God is that he give me the strength to be rid of it as soon as possible, to free some space—I do need free time, and not for pedagogical, but for other, more pressing matters" (August 25, 1875; 1:215). The institution of literature disgusted him. What is more, Tolstoy was disgusted by the novel itself, his "dreary vulgar Anna" (*skuchnaia poshlaia A*). (He often wrote the book's title abbreviated and without quotation marks, like a personal name.) It is an uncanny coincidence that during his previous crisis, Tolstoy had called "Family Happiness," whose main character is named Maria, "my Anna" and "this disgusting composition."

He found the writing profession (which stimulated vanity) morally dangerous: "The rank of writer is loathsome; it's depraving" (April 8–9, 1876; 1:259).

In the fall of 1875, Tolstoy turned from his "pedagogical *profession de foi*" to philosophical and theological reflections on the meaning of life and, especially, death. He chose letters as his main medium: his correspondence with Strakhov—the subject of the next chapter.

After this decisive crisis, following his *Confession,* Tolstoy started working on a treatise that (he hoped) would finally define his view of art. As Tolstoy himself claimed, it took him fifteen years to produce *What Is Art?* (Chto takoe iskusstvo, 1897).[25] Rooted in his pedagogical experiments with peasant children in the early 1860s, this aesthetic treatise consigns his own fiction to the category of bad art.[26]

"To Tell One's Faith Is Impossible. . . . How to Tell That Which I Live By. I'll Tell You, All the Same. . . ." Tolstoy in His Correspondence

Among Leo Tolstoy's voluminous letters, his correspondence with Nikolai Strakhov in the years 1874–79 stands out for its intensity, intimacy, reciprocity, and confessional nature. As a literary critic and philosophical writer, Nikolai Nikolaevich Strakhov (1828–96) participated in the major intellectual debates and publishing ventures of his time. In his prodigious role as editor, private correspondent, and confidant, he served as a conveyor of diverse ideas and a mediator between disparate people. (He served as a link between Tolstoy and Dostoevsky, who never met.)[1] What Strakhov offered Tolstoy was his philosophical erudition (over the years he authored a number of studies popularizing Western philosophy). He also explicitly offered his special ability, and need, to "enter into other people's interests and thoughts" (1:207).[2] Tolstoy insisted on reciprocating. At his urging, in spring 1875 (after four years of friendship), Strakhov confessed that he had been desperately searching for a "cause" in life (April 22, 1875; 1:207). Tolstoy pressed the matter: "Your spiritual condition has been revealed to me a little, and I want all the more to penetrate it further" (May 5, 1875; 1:211). He suspected that they were both yearning for faith. Strakhov eventually admitted to the same desire that Tolstoy himself had experienced of late: to visit the monastery Optina Pustyn' and its hermit "elders" (*startsy*, Orthodox spiritual advisers) (1:211). When they saw each other face to face, at Yasnaya Polyana in late September 1875, Tolstoy felt a "remarkable spiritual affinity" between them. In the letters that followed, he urged Strakhov to join him in an urgent task: to "elucidate and define one's religious worldview" (October 26, 1875; 1:222).

Tolstoy felt that they both were at a crossroads: suspended, like many of their contemporaries, between "Christian belief" and "nihilistic materialism" and, in their individual life journeys, between life and death, they had a common duty to speak out so as to "help those who are in the same miserable lonely condition." Strakhov responded that he would follow Tolstoy's advice and do what he could (November 4, 1875; 1:224). Tolstoy sealed their pact: "I rejoice at your plan and challenge you to a correspondence." He immediately added: "My God, if only somebody would finish A. Karenina for me!" (November 8–9, 1875; 1:226).

"What Is My Life? What Am I?": Tolstoy's Philosophical Dialogue with Nikolai Strakhov

At Tolstoy's instigation, Strakhov opened their conversation. A semi-professional philosopher (whose philosophical knowledge clearly impressed Tolstoy), he used Kant's three fundamental questions to set the agenda: 1. What can I know? 2. What ought I to do? 3. What may I hope for? (*Critique of Pure Reason*, A 805/B 833). For him, the second question was the most important: indifferent (as he wrote) to the issue of the immortality of the soul, Strakhov wanted to know "what is to be done" or, "translated into Christian language, how to save one's soul" (November 16, 1875; 1:228). Like many a Russian intellectual, Strakhov sought specific instructions for "active involvement in life" (his words), but unlike others, he approached the matter in a religious key.

Tolstoy responded that of Kant's three questions, he was most interested in the last: "What may we hope for?" For him, this was clearly a question about the future, eternal life of the soul. But Tolstoy believed that all three questions were inextricably linked into one: "What is my life? What am I?" (November 30, 1875; 1:230).

Some twenty years earlier, in his diary, the young Tolstoy had asked himself "What am I?" Then, he answered in biographical and moral-psychological terms ("I am one of the four sons of a retired Lieutenant Colonel, left at the age of seven without parents. . . . I am ugly, awkward, uncouth, untidy, and socially unskilled. . . ." 47:9). But now this was a question not so much about his own character or his own life as about the nature of man in his relations to God: "What am I?" demanded, first and foremost, not a biographical but a theological exploration.

Commenting that it might seem irresponsible to address such questions "on two sheets of note-paper," Tolstoy added that he would have done the same thing even if he were writing not "a letter to an intimate friend" but a "*profession de foi* to which the whole of humankind attended" (1:230).

Then Tolstoy made what he called a "digression on method" (1:230–35). In brief, he tried to say that a "scientific method" that relied on logical reasoning was inapplicable to "true" philosophy (such as Plato's), which was concerned with the meaning of human life and death. True philosophy relied on "harmony" rather than logic, on "the linking of disparate notions into a single whole," which convinced "instantly," without "deductions and proofs" (November 30, 1875; 1:234). He seemed to hope that such a "method" could be found in the course of their dialogue.

Appended to the November 30 letter was "an introduction of sorts" (transcribed by a copyist) to an "as yet unwritten philosophical work." Entitled "Why Do I Write?" (*Dlia chego ia pishu?*), it addressed the question of purpose. Tolstoy starts in the first person and the autobiographical mode: "I'm forty-seven years old. . . . I feel that old age has set in. Old age is what I call that inner, spiritual condition in which all the world's external phenomena have lost interest for me. . . . If a sorceress were to appear before me and ask me what I desired, I would not be able to express one single wish" (1:236). He speaks in metaphor: he has gone "up the mountain," reached the "summit," and "started the descent." What next? This much seemed clear: death (1:236). Having considered, and rejected, the idea that life might be inherently meaningless (the idea, he noted, that had led Descartes to seek a proof of God's existence), he started searching for a view on life that would relieve this sense of meaninglessness. The purpose of his writing was "to tell how it was that I passed from a state of hopelessness and despair to an explanation for myself of the meaning of life" (November 30, 1875; 1:237). (Several years later, in his *Confession*, Tolstoy would use similar language.)

At this point, the copied manuscript comes to an end. Resuming his letter (in his own hand), Tolstoy commented that he could not give the rest to the copyist. The text that followed argued that while these questions were fully answered by religion, "with the knowledge we possess, it is impossible for us to believe in the principles of religion." Exposure to such material "could have led the copyist into temptation" (1:237).

As Tolstoy made clear, he started writing about himself at the very moment of transition (from the state of hopelessness to uncertain groping for meaning) and in the presence of others (his correspondent as well as the copyist). He focused on the *how*: on method. The process of writing gave expression to those changes that occurred in him over time.

Tolstoy concluded his first philosophical letter by inviting Strakhov to respond. The philosophical method, he reiterated, rests on the harmonious linking of disparate notions into a single whole: He awaited Strakhov's "responses and objections" in order to demonstrate the harmony in the assembly of his "religious (philosophical) views" (November 30, 1875; 1:239).

Strakhov responded that in his digression on method, Tolstoy seemed to be saying that science employed "analysis" (division of the whole into parts), while philosophy strove for "synthesis" (December 25, 1875; 1:240–41). Tolstoy retorted that he did not agree with this simple "substitution of terms," and he urged Strakhov to respond to his next letter, which would go out in a few days (January 1–2, 1876; 1:243). But it took Tolstoy several weeks to complete it. In the meantime, he returned to *Anna Karenina*, reading the proofs (1:250).

Tolstoy's long-delayed second philosophical letter, mailed on February 14–15, 1876, contained an unfinished essay, "On the Soul and Its Life Outside of the Life That is Known and Understood by Us" (*O dushe i zhizni ee vne izvestnoi i poniatnoi nam zhizni*).[3] Turning to a different mode—not spiritual autobiography but abstract philosophy—Tolstoy again started with the word "I": "~~I exist~~ . . .") (PSS 17:340; crossout in original). (He may have been inspired by Rousseau's variations on Descartes in "Profession de foi du vicaire Savoyard": "But who am I? . . . I exist, and I have senses by which I am affected. This is the first truth that strikes me. . . .")[4] Having crossed out this statement, he made an attempt to approach the problem from the vantage point of his antagonists, the materialists: I live and, as I know from experience, I will die; nothing remains, then, but dead matter (PSS 17:351–52). (Tolstoy borrowed this theme, the division between the living and the non-living, from Strakhov's 1872 book *The World as a Whole*, a collection of essays written in the form of letters.)[5]

To respond to this argument, he tried to define the notion of "soul." But how would one define that which is larger than both the living and the dead, the "I" and the "non-I"? After many pages, Tolstoy returned to his initial point: What am I? He mused: "I don't know to what extent Descartes' formulation is accurate: I think, therefore I live; but I know that if I say—*I know myself above all, that I live*—this cannot be inaccurate" (PSS 17:351; emphasis in original). In the end, his attempt to define the "soul" failed.

It was not easy for Strakhov to engage in a philosophical dialogue with the man he venerated. When he finally forced himself to respond, he contextualized Tolstoy's main arguments in the language of Western philosophy: "Your letter is an attempt to tread the same path as Descartes, Fichte, Schelling, Hegel, Schopenhauer. They began in precisely the same way, from themselves, from *Cogito ergo sum*, from the 'I,' from the consciousness of the will—and from there derived their understanding of all else that exists." In this way, he said, we would begin and end with the "conscious I," we would remain locked in a circular reasoning process. Strakhov felt that retracing the steps of post-Cartesian philosophy from its starting point in the thinking subject would not bring what both men desired: something that lay beyond human reason and beyond the human subject (April 8, 1876; 1:256–67). Much was at stake for Tolstoy's learned correspondent: "Your attempts both tempt and frighten me. If you fail, if you feel doubts, this will be worse for me than my own failures and doubts. Because I believe in you; I expect revelations from you, like those revelations that I have found, in such quantity and such power, in your poetic works" (1:257). It was then that Strakhov told Tolstoy that the form he had chosen to express his view on life did not show him at his best: "You are trying to contain your views in the formulas of general knowledge. I am certain that the results . . . will be one hundred times more impov erished than . . . your poetic meditations. Consider, for instance, whether I can place the view on life diffused in your [literary works] above what Schopenhauer or Hegel or anyone else has to say about life?" (April 8, 1876; 1:257). He turned the conversation to readers' reactions to the published in- stallments of Tolstoy's novel (Chapters 7–20 of Part Five appeared in April): "*Anna Karenina* is arousing admiration and rancor such as never before in literature" (1:258).

But Tolstoy did not want to hear praise for *Anna Karenina* (1:259). As for Strakhov's response to his philosophical letter, he again rejected his inter- locutor's interpretations, but he hoped that Strakhov will nevertheless un- derstand him: "I am afraid that I cannot say what I want to. . . . I hope that you will understand even that which is ill expressed." Tolstoy made another attempt to make himself clear, naming the one principle that embraced "ev- erything" (the living and the dead, the "I" and the "non-I"), namely: "the living God and the God of love" (April 14, 1876; 1:261).

Strakhov began his response immediately, but he mailed his unfinished "*philosophical letter*" (1:27; emphasis in original) much later, as an addendum to a mundane letter of May 8, 1876: "You see in the world the living God and feel his love. Now your meaning is clear to me, and I can, I feel, tell you frankly that it can be developed logically in the same strict form as other phil- osophical systems possess. It will be a pantheism, the fundamental principle of which will be love, just as the will is for Schopenhauer, as thought is for Hegel" (1:263). Tolstoy did not respond. He would resume their philosophi- cal correspondence only six months later (November 12–13, 1876; 1:291). In the summer of 1876, Strakhov twice visited Yasnaya Polyana, where the two men continued their philosophical conversations in person, but we do not know what was said.

At this point, the correspondence appears to have reached a dead end: Mounting philosophical propositions did not seem to bring Tolstoy any closer to answering questions about the meaning of life and death. Moreover, he did not seem encouraged by Strakhov's responses—his learned friend's attempts to rephrase his reflections in the language of professional philosophy, to relate them to existing traditions.

While the regular exchange of the philosophical letters proper came to a halt, another topic came to the fore in their continuing correspondence: *Anna Karenina*. Over the course of the year, Strakhov again and again tried to turn the conversation to Tolstoy's unfinished novel.

"I Wish that You, Instead of Reading *Anna Kar[enina]*, Would Finish It. . . ."

Tolstoy was increasingly irritated by Strakhov's exhortations to return to *Anna Karenina*. He reproached Strakhov, who continued to write literary criticism, for "paying tribute to Petersburg and to *littérature*" (January 1–2, 1876; 1:244). (Tolstoy expressed his disdain for the institution by using the French spelling.) Literature—an institution comprised of professional authors, publishers, critics, and foundations—disgusted him, and he found the writing profession morally dangerous because readers' praise corrupted the author by fueling his vanity (1:259). Strakhov responded with intense emotion: "You are losing your usual calm and, it seems, you want me to advise you to cease printing Anna Karenina and leave the thousands of readers who are all asking and waiting for how it will end cruelly in the dark? . . . You've worked me up into such a state of agitation, as if I had to write the end of the novel myself" (late April 1876; 1:264–65). Strakhov also reproached Tolstoy for failing to respond to the reflections on the novel that he had shared in his letters: Did he correctly understand the book's "idea"? (1: 264).[6] Tolstoy finally rose to Strakhov's challenge: "[Y]our opinion of my novel holds true, but this is not everything—that is, it's all true, but what you've said is not everything that I wanted to say" (1:266). What he wrote next has often been cited by scholars as Tolstoy's aesthetic credo:

> But if I were to try to say in words everything that I intended to express in my novel, I would have to write the same novel I wrote from the beginning. . . . In everything, or nearly everything I have written, I have been guided by the need to gather together ideas which for the purpose of self-expression were interconnected; but every idea expressed

separately in words loses its meaning and is terribly impoverished when taken by itself out of the connection in which it occurs. The connection itself is made up, I think, not by the idea, but by something else, and it is impossible to express the basis of this connection directly in words. It can only be expressed indirectly—by words describing characters, actions and situations.

He gave an example: the scene of Vronsky's suicide, highly praised by Strakhov. When Tolstoy was revising this chapter, Vronsky, "completely unexpectedly" for him, the author, "but quite decidedly, proceeded to shoot himself" (April 26, 1876; 1:267). Tolstoy then leveled his anger at literary critics: "And if critics now already understand what I want to say . . . then I congratulate them and can confidently assure them *qu'ils en savent plus long que moi* [that they know more than I do]" (April 26, 1876; 1:267 68).[7]

Twentieth-century literary critics tend to read this much-quoted formula as a claim of art's superiority over other forms of expression, affirming art's ability—and Tolstoy's—to produce inexhaustible meaning, perhaps to express the inexpressible. But at precisely the time Tolstoy coined this formula, he was considering retreating from literature and abandoning *Anna Karenina*. In this context, we may read Tolstoy's words somewhat differently: as an admission of art's inherent inability to deliver a clear message and a complaint about the author's lack of control over his text. Indeed, rather than struggle with the vicissitudes of artistic form, Tolstoy now wanted to find a form of expression that would allow him to say, in words, what he wanted to, would allow him to say "I," and would convince instantly. It seemed to him that philosophical discourse, while it also required careful "linking," offered such a possibility. But he had not yet found a "method" that held such power.

Rather than give in to his friend's insistent appeals to return to literature, Tolstoy tried to convince Strakhov to follow his example: "Give up literature altogether and write philosophical books. Who else is there? Who else will say what we think?" (November 12, 1876; 1:293). But Tolstoy must have known that the real problem was *how*: how to put what one thought into words, either in a novel or in any other form? While Strakhov begged him not to leave thousands of readers in the dark, Tolstoy himself did not know "how it would all end." Addressing Strakhov, he grumbled: "I wish that you, instead of reading *Anna Kar[enina]*, would finish it, and rescue me from this sword of Damocles" (July 31, 1876; 1:276).

After the April 1876 issues, the publication of *Anna Karenina* came to a halt. At the end of July, still nothing had appeared in press. The April installment had ended with the all-important chapter describing the death of

Levin's brother, Nikolai, the only chapter in the whole novel to have a title: "Death." With this chapter, autobiographical material started to play a larger and larger role in the novel. In relating the death of his character's brother, Tolstoy (as scholars have noted) drew on the most painful experiences of his own life: the death of his brothers, Dmitrii in 1856 and Nikolai in 1860. What is more, he wrote from his own concurrent emotional experience: his increasing preoccupation with death and his desperate longing for faith.

When he did finish the novel (in April 1877), Tolstoy ran into difficulties with the publication of the last installment, which added to his frustration with the institution of literature. The story is well known. In brief, Mikhail Katkov, the editor and publisher of the journal *Russian Herald* (Russkii vestnik), in which *Anna Karenina* had appeared in installments since January 1875, refused to publish Tolstoy's epilogue because of its politically troublesome criticism of the Balkan war. Instead, in the May 1877 issue of the journal, the publisher issued a brief statement to the effect that, while the author still planned to add a short epilogue, with the death of the heroine, Anna, the novel was basically finished; the rest of the characters were alive and well. Strakhov helped the enraged Tolstoy to publish the epilogue as a separate brochure, which appeared in July 1877. The epilogue was of the utmost importance to Tolstoy: It focused on the philosophizing of his increasingly autobiographical character Levin, culminating in his conversion to a yet-inexpressible faith. Tolstoy then entrusted Strakhov with the task of preparing the first book edition of the novel, in which the epilogue turned into Part Eight, making Levin's philosophizing an integral part of the novel.[a] As their philosophical correspondence went on, Strakhov was busy reading the proofs and suggesting revisions (the book appeared in 1878). In a way, he really did finish *Anna Karenina* for Tolstoy.[8]

Immediately after the completion of the novel, in late July 1877, the two men made their long-planned pilgrimage to the monastic community Optina Pustyn', whose members were known to advise laymen and even hear their private (non-sacramental) confessions.[9] By all accounts, the two friends discussed their personal difficulties in embracing faith with the elders. (One of them, Father Pimen, fell asleep during the debate, which Tolstoy found especially inspiring, as we will see.)[10]

But with all that had been said and done, Tolstoy continued his desperate search. His autobiographical character Levin (whose surname was derived

---

[a] Of all the readers' reactions to *Anna Karenina* that Strakhov reported to Tolstoy, there was one that brought him joy: This reader was deeply affected in his own thoughts not by the "purely novelistic part" but "by L. N.'s philosophy" or, as Strakhov explained, by "Levin's philosophizing" (1:363).

from Tolstoy's own Christian name) finds a solution to his crisis: not in the kind of faith that could be expressed in a formula or credo but in a faith that filled his heart, as a "sensation." But Leo (Lev) Tolstoy, the author who refrained from clearly articulating Levin's newly found faith in words, did not find a solution to his personal crisis. Obviously, Tolstoy was unable to share his character's conviction that there was "no need to speak." In the epilogue to the novel, Levin concluded that faith was "a mystery needed and valued by me alone and inexpressible in words." But Tolstoy, in his nonfiction, was still searching for the verbal means of speaking about his faith to others.

After all, with everything the author and the character shared, there was an important difference: Levin is not a writer; he has not written *War and Peace* and *Anna Karenina*.[11] The gentleman-farmer might accept, for himself alone, a faith inexpressible in words, but not Tolstoy—the man who, even when writing a letter to an intimate friend, felt that he was reciting a *profession de foi* to which the whole of humankind attended (1:230).

"In the Form of Catechism," "In the Form of a Dialogue"

There were, of course, established forms for expressing faith. In November 1877 (not long after the completion of *Anna Karenina*), Tolstoy wrote to Strakhov that he had heard a priest teaching his children a lesson in Orthodox catechism and, finding it odious and unconvincing, tried to write his own: "to express, in the form of catechism, what I believe in" (1:374). This attempt, too, showed Tolstoy how "hard" it was; he even feared that, for him, it might be "impossible." As often happened in these years, he felt overcome with despair (November 6, 1877; 1:374).

Tolstoy's "Christian Catechism" (*Khristianskii katikhizis*) opens with a formula of his personal creed: "I believe in the one true holy church, living in the hearts of all men and on all the earth" (PSS 17:363). (This sounds like an echo of "Profession de foi du vicaire Savoyard.") But when Tolstoy passed to the standard sequence of questions and answers, he found himself in difficulty. The first question ("What is necessary for the soul's salvation?") found a clear answer ("A clear definition of what we believe in"). But the next question—"What is faith?"—led to a deadlock (PSS 17:364). The Catechism remained unfinished.

There is a rough draft of a yet another unfinished piece, "A definition of religion-faith" (*Opredelenie religii-very*). In this fragment, Tolstoy coined a new term, "religion-faith," and he focused on the word itself: "the word religion-faith is the word. . . ."[12] "Clear and unquestionable" as it might be for believers, for those who did not believe (or "thought that they did not believe"), this word needed definition (PSS 17:357). The untidy piece of paper (torn and crumpled as if discarded in despair) runs less than half a page and ends in a half phrase (PSS 17:781; undated).

After these failures, Tolstoy embarked on an extensive reading of the works that "define religion, faith." Strakhov—who was employed at the Imperial Public Library in St. Petersburg—sent him books. In late November, Tolstoy reported that he was in the process of assembling a set of historical and philosophical studies of religion, including D. F. Strauss, Ernest Renan, Max Müller (whose study included information on non-Western religions, in particular the Vedanta tradition of India), Émile Burnouf (also known for bringing Vedantic and Buddhist thought to Western Europe), and Vladimir Soloviev (December 17–18, 1877; 1:385). Tolstoy asked about Lao Tzu (Laozi), whom Strakhov knew from a French source, and about Hindu, Buddhist, and Iranian religious thought. Two weeks later, he acknowledged that he felt "lost" in the thoughts of others (January 3, 1878; 1:389).

Still another attempt to define his faith was a literary dialogue, entitled "Interlocutors" (*Sobesedniki*), which Tolstoy started on December 20, 1877. In form, Tolstoy's piece resembles a Platonic dialogue. It is a conversation involving seven participants who debate one topic: What is faith? Tolstoy defined the participants by their social roles and ideological positions, suggesting concrete prototypes: a "healthy idealist philosopher," aged forty-two ("Fet—Strakhov—Schopenhauer—Kant"); a "natural scientist," who speaks for progress, aged thirty-seven ("Virchow—Dubois Raimond—Tyndall—Mill"); a "positivist," aged thirty-five ("Bibikov"); a "clever priest" who denies reason, aged fifty-six; a "dialectical thinker" who justifies faith by sophisms, aged fifty ("Khomiakov—Urusov"); a "monk," aged seventy ("Father Pimen . . . sleeps"); and, finally, the "I," aged forty-nine and named "Ivan Il'ich."[13] Here we gain a clue to what Tolstoy may have seen in his real-life correspondent, Strakhov (an idealist approximating Kant or Schopenhauer). For his imaginary dialogue, however, Tolstoy expanded the team of interlocutors.

The "priest" and "monk" are clearly based on the elders Tolstoy had met during his recent pilgrimage with Strakhov to Optina Pustyn', where he was especially impressed with the sincerity and simplicity of Father Pimen.

The participants in Tolstoy's dialogue discuss whether or not faith might be justified by different types of knowledge—science, pure reason (according to Kant), "dialectical reason," and experience (*opyt*). The "I" (Ivan Il'ich) initially attempts a definition of faith, tries to circumvent the arguments of his interlocutors, momentarily insists on the "subjective ethical principle," and finally "comes over shy and finds himself in a pitiful situation" (PSS 17:371).

Exactly a year later, December 20, 1878, Tolstoy returned to his unfinished dialogue, now reworking it as an interchange between two interlocutors. After several pages, Tolstoy stopped and addressed himself: "I wanted to express the thought that had come to me directly in the form of a dialogue and I got into a muddle" (PSS 17:373). He continued in a diary of sorts, with dated entries, asking himself again and again, "Where is the source of faith?" "What am I?" Like his other such projects, the dialogue was a failure.

In an April 1878 letter to Strakhov, Tolstoy described how he had tried to access faith by yet other means: at Easter, he had participated in the long-neglected Orthodox rites. In the same breath he reported that he had read the Gospels and Renan's *Vie de Jésus* (1:429). But nothing helped. The ritual repelled him. The Gospels, rather than telling the story of Christ and his teaching, indulged in miracles that were hard to believe. Renan, on the other hand, presented Christ as a man "who definitely worked up a sweat and went to the loo" (1:430). Both ways were unacceptable.

To summarize, for more than three years now, Tolstoy had been trying to elucidate his religious views or define his *profession de foi*, but all of his attempts—an intimate correspondence with a like-minded friend, a philosophical essay, a catechism, a literary-philosophical dialogue—came to naught. His correspondent, Strakhov, was implicated in many of these attempts, and he heard Tolstoy's confessional reflections on his attempts to define his faith, his frustration with *Anna Karenina*, his disillusionment with *littérature*, and his despair.

Tolstoy confided his struggles with faith to yet another trusted friend, his longtime confidante Alexandra Tolstaya. To her, he described his relations with Strakhov and explained the reason for their difficulties: "I have a friend, Strakhov, a scholar and one of the best people I know. We are very much alike in our religious views: we are both convinced that philosophy provides nothing, that one cannot live without religion, but we are unable to believe. This year we plan to go to Optina Pustyn'. There, I will tell the monks about all the reasons for which I cannot believe" (February 5–9, 1877; 62:311). This is a remarkable admission: both Tolstoy and his learned friend lacked the immediate experience of faith.

To Tell One's Life

In January 1878, Tolstoy sent Strakhov a brief private report entitled "On Searching for Faith" (*Ob iskanii very*). He returned to the initial Kantian questions posed in November 1875, reiterated that all three could be easily expressed by one—"What am I?"—and affirmed his conviction that "reason did not, and could not, say anything in response." He who sought answers to such questions, Tolstoy noted, was not alone. Billions of people have been tormented by these questions and have received vague answers in the depth of their souls. These answers lay in religion. That much was clear. But when one tries to formulate such answers in words, they seem meaningless. What follows this conclusion is a remarkable formulation about the inability of language to offer solutions to the problems of life: Such answers are "meaningless simply by virtue of the fact that they are expressed by the word. . . . As expression, as form, they are meaningless, but as content, they alone are the truth." But the question remained: how, then, to access that "truth" that lies apart from words? People, Tolstoy now claimed, give their answers "not by words, the instrument of reason . . . but by their whole lives, by their acts, of which the word is only one part" (January 27, 1878; 1:399).

Strakhov responded that he did not share Tolstoy's trust in religion: He could not even read the Gospels, finding them unclear (February 3, 1878; 1:402). Tolstoy sadly acknowledged: "I see that my way is not your way" (February 7, 1878; 1:405). Two months later, he expressed his disappointment in his fellow traveler: In all this time, Strakhov had not covered much distance on his way to faith (April 8, 1878; 1:423). Strakhov eagerly admitted his failures: Tolstoy expected something from him but "got nothing"; he proved to be incapable of firm belief: "Yes, such am I. . . ." (April 11, 1878; 1:428). Still, he worked hard to research various existing views on religion in books. Tolstoy responded that it was precisely this immersion in other people's views that was to blame (1:429). Then, he made another demand on Strakhov: "You've lived through two thirds of your life. What has guided you [*chem vy rukovodilis'*], how have you known what is good and what is evil? This is what counts—tell your own self and tell us. . . ." (April 17–18, 1878; 1:429). With this, Tolstoy embarked on a new attempt: to profess one's faith by speaking about one's life.

Strakhov did try to meet Tolstoy's new expectations; first he rephrased Tolstoy's question: "You ask me: how have I lived up to this point?" His answer—his "confession"—focused on his inability to engage actively in life: "You ask me: how have I lived up to this point? Well this is how: I have never really lived. . . ." He then hesitantly develops this proposition: I have lived for no reason. I didn't so much live as submit to life or accepted life . . . I have lived in vain, that is, I haven't lived. Strakhov concludes: "Here is my confession to you" (April 25, 1878; 1:432–33).

But Tolstoy was not satisfied. He made it clear that this was not what he expected, and he brought up the question of faith: "I hope that we shall be able to discuss the subject of our correspondence in person. In brief, what's strange to me is why you are not a believer. And this is just what I've been saying, though probably awkwardly and not so clearly" (May 5–6, 1878; 1:434). In the weeks that followed, Tolstoy kept insisting but remained vague about what it was that he expected from his correspondent: "I keep on at you about something that's tricky: give me a straight answer—how do you know that which has guided [*to, chem vy rukovodilis'*] and what guides you now in life?" (May 23–24, 1878; 1:439). A strange kind of "misunderstanding" had arisen between them (Tolstoy's word) (1:429).

In his next philosophical letter, Tolstoy responded to Strakhov's newly published philosophical study *On the Fundamental Concepts of Psychology* (*Ob osnovnykh poniatiiakh psikhologii*, 1878). Strakhov used the word *psychology* in its initial meaning: "the study of the soul." He focused mainly on Descartes and the implications of his famous proposition, "*Ego cogito, ergo sum.*" (Strakhov spells out the "ego" in the Latin formula generally known as *Cogito, ergo sum.*)[14] Descartes meant to emphasize not "thought," Strakhov claimed, but "soul." In Strakhov's reading, *Cogito, ergo sum* translates as: I am the soul. Subsequently, German philosophers distorted the meaning of this formula by reading the "cogito" as "I think," which gave rise to a whole philosophical path that privileged reason. From this point of view, Strakhov rejected both the German philosophical tradition and contemporary empirical ("materialist") psychology. It seems that Strakhov, his philosophical erudition notwithstanding, was now under Tolstoy's spell. Like Tolstoy at the onset of their correspondence, he was trying to define the notion of the soul. And he rewrote Descartes's definition of self, which forms the foundation of the whole system of modern Western metaphysics and epistemology, by replacing "thought" with "soul."[15]

Tolstoy read Strakhov's treatise with intense attention. He felt that Strakhov had proved "the falsity of Kant's and Schopenhauer's idealism as well as the falsity of materialism." What is more, Strakhov had defined the soul *en passant* ("as if incidentally"), which (Tolstoy noted) was the strongest and most convincing way to make a point. And yet Tolstoy felt that, on the whole, Strakhov was on the wrong track:

> Your merit lies in the fact that you have proved that philosophy—thought—cannot, in any manner, serve as the foundation for spiritual life, but your error lies in the fact that you do not admit that it is necessary that these foundations (if foundations are what they are) do exist . . . [those foundations which we] cannot possibly gain by reason, or by our very nature, and which are therefore given to us. It is in this sense

that I ask you: what do you live by—and you, about the most important thing, say in jest, mistakenly: I do not live. (May 29, 1878; 1:447)

But he again was unable to explain what exactly he meant by his insistent
question, "What do you live by?"

In the meantime, Tolstoy tried to tell his own life. In May 1878, he started
working on an autobiographical piece of sorts, calling it "My Life" (*Moia
zhizn'*). But this attempt remained unfinished: Tolstoy could not progress
beyond a few memories from his early childhood. ("My Life" and Tolstoy's
other autobiographical works are discussed in chapter 4.)

So, what did it mean to write one's "life"? Obviously, Tolstoy could not
give a straight answer. A clue may be found in his phraseology. He was not
asking, "How have you lived?" (as Strakhov took it) but rather, "What have
you lived by?" (*chem*). This formula can be found in Tolstoy's later writings,
most prominently in the introductory lines to his own translation and revision of the Gospels (written around 1880): "When I was led by reason into
despair and denial of life, I, looking at the people living around me, became
convinced that . . . people lived and live by faith [*liudi zhili i zhivut veroi*]"
(24:9). The phrase also appears in the title of one of Tolstoy's religious-
moralistic fables, "What People Live by?" (*Chem liudi zhivy*, 1881). Were we
to give a "clear" answer (something that, in his letters to Strakhov, Tolstoy
could not do or refrained from doing), it would be: To tell one's life means to
tell one's faith (that is, to tell one's faith one has to tell one's life).

The next step in their dialogue took place in a face-to-face meeting in
August 1878, which made Tolstoy's demands clearer to Strakhov. Returning
from his visit, Strakhov wrote to Tolstoy that, on his way back from Yasnaya
Polyana, he had decided to take up Tolstoy's challenge to tell his life, but not
as a "biography": "I will write *Instead of a Confession* and dedicate it to you"
(August 29, 1878; 1:458). Two weeks later, Strakhov confirmed his intention
to write a "not-autobiography":

But what value, what meaning does *my life* have? . . . In what tone is it to be
written? I could, I think, express a feeling of disgust most strongly of all:

> And I, repulsed, read the story of my life,
> I shudder and I curse . . .

> И, с отвращением читая жизнь мою,
> Я трепещу и проклинаю . . .
> (September 14, 1878; 1:463)

(Strakhov borrows lines from Pushkin's 1828 poem "Reminiscence" [*Vospom-inanie*]).

He also affirmed that Tolstoy was the sole addressee of his alternative confession: "I am prepared to write this for you, but for others—I wouldn't see the point" (September 14, 1878; 1:463). But Tolstoy declined. He was in such a troubled mental state—"not in himself"—that he could not properly respond to his friend's letter, much less hear a confession (October 27, 1878; 1:475).

A year later, the two friends were still discussing their plan to exchange self-definitions. This time, echoing Strakhov, Tolstoy affirmed that self-disgust was the most appropriate emotional key in which to tell one's life story for the benefit of others: "Write your life story; I still want to do the same thing. But we just need to set this up so as to arouse disgust for our lives in all our readers" (November 1–2, 1879; 2:540).

Thus, in 1879, it would seem, Tolstoy had in mind not a *profession de foi*, but a confession of sins and faults.

In response to Tolstoy's latest exhortations, Strakhov once again shared with Tolstoy his sense of uncertainty and clouded judgment: "It's very hard for me to judge my life, not just the most recent events, but also the most distant ones. Sometimes my life appears vulgar to me, sometimes heroic, sometimes moving, sometimes repulsive, sometimes unhappy to the point of despair, other times joyful. . . . These oscillations cause me great distress: I can't get any truth from myself! And it doesn't happen just in my reminiscences, but every day in all my affairs. I don't feel anything purely or directly, everything in me splits into two" (November 17, 1879; 2:541). Tolstoy reacted with a strong moral admonition. He took Strakhov's ambivalence as an inability to discriminate between good and evil: "You write as if to challenge me. And I know very well that you value my opinion, as I do yours, and so I'll tell you all I think. . . . The other is more visible than oneself. And I see you clearly. Your letter distressed me greatly. I have felt a lot and thought it over a lot. I think you are spiritually ill. . . . And it is impossible for you to write your life story. You don't know what is good and what is bad in it. And one needs to know." But he realized that he might have gone too far: "I don't think I will send this. I am very busy with work for myself, which I will never publish. Forgive me" (November 19–22, 1879; 2:545–46). This letter, indeed, remained unsent. The one Tolstoy sent instead focused on his own ongoing work.

Almost five years had passed since Tolstoy had "penetrated" his friend's soul (as he put it in his letter of May 5, 1875). In December 1879, he reevaluated his initial hopes that an interpenetration of two kindred souls would bring each to a higher state of self-awareness: "I was glad to look into your soul, since you opened it to me; but it has been distressing me that you are so unhappy, so troubled. I did not expect that. . . . You were not able to say what you have inside, and something incomprehensible came out. But you must not write your life story. You will not be able to" (December 11–12, 1879; 2:550). Before, he had urged Strakhov to speak out; now he was trying to shut him up.

Rousseau and His Profession/Confession

Let us pause to introduce a cultural precedent: Rousseau's attempt to define his *profession de foi*, which provides an essential context for understanding Tolstoy's endeavors.

In many ways, Tolstoy's position toward religion and faith in the nineteenth century was parallel to Jean-Jacques Rousseau's in the eighteenth. Indeed, Rousseau, too, placed himself between the two parties of his time, those who relied on reason and those who relied on the church, rejecting both: He, too, could not stand the materialists, and he located faith outside of the church, in the hearts of men.[16]

What is more, at a pivotal point in his life, Rousseau decided to abandon literature, and above all the profession of writer, with all the social falsity it entails. Holding pedagogy in higher esteem, he embarked on a pedagogical novel, *Émile, ou de l'éducation*, devoting its core part, "Profession de foi du vicaire Savoyard" (1762), to religion. This work considers a catechism lesson, taught to children by a pedantic priest, to be a "heart-breaking stupidity," better replaced with a confession of personal faith. Asking "What am I?" the narrator takes himself—a sense of his own being (beginning with the formula "I exist")—as the fundamental truth and the starting point of reasoning about the world.[17]

Rousseau's "Profession de foi du vicaire Savoyard" had a formative influence on Tolstoy's ideas about religion. (As he once put it, "Rousseau and the Gospel have been the two great and beneficent influences of my life.")[18] While the name of Rousseau does not appear in Tolstoy's writings on faith in 1874–79, his presence, especially that of "Profession de foi du vicaire Savoyard," is palpable. (The parallel, of course, is not complete: For one thing, Tolstoy did not follow Rousseau in claiming his senses as the foundation of truth; neither did he follow Rousseau in all aspects of his views on religion.) Below, I will focus on one concern that they shared: how to tell one's personal faith to others.

The purpose of this excursus is not limited to establishing a direct link between Tolstoy and Rousseau. It hardly needs saying that Rousseau, in the "Profession de foi du vicaire Savoyard" as well as in the *Confessions* and its sequels, provided articles of faith and strategies of self-expression that were subsequently used by generations of modern people, especially those who felt the need to formulate a religious belief apart from the established religion.

Scholars have sought the secret of Rousseau's impact in his ingenious use of form, genre, and ways of communicating with the reader, and I will rely on one such work.[19] To summarize a complex analysis in brief: The text of the "Profession de foi" carefully situated within *Émile* shows the hero, a "young man," in a conversation with his mentor, the Vicar, who not only entrusts his young friend with the profession of his personal faith but also "opens his soul," confessing intimate facts of his life, mainly his relationship to the church, religion, and faith. As the introductory narrative to the "Profession de foi" makes clear, before their decisive conversation the two friends routinely engaged in a reciprocal exchange of confessions. Thus, Rousseau's text uses two overlapping forms, the profession of faith and the confession of sins. And after the Savoyard Vicar makes his profession/confession to his friend, the latter comes to share his noncanonical faith. In the end, Rousseau's "Profession de foi" "achieves both a secularization of the profession of faith" (replacing it with a conversation about God between friends) and "a sacralization of the intimate, confessional dialogue," endowing it with the promise of faith and salvation.[20] Staged as a dialogue between two characters, this text invites the reader to enter into a similar dialogue with the author. It has been argued that after Rousseau (of course, not only "Profession de foi du vicaire Savoyard" but also his later *Confessions*), the story of religious confession and conversion was transformed into a secular autobiographical narrative. Thus, his "Profession de foi" pointedly addresses the problems of life (one's outlook onto the world) traditionally treated by religion in a secular fashion. What the "cultural work" performed by Rousseau ultimately achieved was a crucial step toward the "displacement of religion in favor of the autonomous sphere of art and aesthetics."[21]

And yet, arguably, neither Rousseau's "Profession du foi" nor many of the secular biographical narratives that followed have cut all of their ties to the initial Christian pattern and its theological meanings.

When, in the mid-1870s, Tolstoy invited his friend Strakhov to a confessional dialogue in which each was supposed to define his personal *profession de foi*, this whole tradition was at his disposal. With this in mind, I now return to Tolstoy in his correspondence with Strakhov.

The Parting of Ways: Tolstoy Writes His *Confession,* and Strakhov Continues to Confess in His Letters to Tolstoy

In a decisive letter of November 22, 1879, Tolstoy described his ongoing work, "not fiction and not for publication" (2:547). In late December 1879, when Strakhov visited him at Yasnaya Polyana, Tolstoy shared this work with his confidant. Scholars believe that this was a preliminary variant of Tolstoy's *Confession.*

When he returned home, Strakhov affirmed his acceptance of Tolstoy's faith, describing the experience of religious conversion:

> Something has as if suddenly dawned on me, and I feel more and more joy and view everything in this new light. I will tell you in all honesty why I was confused earlier, and why your present idea seems so new to me. Individual immortality in the form in which it is usually presented always seemed so incomprehensible and savage to me; in just the same way, the mystical rapture reached by the majority of religious people who talk in almost the same terms as you has always been abhorrent to me. But you have avoided both of these; acute as may be the movements of your soul, you do not seek salvation in self-oblivion or immobilization, but in clear and living consciousness. My God, how good is this! When I remember you, all your tastes, habits, pursuits, when I remember that unfailing, vehemently strong disgust of yours for forms of falsity in life, which resounds through all your writings and is reflected in all of your life, then I begin to understand how you have finally arrived at your present point of view. It could only be attained through strength of the soul, only through that long and arduous work to which you have devoted yourself. Please do not chastise me for praising you; I need to believe in you, this faith is my support. I've long called you the most complete and consistent writer; but above and beyond that, you are the most complete and consistent man. I am convinced of that by my reason and by my love for you; I will hold on to you and hope that I am saved. (January 8, 1880; 2:552)

It seems that Tolstoy's profession of faith—a faith devoid of belief in individual immortality—and, still more, the example of Tolstoy's life finally allowed Strakhov to believe. He addressed Tolstoy as his confessor and savior. Tolstoy—a layman—became for Strakhov a kind of holy elder, like those the two friends had visited in Optina Pustyn'.[22]

As to the work in which Tolstoy was then involved, Strakhov alone was taken into Tolstoy's confidence, and he found a way to tell others without betraying this trust: "I *usually* say that you are writing a story of your relations to religion, a story that cannot appear in press." He also said that Tolstoy had reached this position by getting closer to the "people" (that is, peasants) (January 8, 1880; 2:553).

Thus, addressing Tolstoy, Strakhov came up, *en passant*, with a simple definition of what it was that Tolstoy was writing as his "life" (a subject on which Tolstoy remained vague): a private history of his relationship to religion.

In the years that followed, Tolstoy and Strakhov continued to correspond, but Tolstoy's letters lost their confessional quality after 1879.

Not so for Strakhov, who continued to address his "confessions" to Tolstoy: "I will speak as if at confession" (November 29, 1881; 2:624); "I need to address God. And so, I want to confess before you. . . ." (May 2, 1895; 2:994). In one such letter, speaking about his own role as a thinker who did not carry his arguments to any conclusion, Strakhov evoked an "illustrious precedent" for such an exchange of thoughts: Plato and his "conversations," which "did not have definitive conclusions." He begged Tolstoy to write at least a few words in response to his "confessions" (August 24, 1892; 2: 911). But Tolstoy had long since withdrawn from this philosophical dialogue.

Strakhov, in letters to his other friend and confidant, Ivan Sergeevich Aksakov, expressed his skepticism about the theological writings Tolstoy produced after 1880. Yet, even when he wrote in a critical mode (addressing one of Tolstoy's critics), Strakhov drew a distinction between Tolstoy's—"poorly written"—professions of faith and the man himself as he knew him in direct and intimate contact: "Everything Tolstoy writes concerning his abstract interpretation of Christianity is *very poorly* written; but his *feelings*, which he is entirely unable to express but of which I have direct knowledge through his facial expression, his tone of voice, his conversations, are imbued with exceptional beauty. There is so much of everything in him; but I am struck, and forever will be struck by his *nature*, the Christian traits of his nature."[23] Here, Strakhov has put his finger on the essence of Tolstoy's struggle with his *profession de foi*: Tolstoy may have been unable to put it into words, but his "life"—his whole being—carried the message of sin, despair, repentance, faith, and salvation.

The correspondence between Tolstoy and Strakhov started at a time when Tolstoy, painfully unable to finish *Anna Karenina*, was eager to abandon *littérature* and the profession of the writer for another sphere and for another, as yet undefined, personal role. He was troubled by the nature of the message that literature delivered. In the course of this four-year philosophical dialogue, he became equally troubled by the shortcomings of philosophical discourse. He was looking for a form of expression that would offer solutions to the questions about the meaning of life: Linked into a "single whole," it would convince instantly. Only such a form of expression (and not a set of philosophical propositions) befits a profession of faith. But, as he came to realize, when one tries to formulate answers to such questions as "what am I?" and "how do I live?" or to tell one's faith, these formulations become meaningless simply by virtue of the fact that they are expressed by words.

The intimate conversation between two friends took the place of confession and profession of faith. In this sense, Tolstoy seemed to reenact Rousseau's "Profession de foi du vicaire Savoyard." But if Rousseau's "Profession de foi" (and Rousseau's later *Confessions*) had inaugurated the new autonomous sphere of art and aesthetics, Tolstoy, more than a century later, tried to do just the opposite: to return personal writing to the religious domain, which alone held a promise of truth.

But in the years 1874–79, "faith" was not yet a creed for Tolstoy: Faith was envisioned as a thing of the future, an end product of ongoing activity or experience. His letters transcribed this experience as it unfolded. I hope to have shown how this correspondence dramatizes the double process of searching for faith and for an expression of such a personal faith that offered answers to the essential problems of life. The two interlocutors may have understood each other better in their face-to-face conversations, aided by facial expression and tone of voice (or so Strakhov thought), but the correspondence, while retaining some of the immediacy of speech, had advantages for Tolstoy. Whether he liked it or not, he thought his life and faith through mostly in writing. In this case, he used a form, correspondence with a friend, that allowed him to convince the other but did not require him to verbalize his final conclusions in any clear way.

This epistolary dialogue proceeded slowly and hesitantly. Tolstoy started in the vaguely autobiographical mode, quickly moved to abstract philosophizing, ran into a deadlock, and returned to the idea of writing his own life. When Tolstoy sought a response to his philosophizing, he invited his interlocutor to object, then rejected Strakhov's objections (made from the point of view of existing philosophical knowledge). He kept insisting on the truth of his convictions, accepted the difficulty of expressing them in words, and demanded nevertheless to be understood. When Tolstoy turned to the autobiographical mode, he started by seeking help from his correspondent by urging him to write *his* life, but, in the end, he withdrew his request.

Attempting two different modes—writing about "faith" and writing about "life"—Tolstoy seems to have hoped to come up with a synthetic form. He posited "faith" as something that was derived from lived experience as well as something that propelled one's life forward. Consequently, to profess one's faith was to tell one's life—not as autobiography but as the story of the development of one's religious convictions. (It was his correspondent, Strakhov, who formulated this principle.)

Throughout the correspondence, Tolstoy was unclear and imprecise—perhaps not only because he found it difficult to express himself but also because he believed that truth and faith eluded verbal expression.

To describe his situation, I will again turn to Tolstoy's correspondence with Alexandra Tolstaya. In February 1880, when his confessional-professional correspondence with Strakhov came to a halt (at least on Tolstoy's part), he tried to exchange professions of faith with his devout cousin. She succeeded, but this did not inspire Tolstoy: "You told your faith only because you said what the church says." For his part, Tolstoy wrote: "To tell one's faith is impossible. . . . How to tell that which I live by? I'll tell you, all the same. . . ." (63:8). I suggest that this same paradoxical position manifests itself in Tolstoy's philosophical correspondence with Strakhov in 1874–79: "How to tell that which I live by? I'll tell you, all the same. . . ."

What next? As we have seen, in 1879 Tolstoy was busy with a long work that would combine the itinerary of personal conversion with the theological principles of his new faith; as he wrote to his confidant, he strained his whole being and suffered from constant headaches. In 1882, contrary to his initial intention, Tolstoy released for publication the first part, under the title *Introduction to an unpublished work*; circulating among readers, this work soon came to be known by another title, *Confession*. He envisioned this first, confessional part as an "introduction" to his yet unpublished (indeed, yet unwritten) theological studies: his profession of faith. (The story of the *Confession* will be told in the next chapter.) Tolstoy's *Confession* invited even those readers who did not enjoy personal intimacy with the author to share in his search for faith and salvation. The relationship between writer and reader held out a promise of salvation.[24] This was not *littérature*.

CHAPTER THREE

Tolstoy's *Confession*: ~~What Am I?~~

Tolstoy Publishes His Confession

In late 1879, Tolstoy (as he wrote to his confidant Nikolai Strakhov) was intensely involved in a work that was not fiction and not for publication. More than two years later, in April 1882, Tolstoy read his work to an old acquaintance, Sergei Iur'ev, the editor of the journal *Russian Thought* (*Russkaia mysl'*), who told him that what he had heard had left an indelible impression on his soul as well as a strong desire to publish Tolstoy's essay (23:520). Contrary to his original intention, Tolstoy submitted his work for publication. Yet, until the very last moment, he could not decide what to call it. On the manuscript that he sent to the typesetters, the title is crossed out: "~~What am I?~~" (~~Что я?~~). The final set of proofs is dated "1879," and it contains a postscript dated "1882."[1] When Tolstoy's essay was typeset for the May 1882 issue, it bore the title *Introduction to an Unpublished Work* (*Vstuplenie k nenapechatannomu sochineniiu*). But before it could appear, the publication was banned by the ecclesiastical censorship, which ordered that the whole print run be burned. However, the work was soon circulating illegally, mostly in lithographed copies of the proofs and hand-copied versions.[2] Before long, family members, friends, editors, and reviewers alike started to call the work "Confession." When it finally appeared in print, in 1884 in Geneva, the title page read: *Confession of Count L. N. Tolstoi. Introduction to an Unpublished Work* (*Ispoved' grafa L. N. Tolstogo. Vstuplenie k nenapechatannomu sochineniiu*). After 1884, Tolstoy, too, called his work the *Confession*.[3]

The Conversion Narrative: Excursus on the Genre

Tolstoy's *Confession* presents the key moments in the religious life of its author-hero: the falling away from the faith in his youth, the adoption of a surrogate religion that supported his adult years, a "stoppage of life" in suicidal despair at the age of fifty, and a long search for God culminating in an "awakening" at the time of writing. Arguably, this story falls into an established form with a long tradition in Christian culture: the conversion narrative. In this sense, the *Confession* is neither a work of fiction nor an autobiography.[4] A brief excursus on the conversion narrative will help to situate Tolstoy's text.

In the Judeo-Christian tradition, the act of conversion is understood as a change in the inner self that restores one's relationship to God: the return of a wayward man to the source.[5] (The concept, it has been noted, has a certain ambiguity: It refers both to the abandoning of one faith for another and to a change to a more exacting attitude toward the faith one already has.)[6] The conversion narrative relies on an autobiographical plot that moves from the origins to the present and includes a hiatus—a break in the continuity of life and self.[7]

The roots of the conversion narrative are usually traced to Augustine's *Confessions*, the text that is often viewed as a general prototype for self-narratives in Western culture, one that cuts across genres and across denominations. A paradoxical effect of the conversion narrative, as established in Augustine's *Confessions*, is that it destabilizes the self. Conversion marks a rift between two "I's". The author who writes the narrative is no longer the person who lived the life it describes.[8] There is a potential disjunction between the "I" that refers to the author, who stands behind the whole narrative, and the shifting "I" of the protagonist, whose identity keeps changing as the narrative progresses through his past life. The very act of writing serves both to separate and to connect the two "I's." Staging the death and resurrection of the self, narratives of conversion may create the effect of speaking from beyond the grave.[9]

In Augustine, the word *confession* has a complex meaning: he "confesses" his sins (*confessio pecati*), as seen from the point of his conversion; he praises the Lord, in the biblical, psalmodic sense (*confessio laudis*); and he "confesses" his faith before mankind.[10] After the *Confessions*, in such theological studies as *On the Trinity* and *The City of God*, confessions are replaced by professions of faith, which Western Christianity was to adopt.[11]

Augustine famously drew attention to the problematic nature of his own self: "And I turned toward myself, and said to myself: 'Who are you?' I replied: 'A man'" (10.6.9). But the crucial question was addressed to God:

"What am I, my God? What is my nature?" (10.17.26). (Throughout his narrative, Augustine consistently follows the "I-Thou" structure.)[12] Augustine's *Confessions* is "prayer, not literature."[13]

The meaning of this double question has been explicated by Hannah Arendt: "In brief, the answer to the question 'Who am I?' is simply: 'You are a man—whatever that may be'; and the answer to the question 'What am I?' can be given only by God who made man. The question about the nature of man is no less a theological question than the question about the nature of God."[14] The answer lies in reestablishing contact with the divine: For a wayward man, a turn to himself is the beginning of an ascent on the road to God and thus a step toward conversion.[15]

Telling his whole life story (in Books 1–7), Augustine is concerned with the relationship between himself in the present, after his conversion to the Christian faith (to be described in Books 8 and 9), and himself in the past, as an infant, child, young man, and adult. He speaks of his infancy and childhood (Book 1), his wayward adolescence (Book 2), and his youth, focusing on the seductions of sexual desire (Book 3) and on another type of seduction—the arts and rhetoric, which are eventually seen as a "false religion" (Book 4). After the death of a close friend, he is plagued by a "sense of being tired of living and scared of dying": "I had become to myself a vast problem" (these words from Book 4 are repeated in Book 10). Books 5 through 7 cover a short span, dwelling on Augustine's associations with the false religion of the Manichaeans and on his secular ambitions. The "birthpangs of conversion" to the true faith, which come to a climax under a fig tree, are described in Book 8, followed by Augustine's experience of his mother's death in Book 9, which allows him to embrace the beneficence of death. The conversion is now complete. In Books 10 and 11, Augustine moves from the biographical narrative to philosophical reflections on memory, time, and eternity, presenting man as the image and likeness of God, and in Books 12 and 13, he interprets the Scriptures in a way that connects faith and the church to the world.

The post-conversion part of the narrative is very different. As one scholar put it, "once conversion has done its work, the past of experience 'catches up' with the present of writing, and narrative retrospection ends"; the post-conversion self moves toward its own effacement *as self*: Life on earth becomes pure expectation of the otherworldly life, which is beyond time, space, and narrative.[16] (In the last four books of the *Confessions*, Augustine presents not his life but an elaborate set of philosophical and theological principles.)

Scholars believe that in the centuries to come, the Augustinian narrative of the self was transformed in texts ranging from Descartes' *Discourse on Method* (frequently treated as a conversion autobiography of sorts, culminating in the formulation of the Cogito) to Puritan and Pietist conversion memoirs in the seventeenth and eighteenth centuries to secularized autobiographical narratives, a trend that begins in the eighteenth century, with Rousseau's *Confessions*.

Puritan narratives plot conversion as a falling away from and return to the faith, and they often focus on the very process of change in the self: The plot usually starts with melancholy and suicidal temptations and leads to an "awakening." Thus, English Puritans describe conversion not as a point in time but as a long journey. After the initial "awakening" begins a trial of mental and physical anguish that may continue for years, even for a lifetime.[17]

Rousseau's *Confessions*, it is often claimed, marks a turning point in the narrative of self: The experience of conversion and the act of confession are now transposed from a religious to a secular mode.[18] For Rousseau—a deist, not an atheist—God is still present in the act of confessing. (What is more, Rousseau imagines himself appearing at the Last Judgment holding the copy of his *Confessions* in his hand.) But "while Augustine, befitting a God-centered view, confessed his soul to God, Rousseau, as a measure of the degree to which the world had become secularized," primarily addresses his fellow men.[19] Like Augustine, Rousseau, in his *Confessions* and its sequels, the *Dialogues* and the *Reveries of the Solitary Walker*, asks: "*Que suis-je moi-même*"? (What am I?).[20] But, unlike Augustine, who addressed this question to God, Rousseau thinks that all he has to do is make his soul into an open book, rendering it transparent to the reader. Rousseau (it has been argued) experiences his true being as his own inner self: an autonomous self. With Rousseau starts a long tradition of modern secularized confession and autobiography.[21]

The act of conversion is still present in Rousseau's *Confessions*, but its result is very different than in Augustine's. The central conversion in Rousseau's narrative is his decision (in the famous episode on the road to Vincennes) to enter the competition that was to launch his literary career. As Rousseau makes clear, under the oak tree he instantly became "another man": an author (one who writes about how the progress of the arts and sciences have contributed to the corruption of man). Thus, his conversion is secular. What is more, it rests on a contradiction.

According to Rousseau the author of the *Confessions*, his turn to writing (and his successful literary debut) was a curse: From that moment he was lost. In writing his *Confessions* to the end, Rousseau disavows years of authorship and abdicates the role of writer. This creates a paradox: Rousseau writes in order to proclaim his renunciation of writing.[22] It has often been claimed that Rousseau's *Confessions* became the text that enabled the subsequent production of secular autobiography. But there is more: Rousseau provided both a way of defining the secular self through autobiographical, literary writing and a way of renouncing the writer's self as inauthentic.[23]

In the end, Rousseau both reaffirmed and transformed the Augustinian pattern of conversion and confession: He created a secular narrative of the self, but in a way that cannot be understood without reference to the religious model.[24] His *Confessions* show both how much the world had changed from Augustine's time to Rousseau's and how much it longed to be the same.[25] It can be argued that this text contains the potential for another reversal: a turn from the secular, literary mode back to the religious mode.

This complex heritage stands behind Tolstoy's work. Indeed, the form of Tolstoy's *Confession* and its (acquired) title invite readers to compare his work to both Augustine's and Rousseau's. Many scholars have made such a comparison, either claiming or denying a direct connection.[26] But we may gain more, I think, by tracing the specific workings of the patterns of the conversion narrative in Tolstoy's text.

With this in mind, let us turn to the text itself. Surveying Tolstoy's *Confession* step by step, I hope to show its narrative structure, with a view to locating Tolstoy in a tradition that rests on two pillars, Augustine and Rousseau.

Tolstoy's *Confession*: Step by Step

> I was baptized and brought up in the Orthodox Christian faith. I was taught it in childhood and throughout my boyhood and youth. But when I abandoned the university at the age of eighteen, I no longer believed any of the things I had been taught. (23:1)[27]

Thus begins Tolstoy's *Confession*. The work features a strong authorial "I," but it becomes clear as the narrative unfolds that there is a complex play between several different kinds of "I." For one thing, as befits a conversion narrative, the authorial, writing "I" is not necessarily the same person as the "I" of the protagonist, whose identity keeps changing over time. What is more, while the "I" mostly draws on biographical facts, one also encounters the allegorical "I" of a conversion narrative. It would be impossible to unravel all the mingled meanings of the narrative "I," but I will point to those strong moments in which the split becomes palpable.[28]

Of the author's childhood, boyhood, and youth, the narrative says next to nothing. Chapter 1 describes his "falling away from the faith" (*otpadenie ot very*), which is common for men of his social circle and level of education. The reasons seem obvious: In our time, religious doctrine has become disconnected from life. Faith "thaws away" under the influence of knowledge and experience that conflict with it, and "a man of our circle and education" can live for ten or twenty years without once remembering that he is living among Christians (23:2). The question arises: What, then, drove *my* life? From his current vantage point, the answer is clear: back then, "my faith . . . or that which I lived by" was a secular belief in self-improvement, but "moral self-improvement" was soon replaced by a "desire to be better not before oneself or before God, but before people" (23:4).[a]

Chapter 2 surveys the ten years of "my youth," listing experiences typical for the whole social class (the landed gentry): "I killed men in war and challenged men to duels in order to kill them. I lost at cards, consumed the labor of the peasants, sentenced them to punishments, lived in lust, and deceived people" (23:5). This sequence of biographical events is then translated into a religious idiom: "Lying, robbery, sexual sins of all kinds, drunkenness, violence, murder—there was no crime I did not commit. . . ." (23:5). A rhetorical operation has effectively converted an autobiographical narrative into a confession of sins.

It should be noted that "sexual deeds of all kinds" (*liubodeianiia vsekh rodov*) play a large role among Tolstoy's sins. In the *Confession,* he does not say much about sexual desire, but elsewhere—in his early and late diaries and in his late fiction—he dwells on this topic incessantly and in considerable detail, ultimately making the complete renunciation of sex (even procreative sex) central to his conversion.

But this is not all. The list of sins continues: "During that time I began to write from vanity, covetousness, and pride" (23:5). (Tolstoy uses the biblical, Church Slavonic vocabulary: *tshcheslavie, korystoliubie, gordost'.*) Writing appears as a product of three of the eight cardinal sins.[29] Indeed, Tolstoy makes clear that this is not the story of his life, which is yet to be told ("Someday I will narrate the touching and instructive history of my life during those ten years of my youth") but a religious act of confession (23:4).

The narrative then tells how, at the age of twenty-six, "I" returned to Petersburg after the war, joined the rank of writers, and adopted their view of life, summarized as follows: "Life in general goes on developing, and in this development we—men of thought—have the chief part; and among men of

---

[a] In one draft, Tolstoy notes, with regret, that, judging by his diaries, his youthful drive for moral self-improvement was informed by "secular writings, ancient and modern," primarily Franklin and Rousseau ("I still have the diaries from that time, which could interest no one, replete with Franklin tables and rules for self-perfection"; 23:488–511).

thought it is we—artists and poets—who have the greatest influence. Our vocation is to teach mankind" (23:5). Tolstoy then switches to a vocabulary loaded with religious connotations: "This faith in the meaning of poetry and in the development of life was a religion, and I was one of its priests [*odnim iz zhretsov*]" (23:6). The word choice (the Russian word *zhrets* refers to pagan priest) makes it clear that, from his present vantage point, faith in literature or art is a pagan cult. So "I" lived for a considerable time, until "I" began to question the "infallibility of this religion." Having begun to "doubt the truth of the authors' creed," "I" became convinced that "almost all the priests of that religion, the writers, were immoral." This led to a split in the self and, as a result, to a loss of the false faith: "These people revolted me, I became revolting to myself, and I realized that that faith was a fraud." Examining his past situation from the vantage point of the present, the writer finds a contradiction: "But strange to say, though I understood this fraud and renounced it, I did not renounce the rank these people gave me: the rank of artist, poet, and teacher" (23:6). He condemns this modern religion as a form of pagan worship, acknowledging his own participation in the cult. The stage is set for his conversion to the true faith, but the time has not yet come.

At this point, Tolstoy pauses for a social commentary: He reflects on the parasitic existence of intellectuals. Thousands of workmen labored day and night printing millions of words "we" produced. And in order to justify this state of affairs "we" devised a theory: "All that exists is reasonable. All that exists develops. And it all develops by means of enlightenment. And enlightenment is measured by the circulation of books and newspapers. [A]nd we who . . . write books and papers, are the most useful and the best of people" (23:7). Here, Tolstoy aims his heavy irony at the theories of progress, specifically at Hegel and Hegelianism.

Chapter 3 covers "my" life between the ages of thirty and fifty. The first trip to Europe bolstered a false faith in "progress." It was momentarily shaken by witnessing two deaths. One was a public execution by guillotine in Paris: "When I saw the head part from the body . . . I understood, not with my mind but with my whole being, that no theory of the reasonableness of our present progress could justify this deed" (23:8). Another was his brother's death: "He fell ill while still young, suffered for more than a year, and died painfully, not understanding why he had lived and still less why he had to die. No theories could give me, or him, any reply to these questions" (23:8). Here, Tolstoy presents death as a major argument against the secular idea of progress. But, at the time, "these were only rare instances of doubt, and I actually continued to live professing a faith only in progress" (23:8).

Next, Tolstoy's narrative comes to his first crisis of faith, when he decided to abandon literature and authorship and turned to teaching peasant children. From his present position, this, too, looks like a fraud: "This work was [more] to my taste because in it I did not have to face the falsity which had become obvious to me when I tried to teach people by literary means. . . . In reality I was revolving around the same insoluble problem, which was: How to teach without knowing what to teach" (23:9). The narrative briefly dwells on a second trip abroad, where the author hoped to learn how to teach from the latest achievements in pedagogy, and a short stint of public service in the year of the peasants' emancipation, 1861. Then, we see how, overcome with despair and despondency, "I" withdrew to the wilderness of the steppe populated by nomads to live an "animal life" (23:10).

These are events with verifiable biographic reference to the author, Leo Tolstoy. But the life of the protagonist is described in the religious discourse of faith and doubt, and it is plotted as a preparation for the crisis yet to come, followed by a decisive turn from false faith to true.

The narrative then quickly covers the next "fifteen years," when family life—marriage, children, and the household—kept "despair and despondency" at bay. But in all these years (the author admits) he "continued to succumb to the temptation of writing" (23:10). (It is not mentioned that Tolstoy wrote *War and Peace* and *Anna Karenina* in these years.)

About "five years ago" (the numbers do not necessarily tally, but Tolstoy marks the passage of time in relation to the presentness of writing), he began to experience moments of perplexity, which recurred more and more often, expressed by the questions "What for? And what comes next?" (23:10).

Chapter 4 starts with the assertion "My life came to a stop" (23:11). This chapter describes the author as a man hiding the rope to keep from hanging himself from the rafters of the room where he undressed alone every night; a man who no longer hunted, lest he should yield to the temptation of putting an end to himself with his gun. And this took place at a time when he ought to have been completely happy (23:12). These details point to the author's (Leo Tolstoy's) biography, but this is also a literary reference, bringing to mind *Anna Karenina* and its character Levin, whose suicidal despair are likely to have been memorable to readers. What is more, this is a confession of yet another sin: *acedia* (melancholia or despair). (In Orthodox Christianity, *acedia*, along with lust, avarice, and vainglory, counts as a capital sin.)[30]

Extended metaphors are then mobilized to describe the situation of the protagonist who has come face to face with his own mortality: We see the "I" as a pilgrim who has ascended the summit of his life, contemplating both its ends; the "I" at the edge of a precipice, hovering in limbo over the abyss; the "I" lost in a forest. At this point, the autobiographical, author-referential "I" seems to have been replaced with the allegorical protagonist of a standard conversion narrative.

An "Oriental fable"—the story of a traveler surprised in the desert by a wild beast—works to illustrate the protagonist's situation. Seeking to save himself from the fierce animal, the traveler jumps into a dry well, but at the bottom of this well he sees a dragon waiting with open mouth to devour him. The unhappy man clings to the branches of a wild bush that grows out of a crack in the wall; while his hands weaken, threatening him with certain death, he licks the drops of honey he finds on the branch of the bush. "This is no fable," the author concludes, "but the literal incontestable truth, which everyone may understand" (23:14). This fable is borrowed from a collection of Orthodox spiritual readings, *Prolog*, which could be found in every Russian household.[31] Fables, parables, and allegories are, of course, common in spiritual autobiographies, such as John Bunyan's *Pilgrim's Progress*, which Tolstoy knew well.[32] Claiming an allegory borrowed from the Christian spiritual literature as "literal" truth, Tolstoy, a modern man and a well-known author, sends a strong signal to his reader: He offers his own life as a paradigm to which every reader can relate.

Chapters 5 to 16 describe, in allegorical terms, the gradual process of change in the self, which constitutes the core of conversion narratives. The protagonist is a lonely pilgrim, a seeker after the meaning of life and death. In chapter 5, he searches in the sciences, "natural" and "speculative," but finds that natural sciences do not pose such essential questions as "What am I?" or "What do I live for?" or "What shall I do?" and that speculative knowledge fails to answer these questions (23:19).

Chapter 6 applies the old metaphor of being lost in the forest to the situation of the modern man, "wandering between the clearings of experimental knowledge . . . and the darkness of speculative knowledge" (23:21). The voice of Ecclesiastes speaks for the protagonist: "Vanity of vanities, says Solomon, vanity of vanities—all is vanity. . . ." (23:23). He summons Solomon, Socrates, Schopenhauer, and Buddha: Their words confirm that life is a senseless evil.

In chapter 7, the protagonist takes his search from the area of abstract knowledge to that of "life." Having observed his contemporaries, he defines four existing solutions. The first is ignorance (not knowing that life is an absurdity); the second is epicureanism ("licking the honey within reach"). The third is suicide ("thankfully, there are means for that: a rope round one's neck, water, a knife to stick into one's heart, or the trains on the railways").

The fourth is to do nothing while knowing the true state of things. The protagonist finds himself in the last category (23:27–28).

In chapter 8, the protagonist abandons the class of educated men to consider the life of the "simple working people" who see the meaning of life not in reason but in a form of knowledge that lies apart from reason. This leads to a paradox: In order to comprehend the meaning of life, one has to renounce reason—the very faculty that seeks the meaning of life.

Chapter 9 addresses this paradox. Retracing the steps of his reasoning, the author-protagonist finds a methodological mistake. He has asked about a meaning that lies apart from time, causality, and space but seeks an answer within time, space, and causality (23:33–34). Up to this point, he has followed in the footsteps of Schopenhauer, but now his last fellow traveler is left behind, and the "allegorical Tolstoy confronts his doubts and his hopes alone."[33] He asks again: "What am I?" And answers: "A part of the infinite" (23:36). The seeker confronts the necessity of faith: Faith is the force we live by (23:35).

In chapter 10, the seeker studies varieties of religions, including Buddhism and Islam, but most of all Christianity; he studies from books as well as from the people around him, including simple, uneducated people. He realizes that it is this faith that must have sustained "the likes of me, Solomon, and Schopenhauer." His life journey takes a decisive turn: "So I went on for about two years, and a revolution (*perevorot*)[b] took place in me which had long been preparing and the dispositions of which had always been in me" (23:40). The conversion seems to have taken place, and yet his journey is far from complete.

Chapter 11 elaborates on the new situation. The author-protagonist decides that his trouble has been not with life in general but with the life of the upper, educated classes, who are social parasites, focused on intellectual activity and art. He sees the truth in the life of simple, uneducated, working people: "I came to love good people, hated myself, and confessed the truth. Now all became clear to me" (23:41).

But in chapter 12, the "revolution" within the protagonist is still not complete. Furthermore, he now realizes that the conversion has been not a point in time but a gradual process. Looking back, he understands that throughout "the year" in which he was every minute driven to suicide, alongside the

---

[b] Here, Tolstoy plays with the etymological meaning of *conversion* (from the verb *convertere*, "to turn around") in its Russian variant, *perevorot*. In his *Confessions*, Augustine worked in a similar way with the root *vert*. Kenneth Burke, *The Rhetoric of Religion* (Boston: Beacon Press, 1961), 63–65, 135.

arguments of Kant and Schopenhauer regarding various philosophical proofs of God's existence, his heart kept languishing with feeling. Like a fledgling fallen from his nest in a tree, he longed for his mother: He longed for God (23:43–44).

The image of the forest and trees then turns from a metaphor into the setting for a real experience: the author-protagonist remembers one day in early spring when he was alone in the forest, listening to its noises. He thought, as he constantly did, about death. He did what he constantly did in these "three years": He sought God. (The chronology seems almost arbitrary, but marking the passing of time is important.) His thoughts went back to this quest. ""Well,' I said to myself, 'granted there is no God, no God that is not my idea, or representation'. . . ." (23:45). (The phrase, of course, recalls Schopenhauer.) And everything died in him. Then, he remembered God and felt that he had come to life again. The seeker then looked back at the cycle of death and rebirth through which he had passed in the years of his quest. The episode in the forest culminates in the sound of an inner voice and the appearance of light: "Why do I look farther? a voice within me asked. He is there: he, without whom one cannot live. . . . After this, the light shone within me and about me brighter than ever, and the light has never left me. . . . Just how or when the change took place I cannot tell" (23:46). This is, of course, the light by which God is manifest within the soul (an image from John 1:9, developed by Augustine).[34] Now the conversion seems to be complete. Indeed, the narrative has come full circle: The seeker has regained faith, "the same faith that had borne me along in my earliest days" (23:46). The last words of chapter 12 are: "and I again began to live" (23:47). (While Tolstoy does not use this formula, he is describing being born again.)

Chapter 13 cancels the seeming finality of conversion. To return to the faith of his childhood and his ancestors means accepting the Orthodox Church, that is, accepting faith steeped in gross contradictions and strange superstitions. The seeker does try "to avoid all arguments and contradictions, and tried to explain as reasonably as possible the precepts of the church" (23:49). Tolstoy does not comment on what is a gross and fatal contradiction: Having decided to avoid idle reasoning, his protagonist is nevertheless trying to explain rationally those principles of faith that, as he earlier claimed, lie apart from reason. The narrative builds up to a new crisis.

Chapter 14 describes how the protagonist attempted to rejoin the Church, culminating in a dramatic moment when he walks toward the altar to partake of the "body and blood of Christ" (to take communion after years of interruption). Approaching the "Gates of Heaven," he is stopped in his tracks by a movement of his own wayward heart (23:51).[35] Things get better when he partakes of the spiritual literature read by uneducated people (among other texts, *Prolog*, where he found the fable of the wanderer in the well). Ignoring the miracles that pervaded them, he treats such stories as fables that carry symbolic meaning ("fables illustrating thoughts," 23:52). But whenever he turns to the doctrines of the educated believers and to their theological books, he feels that he is approaching an abyss.

Chapter 15 starts with a remarkable confession: "How often I envied the peasants their illiteracy and lack of learning!" (23:52). The reason is clear: Because of their ignorance, the peasants could accept those precepts of faith that spelled utter nonsense to the Tolstoy of the *Confession*. Though he does not say this explicitly, Tolstoy has reached an important conclusion: Faith may be incompatible with reason and education.

The narrative then describes how the seeker lived for three more years: "in the situation of a catechumen" (23:53). This metaphor places him, a modern man, in the position of a convert from the first years of Christianity, in pre-Constantinian Rome.

At the outset of chapter 16, the seeker renounces the church and established religion. He is about to embark on the task of formulating the principles of Christian faith anew, as if from scratch. The results of this labor will be presented in the parts of his work that are still to follow. This promise concludes the main narrative.

"This," Tolstoy comments, stepping outside of his narrative, "was written three years ago" (23:57). What follows is a postscript added in April 1882, when Tolstoy was preparing his work for publication. The postscript relates a dream:

> Now a few days ago, when revising this for publication and returning to the line of thought and to the feelings I had when I was living through all of it, I had a dream.

The narrative provides a painstakingly detailed description of the dream:

> I dreamt that I lay on a bed. . . . And observing my bed, I see I am lying on plaited string supports attached to its sides: my feet are resting on one such support, my calves on another, and my legs feel uncomfortable. (23:57)

The dreamer realizes, with horror, that his body is precariously suspended over a bottomless abyss. This, it occurs to him, cannot be real:

It is a dream. Wake up! I try to arouse myself but cannot do so. "What am I to do? What am I to do?" I ask myself, and I look upwards. Above, there is also an abyss. (23:58)

When he looks up, into the "infinite space" of the "abyss" above him, the dreamer feels calm and safe. What is more, he discovers that he is not alone:

As happens in dreams, a voice says: "Notice this, this is it!" And I look more and more into the infinite above me and feel that I am becoming calm. (23:58)

The dreamer now understands his position:

And then, as happens in dreams, I imagine the mechanism by means of which I am held; a very natural, intelligible, and sure means, though to one awake that mechanism has no sense. I am even surprised, in my dream, that I did not understand it sooner. It appears that at my head there is a pillar. . . . From the pillar a loop is hung very ingeniously and yet simply . . . so there could be no question of falling. (23:59)

This dream evokes the situation of the pilgrim suspended in a well from the fable related in chapter 4 of Tolstoy's *Confession*, replaying it to a happy end. It becomes clear to the dreamer that he is saved. He hears a voice that commands him to be a witness to this salvation:

And it seems as if someone says to me: "See that you remember." And I woke up. (23:59)

These words conclude Tolstoy's *Confession*.

At this point, the protagonist meets the author: The allegorical "I" of the conversion narrative merges with the biographical Tolstoy. What is more, experience and allegory have been fused. Were the author to sign here, "Leo Tolstoy," the name would be identical with both the "I" of the protagonist, who has completed his journey, and the "I" of the author, who has completed his narrative.

But the effect of this postscript does not stop here. It is significant that Tolstoy concludes his work with a dream rather than with an argument. Before he relates the dream, he explains: "This dream expressed in condensed form all that I had experienced and described, and I think therefore that, for those who have understood me, a description of this dream will refresh and elucidate and unify what has been set forth at such length in the foregoing pages" (23:57). Tolstoy returns here to the problem he first confronted in his philosophical correspondence with Nikolai Strakhov. It is the problem of the inexpressible ("to tell one's faith is impossible"). Reason does not offer solutions to the essential problems of life. "True philosophy," which is concerned with the "meaning of life," cannot possibly rely on logic, on "deductions and proofs"; one has to find a form of expression that rests on "the linking of disparate notions into a single whole," which convinces instantly.[36] Concluding his conversion narrative, Tolstoy abandons the language of reason in favor of the dream narrative. His dream conveys meaning mainly in symbolic images, which show, rather than tell, the truth. And this dream is not fiction. As Tolstoy told his secretary (who recorded this conversation in his diary): "I indeed saw this, I did not make this up."[37] (We have no reason to distrust Tolstoy: As his diaries indicate, he had quite a few allegorical dreams.) Tolstoy submits his dream, this evidence of his spiritual activity, as an emblem that expresses everything he "experienced and described." Thus, his *Confession* concludes with a move that replaces the narrative.

Tolstoy's *Confession* Related to Rousseau's and Augustine's

What is the place of Tolstoy's *Confession* in the tradition of conversion and confession whose pillars are Augustine and Rousseau?

To recapitulate, in the late eighteenth century, Rousseau had converted the Augustinian religious act of "confessing" into a secular literary practice while retaining the conversion plot and the word *confession*. With Tolstoy's *Confession*, I would argue, another revolution takes place. Tolstoy the protagonist converts to faith in God; Tolstoy the author converts the narrative of the self back to its religious meaning, as defined in Augustine's *Confessions*. Like Augustine, Tolstoy is confessing in a religious sense (and more than one): He is providing a testimony of his sins (hence the shocking insistence that the pursuits of his youth, common to many, were tantamount to a violation of the basic Christian commandments), and he is laying the foundations for a confession of his new faith (the *Confession* is an "introduction" to a theological work).

It should be noted that autobiographies centered on the author's uneasy relationship to religion were quite prominent in Victorian literature, across Europe. It suffices to recall James Anthony Froude's *The Nemesis of Faith* (1849), which tells the story of a tragic loss of faith; John Henry Newman's *Apologia Pro Vita Sua* (1864), describing the loss of false (Anglican) religion followed by a conversion to the restored truth of Catholicism; and the memoirs of the reformist theologian Ernst Renan, *Souvenirs d'enfance et de jeunesse* (1883), describing his loss of faith and search for another (which remains incomplete).[38]

And yet Tolstoy's *Confession* stands out among these works in its radical departure from the modern autobiography. Tolstoy does more than proclaim his return to faith (some of his contemporaries did this as well): He also proclaims his abdication of the rank of writer. What is more, he marks the beginning of a journey toward the renunciation of selfhood. Relying on seeds of doubt in the secularization of writing (the doubts that Rousseau himself had planted), Tolstoy renounces the literary form of modern autobiography. For Tolstoy, his *Confession* is not "literature."

Of course, Tolstoy's narrative is still a modern text. For one thing, his *Confession* is a fall-and-conversion narrative mapped historically and socially: It explicitly speaks about the situation of a man of his time, his class, and his education. A conversion narrative created in the image of Augustine's, Tolstoy's narrative is adapted for the needs of a modern man who has followed in the footsteps of Rousseau: a secular man who is equipped with elaborate literary forms, to which Tolstoy, as a fiction writer, himself had made a contribution, but who faces death without the protection of faith. And Tolstoy's profession of his new faith (soon to be provided) would present theological principles acceptable to this modern man.

In a historical perspective, Tolstoy's work is retrogressive: It attempts to go back to the original state. (It should be noted that, in this, Tolstoy followed Rousseau, who taught that mankind should move back, not forward.) But Tolstoy's *Confession* goes back in a way that takes full benefit of hindsight (of what transpired since Rousseau's revolution).

Of course, there are also significant differences between Tolstoy's *Confession* and Augustine's. Among other things, in this work, focused as it is on reproducing the generic pattern of the conversion narrative, Tolstoy, unlike Augustine, does not even purport to provide philosophical reflections on self and memory. (Tolstoy attempted to do this in equally "retrogressive" works of a different autobiographical genre, "My Life" and "Reminiscences," which will be discussed in the next chapter.)

After *Confession*: "Presenting Christ's Teaching as Something New after 1,800 Years of Christianity"

Tolstoy's *Confession* provided an account of his life and thought that led its author to the "conviction that truth lies in the Christian teaching" (23:519), but, as he made clear, his was a conversion that required a revision of the Christian teaching, one to be undertaken in a yet-unpublished, yet-unfinished work. By spring 1882, when Tolstoy decided to publish his confession, he was pursuing several lines of investigation in canonical theology, biblical exegesis, and the social critique of religion. The results were eventually released as three separate books. The *Critique of Dogmatic Theology* (*Issledovanie dogmaticheskogo bogosloviia*), written in 1879–80 and 1884, meticulously surveys and vehemently denounces the theological principles and liturgical practices of the "dead church" (specifically, but not exclusively, the Russian Orthodox Church), including the doctrine of the Trinity and the dogma of Christ's divinity. *The Four Gospels Harmonized and Translated* (*Soedinenie i perevod chetyrekh Evangelii*), written mostly in 1880, critiques all previous interpretations, Orthodox, Catholic, Protestant, and secular (such as Renan's), and offers Tolstoy's own translation and adaptation of Christ's story, stripped of miracles and purged of textual and biographical contradictions. There is also a condensed version, *The Gospel in Brief* (*Kratkoe izlozhenie Evangeliia*). Finally, *What I Believe?* (*V chem moia vera?*), written in 1883–84, presents Christ's teaching as a practical guide for individual conduct (derived from the Sermon on the Mount), which, if followed to the letter, would bring about the Kingdom of God in modern society.

All of these works, banned by censorship, were published (without the author's control) outside Russia, following a period of illegal circulation in hand-copied manuscripts and handcrafted editions. Some appeared in French or English before they were printed in Russian. There was at least one work, *The Four Gospels*, which Tolstoy did not consider finished at the time of its release. *The Gospel in Brief* was first released in 1881 as a condensed and abbreviated version created by Tolstoy's disciples. In each case, the text remained fluid, morphing from edition to edition. Over the years, *Confession* appeared in compilations with one or another work of this series, often under a title that marked it as an introduction to the exposition of the theological principles of Tolstoy's new Christianity.[39]

I pause here to make a comment that may help to clarify Tolstoy's plan. The Tolstoy archive contains a notebook of more than a hundred (barely legible) handwritten pages; this continuous narrative is loosely divided into five sections or chapters. Chapter 1 uses the biographical "I" to relate the condition of Tolstoy's "soul" at the moment when he looked back at his life and started thinking about his faith. Chapters 2 and 3 provide a critique of canonical theology. In chapter 4, Tolstoy again relates the evolution of his religious thought. Finally, in chapter 5, which occupies three quarters of the notebook, Tolstoy retells, for clarity, all four Gospels. In conclusion, Tolstoy tries to formulate the main precepts of his faith and to offer his critique of contemporary society from this point of view. This manuscript suggests that what eventually became a series of four works (from the *Confession* to *What I Believe?*) may have been conceived as one text.[40]

In the end, Tolstoy's core writings on religion (to which his *Confession* served as an introduction), along with scores of other tracts, essays, and pamphlets that appeared in later years, repeating and extending his core tenets, did nothing less than advance Tolstoy's own brand of Christianity. Detailed discussion of Tolstoy's theology lies beyond the immediate goals of this book, focused on the workings of the narrative of self, and it would be impossible to do justice to this vast topic, which has already been treated by many scholars.[41] In brief, this is a Christianity purged of everything (in theology, liturgy, and the story of Jesus Christ) that is not compatible with reason—a faculty that Tolstoy, hard as he tried, proved unable to shake off. Tolstoy rejected the authority of the church, and he found himself in a difficult relationship to Christ.[42] Thus, he embraced the teaching but not the sanctity of the life, death, and resurrection of Jesus.[c] Tolstoy's teaching, unlike Christ's, did not promise individual immortality (in the form of resurrection of the flesh). In this sense, Tolstoy is a deist, in the tradition of the Enlightenment.

He found the key to true religion in the Christian "law of love," understood both as a practical guide to social action (the love of one's brother) and as a metaphysical principle of man's unity with God. The philosophical implications of Tolstoy's interpretation of Christianity include his rejection of a temporal understanding of life: The true life is life in the present. The social and political implications stem from the emphasis on Christ's repudiation of "the law of an eye for an eye," which Tolstoy interpreted as a radical prohibition against all kinds of violence and coercion. This line of thought culminated in Tolstoy's principle of nonresistance to evil (to be discussed in chapter 5). Applied consistently to all social situations, this principle, Tolstoy thought, would lead to nothing less than the Kingdom of God on earth. In this way, he had reconnected Christianity to the practical tasks of living and dying in contemporary society.

To return to our immediate subject: Written in the first person, from the deliberately naive position of a man seeking personal understanding of

---

[c] Revealing in this respect is Tolstoy's blasphemous witticism, reported by a memoirist: "What interest is there in knowing that Christ went out to relieve himself? What do I care that he was resurrected? So he was resurrected—good for him! For me the important question is what am I to do, how am I to live." This *bon mot*, based on puns, works best in Russian: "Какой интерес знать, что Христос ходил на двор? Какое мне дело, что он воскрес? Воскрес—ну и Господь с ним! Для меня важен вопрос, что мне делать, как мне жить" (24:980; cited by Hugh McLean, 123).

Christian teachings, Tolstoy's theological tracts were part and parcel of his larger attempts to look for "answers to the question, what am I, what is God" (24:17). (This is how Tolstoy himself described his efforts in the introduction to his *Four Gospels Harmonized*.) It is to this end that he reread and rewrote the Scriptures. The two questions—"What am I?" and "What is God?"— were now fused into one and answered via theological, not autobiographical, studies. Like Augustine, in his *Confessions* and subsequent works on dogmatic theology, Tolstoy supplemented the story of his life (his conversion) with the theological foundations of a faith that he offered to others. For both authors, "confessions" were followed by "professions."

The parallel is not as far-fetched as it might seem: Like Augustine some fifteen centuries before him, Tolstoy purported to create, or recreate, the Christian doctrine. Religion, he felt, had become divorced from life, failing to serve the needs of contemporary men. As Tolstoy said (in the introduction to *What I Believe?*), he found himself in the strange situation of "presenting Christ's teaching . . . as something new after 1,800 years of Christianity" (23:335).

From a biographical perspective, the *Confession* responds to a double impulse to separate the two "I's" (the man whose life came to a stop and the man who is confessing) and to mediate between them, to mediate between the past and the future. As a classic conversion narrative, Tolstoy's *Confession* achieves a paradoxical effect: It creates a rift between the "I" who writes the narrative and the "I" who has lived the life it describes. At the end, with the "awakening," the former "I" catches up with the present of writing. But once the work of conversion is done, the "I" moves toward its own dissolution as self: The new, post-conversion self is beyond time and beyond narrative. Of course, Tolstoy's *Confession* receives its meaning from his previous reputation as a writer, but it signals a decisive change not only in his idea of the self but also in his concept of authorship. There is a separation between the "I" who is a writer (a member of a pagan cult of sorts) and the new, post-conversion "I." With his *Confession*, Tolstoy distanced himself from his career as an author of fiction. What is more, identifying the cult of the arts as a false religion, he renounced the institution of literature and the secular literary form.

From a historical perspective, Tolstoy tries to reverse the course of secularization: He resacralizes the autobiographical form inaugurated by Rousseau in his *Confessions* and tries to return this form to its roots in Augustine's *Confessions*.

Soon after the *Confession*, Tolstoy resumed, after a long interruption, his diaries, in which his personal struggle with "Who am I, what am I?"

continued, on a daily basis. As we will see (in the last chapter of this book), Tolstoy in his late diaries embarked on the impossible task of describing the form of self that lies beyond narrative. The older he got, the more he longed to stop being not only a writer but also an individual, to shed his self and his body so that he could be one with God. But, of course, Tolstoy continued to write: Contrary to his professed intentions, he would produce more fiction. He would even attempt to write a memoir or autobiography. The next chapter will turn to this topic.

Coda: Tolstoy's Influence

We do know that for quite a few people reading *Confession* and Tolstoy's subsequent religious writings would lead to a full religious conversion, similar to that experienced by Strakhov in Yasnaya Polyana in December 1879 (described in chapter 2).

Such was the story of Pavel Ivanovich Biriukov (1860–1931), who was a successful naval officer until he read Tolstoy. His fate was sealed by the emotional impact of a face-to-face meeting with the "prophet" in 1884. He eventually left military service and spent the rest of his life proselytizing Tolstoy's works. (Biriukov became personally close to Tolstoy and wrote an authorized biography, *Biografiia L'va Nikolaevicha Tolstogo*, published in four volumes between 1901 and 1923.) This is how Biriukov described his conversion: "The reading of Tolstoy's religious writings, first of all, *Confession* and *What I Believe*, immediately captivated me and put my life on a new track. What is more, these unparalleled works built a bridge over the abyss that I then faced in trepidation and allowed me to continue the path of life." (Biriukov adopts the symbolic vocabulary of Tolstoy's own confessional writings, including the image of the abyss, featured in the dream that concludes the *Confession*.)[43]

My other example concerns a person who lived far away from Tolstoy. Tolstoy's religious writings are believed to have had an enormous influence on Ludwig Wittgenstein (1889–1951). It was in August 1914, as a volunteer enlisted in the Austrian army in Galicia that the young Wittgenstein (as the story goes) "entered a bookshop, where he could find only one book: Tolstoy's *Gospel in Brief*. The book captivated him. . . . [H]e carried it wherever he went, and read it so often that he came to know whole passages of it by heart." He recommended Tolstoy's *Gospel* to people in distress. He later claimed that Tolstoy's *Gospel* had virtually "kept him alive." Facing the advancing Russians, Wittgenstein thought about death (which he believed was imminent).

As he wrote in his diary, "may I die a good death, attending myself." Thinking in Plato's terms, he was consciously striving to separate his spirit from his body (his body, he mused, belonged to the "external world," and "his soul must inhabit an entirely different realm"). Tolstoy's *Gospel* helped the young philosopher, who had lost faith in God during his school years, to become a believer. The ground for his thoughts about the spiritual value of facing death (and about the value of conversion) might have been prepared by his reading (in 1912) of William James's *Varieties of Religious Experience*—a work that includes a discussion of Tolstoy's conversion and his *Confession*. Tolstoy's influence played a role in Wittgenstein's decision to live among the rural poor and to teach peasant children (which did not go well) as well as in his later move to give up his enormous fortune (which resulted in his spending the rest of his life under conditions of extreme austerity).[44]

It has also been claimed that Tolstoy influenced Wittgenstein's philosophical views on the limits of language and his doubts in the efficacy of philosophy. Indeed, Wittgenstein's *Tractatus Logico-Philosophicus* has been shown to have parallels with Tolstoy's *Confession*. These parallels include Wittgenstein's treatment of the "problems of life," which (*Tractatus* argues) are not resolved by answers to scientific questions, and his general distrust of the meaning of language utterances. The parallels between Tolstoy and Wittgenstein appear still stronger when we consider Tolstoy's musings on the limitations of "the word" in expressing answers to the fundamental problems of life that appear in his private correspondence with Strakhov ("such answers are meaningless simply by virtue of the fact that they are expressed by the word," 1:399). Going entirely by the *Confession* (Tolstoy's private correspondence remains known mostly to Tolstoy scholars), some Wittgenstein scholars hear Tolstoyan echoes in Wittgenstein's central proposition on the inexpressible—something that "shows" itself but cannot be said, or the famous exhortation that concludes the *Tractatus*: "Whereof one cannot speak, thereof one must be silent." One such scholar has linked Wittgenstein's distinction between saying and showing and his emphasis on the importance of understanding the author's intentions (rather than the content of a book) with the prominent conclusion of Tolstoy's *Confession*. When Tolstoy concludes his book with a dream rather than with an argument, he "directs his reader away from the argument of the book as its proper result" and toward its influence on the reader. This is underscored by Tolstoy's own remark: "for those who have understood me, a description of this dream will refresh and elucidate and unify what has been set forth at such length in the foregoing pages." But there is (as it has been pointed out) an important difference between the two works: Wittgenstein intensely attempts "to head off the impulse that Tolstoy ultimately could not resist, namely, to speak where one cannot."[45]

The situation brings to mind the statement Tolstoy made privately (in a letter) in 1880: "To tell one's faith is impossible. . . . How to tell that which I live by. I'll tell you, all the same. . . ." (63:8). But in the years that followed the *Confession*, in his diaries, Tolstoy would speak about his growing desire to remain silent. As he once put it, "If this were not a contradiction, to write about the necessity to be silent, I would have written: *I can be silent. I cannot be silent.* I wish I could live by God alone. . . ." (January 6, 1909; 57:6).

CHAPTER FOUR

"To Write *My Life*": Tolstoy Tries, and Fails, to Produce a Memoir or Autobiography

Over the years, Tolstoy told his life in different forms. He did try, and more than once, to write his autobiography or memoirs but proved unable to complete any of these projects. How did he approach this task, and why did he fail?

The Author Biography

Let us start with the project that Tolstoy did bring to completion. In 1878, Nikolai Strakhov (the writer's intimate friend, editor, and correspondent) prepared selections from Tolstoy's fiction for the anthology *The Russian Library* (*Russkaia biblioteka*).[1] Acting on behalf of the publisher, Strakhov asked Tolstoy to provide biographical information. Tolstoy's wife took this task upon herself, and she was ready to send off the author biography, when Tolstoy intervened. As he wrote to Strakhov, the biography (based on the perusal of his letters and diaries) "turned out splendidly," but it was suitable "for me, and for me alone": "It is interesting for me to reconstruct my life in memory. And if God gives me life and I do some day decide to write my story, this will serve as a wonderful outline for me; but it is unthinkable to release this to the public" (November 22–23, 1878).[2] A few days later (exactly three months after his fiftieth birthday), Tolstoy sent Strakhov another letter, which contained a brief biography based on "facts." Embedded in a letter to the editor, this biography opens with the date of writing: "November

27–28, 1878. Yasnaya Polyana." Then, Tolstoy started: "Count Lev Nikolae-vich Tolstoy was born on August 28, 1828, in the village Yasnaya Polyana of the Krapivenskii district in the province of Tula, the hereditary estate of his mother, Princess Volkonskaya. . . ." Tolstoy follows the narrative outline of the biography, that is, a chronological narrative that presents his life as a list of dates, names, places, battles, and work titles: "In 1851 he went with brother Nikolai to the Caucasus . . . he joined . . . the 4th Battery of the 20th Artillery Brigade, which was housed in the village Starogladovskaya on the river Terek. In the Caucasus Count Tolstoy for the first time stated to write in novelistic form. He planned a large novel, the beginning of which comprised his *Child-hood*, *Boyhood* and *Youth*. . . ." He appears here not only as an author but also as the scion of a noble Russian family who served his country in war and in peace. The life story starts slowly, providing much detail about his family origins, childhood, boyhood, and youth, but moves much faster as his life un-folds. But only three brief sentences cover the crucial sixteen years (1862–78) in which Tolstoy fathered six children and authored two major novels (which are mentioned alongside his primers for peasant children):

> In 1862 Count L. N. Tolstoy married in Moscow Sofia Andreevna Bers. . . From that time on, he has been living permanently on his es-tate, Yasnaya Polyana, engaged in the education of his six children.
>   In these sixteen years, *War and Peace*, *The ABC* and *Primer for Reading*, and *Anna Karenina* were written.[3]

At the end, the narrative switches from the past ("was born," "joined," "start-ed to write," "married") to the present tense. The time and place of Tolstoy's recent life are frozen in the present: "From that time on, he has been living permanently on his estate, Yasnaya Polyana."

"My Life": "On the Basis of My Own Memories"

In 1878, Tolstoy made another attempt to describe his life. Recall that at the time he was involved in a philosophical correspondence with Nikolai Stra-khov that was focused on formulating their respective professions of faith and that in April he gave a new direction to their reciprocal search for self-definition, suggesting to Strakhov: "Write your life story. I want to do the same thing."[4] Scholars think that these plans eventually found fulfillment in Tolstoy's *Confession*, written approximately between late 1879 and 1882. But this is not all: He tried different modes and genres. The text I am about to describe is very different from the *Confession*, which follows an established pattern of the conversion narrative and features an allegorical self.

On May 22, 1878, Tolstoy noted in his recently resumed diary: "I started to write '*svoiu zhizn*'" (48:70). (Within days he would abandon the diary, which would not be resumed until 1881.) The key phrase is underlined and put in quotation marks. What does it mean to write one's own life?

The manuscript, entitled "My Life," opens with the date on which he started to write, anchoring his narrative in the present: "May 5, 1878." The first step came easily: "I was born in Yasnaya Polyana in the Krapivenskii district of the province of Tula on August 28, 1828" (23:469).[5] Then, Tolstoy paused to comment on his writing: "This is the first and the last comment I make about my life that is not based on my own memories" (23:469). As this aside suggests, this time, he found the narrative outline of the biography unsuitable. Indeed, the autobiographer could not write "I was born . . ." any more than he could write "I died."[6]

Tolstoy then made another comment on method, focusing on the difficulties of capturing the essence of one's life: to describe the external events that had led to the situation in which he found himself at the time (three months before his fiftieth birthday) would be much too easy; to describe what had made up his "soul" would be much too hard (23:469n). Tolstoy decided that he would consistently describe the "impressions" produced upon his mind by what he had experienced over the course of fifty years. He would refrain from making any inferences about the effects, or influence, that one circumstance or another had had on him but rather would describe what he had felt, inevitably choosing what left "stronger imprints" on his memory (23:469).

Like many of Tolstoy's life writings (beginning with his attempt, in 1851, to write a complete history of one day, "A History of Yesterday"), this was an experiment: He decided to write his life based solely on his memories. Where would the narrative take him?

Tolstoy started chronologically, with the first five years of his life: he named the first section "1828–1833" and proceeded to report his earliest memories. But first he noted that he could not arrange these memories in chronological order, not knowing what came before and what after, and, what is more, he did not even know whether what he remembered had happened "in a dream or in waking life." The first memory, described with astounding precision and insight, relates to the moral suffering of a swaddled infant:

I am bound; I wish to free my arms, but I can't do it. I scream and cry, and my cries are unpleasant even to myself but I cannot stop. Somebody bends down over me. . . . All of it is in half light, but I remember that there are two people and my cries affect them, they are disturbed by my cries, but do not unbind me as I want and I cry yet louder. They think that this is necessary (that I should be bound), whereas I know that it is not necessary, and I want to prove this to them, and I burst into a scream that is repulsive to me, but irrepressible. (23:470)

Tolstoy then admits that this memory, suggestive as it is of a very young infant, might be a product of several experiences, including a later episode, but he insists on the complete authenticity of the remembered "impressions":

> I do not know and will never know what it was: whether I was swaddled when a babe at the breast and tried to get my arms free, or whether I was swaddled when more than a year old, in order that I should not scratch a rash, or whether, as happens in dreams, I have collected many different impressions into this one memory, but it is certain that this was the first and the strongest impression of my life. And it is not my cries that are memorable to me, not my suffering, but the complexity and contradictions of the impression. I desire freedom, it interferes with no one else, and they are tormenting me. They're sorry for me, and they bind me, but I, who need everything, am weak, and they are strong. (23:470)

In this remarkable record, Tolstoy provides a clear example of what Sigmund Freud, using his own childhood memories, would describe two decades later as a psychological phenomenon: "screen memories." I will digress to compare Tolstoy's effort to Freud's.

As Freud put it, recollections of this sort are usually short, vivid scenes, constructed unconsciously, "almost like works of fiction" (Freud's phrase), and they amalgamate into one picture different impressions, including "residues of memories relating to later life." The subject sees himself as a child: He observes the child from the outside, but with the knowledge that the child is himself. Such memories serve as a "screen" onto which one projects later experiences. Thus, screen memories reflect not only what one purports to remember but also the concerns of the moment in which the "memories" were retrieved, verbalized, and recorded. In this sense, Freud called such memories "retrogressive": Operating from the vantage point of the present, one's mind moves backward (and pushes emblematic images of one's life to the distant past). But this does not mean, Freud insists, that these memories are not genuine: They are memories not *from* one's childhood but *relating to* one's childhood, and this may be all that we possess.[7]

In Tolstoy's case, we can read this memory of childhood as an emblem of the problems that preoccupied the fifty-year-old Tolstoy. The scene with the swaddled infant speaks about the dialectical condition of freedom and restraint, as defined in the reciprocal relationship of "I" and "they," and it shows the inherent inequality of power.

What is more, in describing his earliest memory, Tolstoy used imagery he may have remembered from reading Rousseau, who laments in *Émile* that subjection and constraint are imposed on man from birth, when he is tied in swaddling clothes, to death, when he is nailed into a coffin. As long as man keeps his human shape, Rousseau concludes, he is constrained by institutions.[8] Reinforced by this literary association, Tolstoy's first memory, furnished as it is with concrete sensory perceptions, is a composite image that speaks about the constraints on freedom that arise in the relationship between self and other. (Freud, it should be noted, also allowed for cultural references in screen memories and dreams.) A whole moral philosophy is projected onto the screen of Tolstoy's first infantile memory.[9]

Hard as he tried, Tolstoy could retrieve only one other memory from his infancy. The second image relates the intense feelings experienced by a naked child who sits in a warm bath, enveloped in a new, strange smell. "The novelty of this sensation" (Tolstoy suggests) led to an "awakening": The child has suddenly become conscious of his own body (and of his nanny's hands; 23:470).[10]

For a contemporary reader, these two scenes are remarkable for their descriptive power as well as for their psychological insight. Indeed, insisting on the authenticity of these infantile "impressions" as well as the complex origin of his recollections, Tolstoy seems to anticipate Freud's concept of construction in memory.

There are both similarities and differences between Tolstoy and Freud. Freud, in 1905, drew attention to the "infantile amnesia" that "hides the beginning of our childhood," and he purported to reconstruct such repressed memories in analysis.[11] He was distrustful of both infantile amnesia and vivid screen memories, claiming that such recollections concealed as much as they revealed. And yet, once they were interpreted, such memories (especially repressed sexual experiences or fantasies) testified to the hidden core of the true (albeit split) self formed early in one's life experience. Tolstoy (like Rousseau before him) insisted, contrary to common sense, on the complete veracity of his infantile memories and impressions. And he would not have subscribed to the idea of an essential self that opens its dark secrets in analysis. There is more: He wanted to remember a still earlier state of being.

Tolstoy was troubled that he could recover only isolated recollections: He could not recall how he was fed from the breast, how he was weaned, how he began to crawl, to walk, to speak. What is more, his observation on the failure of infantile memory led him to formulate a philosophical question about his origins: "When did I begin? When did I begin to live? And why is it a joy to me to imagine myself back then, while it used to be dreadful—as it is still dreadful to many people to imagine oneself then, at the time when I will again enter that state of death of which there will be no memories that can be expressed in words" (23:470). With these questions, Tolstoy evoked an age-old question (which goes back to Plato and Augustine): Does the self retain a memory of existence before birth and after death? Like Augustine before him, Tolstoy, a modern man, took the limitations of his memory not as a psychological phenomenon in need of analysis (as Freud would) but as a distant echo of the condition that the "I" inhabited before birth and would inhabit at the other end. The process of remembering led him to far-reaching questions: What, then, is "I"? When did it begin? When will it end? Within a few pages covering the first five years of his life, a modern autobiography gave way to theology of the self in the Augustinian mode.

The next section, "1833–1834," presented Tolstoy with other, technical difficulties: Approaching the sixth year of his life, he noted that there were too many memories, and it was difficult to separate, combine, and arrange them in time as an ordered chain of events.

He felt that in this as well as other respects, his early memories seemed similar to dreams. Focusing on a vivid memory from his sixth year, Tolstoy explored the analogy further: "I wake up, and my brothers' beds, my brothers themselves, who have already gotten up or are getting up, Fedor Ivanovich in his robe, Nikolai (our orderly), the room, the sunshine, the stoker, the wash basins, water, everything that I see and hear—all of this is only a change of dream" (23:473). These images hark back to the famous scene of awakening that opens Tolstoy's *Childhood*. But while then (in 1852), Tolstoy had used such a scene as a starting point for a novelistic plot, now (in 1878), it led him to a metaphysical question: how to distinguish between life and dreams? Tolstoy decided that, in the end, there was no difference between "nighttime dreams" and "daytime dreams." (This idea has a long philosophical lineage.)

In one's "nighttime dreams" one sees only what has been experienced in real life. From this it follows that what Tolstoy called "daytime dreams" (that is, impressions or memories of one's real life) might originate in another space, beyond this life (23:473). Thus, trying to capture memories of his childhood, Tolstoy stumbled upon religious questions about the origins and limits of individual life.

With these reflections, Tolstoy's first attempt to write his own life came to an abrupt end, practically in mid-sentence.[12] In the end, it proved impossible to write a story of one's life based exclusively on firsthand memories. For one thing, scattered recollections did not add up to an ordered, continuous narrative or story. What is more, Tolstoy did not always know what was real (what he remembered could have happened in a dream). Finally, Tolstoy seems to have felt that his memories did not adequately represent his true "I," omitting the crucial period before his birth.

"Reminiscences": "More Useful Than All That Artistic Prattle with Which the Twelve Volumes of My Works Are Filled"

Tolstoy returned to his intention to write his "life" only in 1901, at the request of his French publisher. Pavel Biriukov, his close associate and disciple, undertook the commission to provide the story of the author's life, and Tolstoy promised to write an autobiography for his use. But his initial eagerness soon gave way to habitual hesitations. This time, they were of a moral nature. When he attempted to write his "reminiscences" or "autobiography" (he used both words)[13] in the weeks preceding his seventy-fourth birthday, he confronted a "horrible" task: "to avoid the Charybdis of self-praise (keeping silent about all that was bad) and the Scylla of cynical frankness about all the abominations of one's life" (73:279). Tolstoy felt (as he explained to Biriukov) that writing with complete openness about his sins and weaknesses, in the footsteps of Rousseau, would be "seductive": "To describe all my odiousness, stupidity, viciousness, vileness—quite truthfully—even more truthfully than Rousseau—that would be a seductive book. People would say: here is a man whom many place high, but look what a scoundrel he was; if so, then for us ordinary folk, God permits it all the more" (August 20, 1902; 73:279). This time, he did not write anything at all.

It was during a serious illness, in December 1902, that, on a sleepless night, Tolstoy started dictating his reminiscences. In the years that followed (until 1906), he produced several installments, which he handed over to Biriukov, who was working on a multi-volume history of Tolstoy's life; it would take him twenty years to complete it.[14] As Tolstoy claimed, he had no intention of publishing his memoirs (74:141). Rather than write his life, he decided to provide raw materials, relegating the task of producing a story to another.

In a brief introduction to his "Reminiscences," Tolstoy (as was his habit) commented on the process: At first, he recalled mostly the good in his life, but during his illness, when his thoughts kept turning to his past, his memories were "horrible" (34:345). To convey his experience, Tolstoy cited Pushkin's famous "Reminiscence" (*Vospominanie*), which centered on the image of reading the book (scroll) of one's life:

> When memory her unending scroll unfolds
> In silence, with sick recoil I read
> The story of my life, and curse myself,
> And bitterly bewail with bitter tears—
> But I do not wash out the woeful lines.[15]

> Воспоминание безмолвно предо мной
> Свой длинный развивает список:
> И, с отвращением читая жизнь мою,
> Я трепещу и проклинаю,
> И горько жалуюсь, и горько слезы лью,
> Но строк печальных не смываю.

In 1878, Strakhov had cited these lines in his letter to Tolstoy, as the two friends discussed their plans for writing their lives. Now Tolstoy himself used them, but instead of "woeful lines," he wanted to say "shameful lines" (34:345). Remembrance was an act of moral reckoning.

Tolstoy read his life with disgust. Still, as he eventually realized, not all of his life was equally disgusting. He outlined four periods: one of innocence (up to the age of fourteen), one of sensuality and vanity (the next twenty years), one of family life and literary success (the next eighteen years, considered "moral" from a "secular point of view"), and, finally, one of self-abnegation, starting with his turn to "spiritual rebirth" and, he hoped, lasting to his death. It was from this vantage point that he now viewed his whole life (34:346–47).

Much was at stake: He wanted to write a story, or history, of his life (*istoriiu zhizni*) in all four periods, hoping that such a book would be more "useful" for people than all of his fiction, more useful "than all that artistic prattle with which the twelve volumes of my works are filled and to which people of our time attribute an undeserved significance" (34:248).

As he embarked on his "Reminiscences," Tolstoy reread his first work of fiction, *Childhood*, and found it "badly" written: It was "literary, insincere." Furthermore, the story was not based solely on biographical fact (34:348). As Tolstoy noted in his 1878 author biography, *Childhood*, *Boyhood*, and *Youth* were conceived as parts of a large novel; he had then called it *The Four Epochs of Life* (*Chetyre epokhi zhizni*), but the fourth part had remained unwritten.

Now, in his old age, he planned to write a fact-based, nonliterary life history, also in four periods, which would replace all of his fiction.

The brief introduction to the "Reminiscences" also includes an entry from Tolstoy's diary, made at the time when, gravely ill, he first confronted the memories of his past: "6 January 1903. I am now suffering the torments of hell: I am calling to mind all the abominations of my former life, and these memories will not leave me, and they poison my life. Usually people regret that the individuality [*lichnost'*] does not retain memory after death. What happiness that it does not! . . . What happiness that reminiscences disappear with death. . . . As things stand, with the annihilation of memory we enter into life with a clean white page upon which one can again write both good and evil" (34:346). As this diary entry reveals, underlying his "Reminiscences" and Tolstoy's earlier effort, "My Life," was the notion of memory that extended beyond the borders of human life.

There were both similarities and differences between "My Life" and the "Reminiscences." In "My Life," the fifty-year-old Tolstoy wondered about the period that had preceded his birth, asking himself, "Where did I begin?" In the "Reminiscences," the older, ailing Tolstoy focuses on another issue: "What will happen when I die?" Moreover, when he started "My Life," Tolstoy regretted the temporal limitations of human memory; now, he rejoices at the fact that personal memories stop at death. In his old age, remembering has come to be a moral burden.

Tolstoy did not seem to notice a contradiction: While rejoicing that individuality and memory disappear with death, he nevertheless imagined that, after death, life-writing might continue, albeit on a blank page. (In other words, death wipes the slate clean but does not bring the end of writing.)

"Reminiscences": "I Cannot Provide a Coherent Description of Events and States of Mind"

"I was born and spent my childhood in the village Yasnaya Polyana." With these words, Tolstoy opened his "Reminiscences" (34:351). He now understood that it would not be possible to proceed solely by way of memory, as he had in "My Life," and he started with the history of his family and ancestors. One thing was especially important: to recover a "spiritual image" (*dukhovnyi oblik*) of his mother, whom he did not remember (she died when he was not yet two years old). When he passed to his actual memories, he decided that he would not speak about "the vague infantile unclear recollections, in which one cannot yet tell reality from dreams" but start with what he clearly remembered.[16] When he later sent his "Reminiscences" to Biriukov, Tolstoy marked the places where his earliest memories, recorded in "My Life," belonged, connecting the two texts into one (34:375).

He described his father (chapter 3), grandmother (chapter 4), his two aunts (chapters 5 and 6), and a female companion of his childhood (chapter 7); then, he came to a pause. Chapter 8 starts with a discussion of his difficulties and hesitations: "The further I proceed in my 'Reminiscences,' the more indecisive I feel about how to write them. I cannot provide a coherent description of events and states of mind (*dushevnye sostoianiia*), because I do not remember the interconnection and the order of these states of mind" (34:372). The phrase *dushevnye sostoianiia*, translated here as "states of mind," is a calque of the French *états d'âme* (sentiments, dispositions), which, in both French and Russian, literally means "states of soul." In the first chapters of his memoir, Tolstoy described such states of soul: vivid scenes, complete with both precise details of the physical setting and an extended account of his emotions. But he felt unable to connect these scenes into a temporal sequence.

On several occasions, he tried to organize his memories in accordance with a spatial pattern, providing mental pictures of domestic spaces, described in minute topographical detail. (Whether or not Tolstoy was aware of the precedents, he was attempting an age-old mnemonic technique: mentally walking through the rooms of a familiar house.) But it soon became clear that it would be impossible to produce a life history by moving through the rooms of his childhood home (34:600).

Tolstoy tried yet another strategy: to order the narrative by describing, one by one, the people who surrounded him in his childhood. This, too, presented difficulties: He could not decide whether to stop with what he had known about members of the household at the time or to include what he now knew (34:372).

In the end, neither impressions of the states of his soul, nor visual images of the house of his childhood, nor a gallery of family portraits would add up to a story, much less a history, of his life. Tolstoy decided: "I will write at random, and without making corrections" (34:372).

As chapter 8 unfolds, he speaks about the family servants, moves to his brothers, starting with Dmitry, then remembers that he has yet to describe the servant Vasily (who figures in the dream of "A History of Yesterday"). Chapter 9 provides loving memories of Dmitry, ending with a guilty disclosure of Tolstoy's negligence and indifference at the time of his death. But before he describes Dmitry's death of consumption in 1856, Tolstoy pauses to make a philosophical comment: "How clear it is to me now that the death of

Dmitry has not destroyed him: he was before I knew him, before he was born, and he is now, after he has died. ~~How, where I don't know~~" (34:383; crossout Tolstoy's). As this comment reveals, as Tolstoy struggled with the technical task of arranging his memories into a narrative sequence, he held on to his hope for the continued existence of some form of self beyond the biological endpoints of individual life.

With the description of Dmitry's death, chapter 9 comes to a halt. Tolstoy noted: "I have abandoned the chronological form of narrating" (34:385). He decided to put his faith in the spontaneous workings of memory. This strategy brought results: "Yes, the Fanfaron Hill. This is one of the most distant and dear and important memories" (34:385).

This was a memory about his older brother Nikolai, from the time when Nikolai (Nikolenka) was ten or eleven years old and Tolstoy was four or five. (This scene has often been cited by Tolstoy's biographers and scholars.)

> He announced to us that he possessed a secret by means of which, when it should be disclosed, all men would become happy: there would be no diseases, no troubles, no one would be angry with anyone, all would love each other, all would become "Ant brothers" [*muraveinye brat'ia*]. He probably meant "Moravian brothers," about whom he had heard or had read, but in our language they were "Ant brothers."[a] . . . We even organized a game of ant brothers, which consisted in our sitting down under chairs, sheltering ourselves with boxes, screening ourselves with handkerchiefs, and, thus crouching in the dark, pressing ourselves against each other. I remember experiencing a special feeling of love and pathos [*umilenie*], and liking this game very much. . . . [The] secret, as he told us, was written by him on a green stick, which he had buried by the road on the edge of a ravine, at which spot, since my body must be buried somewhere, I have asked to be buried in memory of Nikolenka. Besides this little stick, there was also a certain Fanfaron Hill up which he said he could lead us, if only we would fulfill all the appointed conditions. . . . (34:386)

Next, Tolstoy's memories took him to his brother Sergei, but he soon returned to "ant brothers" to comment on the "state of soul" he experienced in this game: It was "the first experience of love, not love of someone in particular, but love for love, love for God" (34:391).

---

[a] The word for ant in Russian is *muravei*; hence the similarity with "Moravian" brothers.

Like Tolstoy's first memory—the suffering and protest of a swaddled infant who feels himself to be a victim of coercion—the image of the ant brotherhood follows the logic of Freud's "screen memories." Complete with vivid visual details and palpable emotions, this scene fuses memories and fantasies of Tolstoy's childhood with his current preoccupations. In his "Reminiscences," Tolstoy made the relevance of this childhood memory to his present situation explicit: "The ideal of ant brothers lovingly cleaving to each other, though not beneath two chairs curtained with handkerchiefs, but under the wide dome of the sky of all mankind, has remained the same for me. As then I believed that there existed a little green stick, on which was written that which could destroy all the evil in men and give them great welfare, so do I now also believe that such a truth exists, and that it will be revealed to men and will give them what it promises" (34:386). Tolstoy added several brief fragmentary memories, ending with another episode in which he was restrained, this time as a small child made to sit on an adult's lap; he experienced a "feeling of imprisonment, unfreedom, coercion" and protested with violent screams. But soon Tolstoy's "Reminiscences" came to an abrupt end, in mid-paragraph.

The whole text runs to some fifty printed pages, and it took Tolstoy more than three years to write them. There was no question of completing the history of all four epochs of his life: Tolstoy was unable to move beyond his early childhood. After 1906 he did not return to his project. Tolstoy's "Reminiscences" were first published (though not in full) in 1911, a year after his death.[17] By that time, these raw materials of his life had been put to use in Biriukov's biography. In the end, Tolstoy's fragmentary memories were incorporated into a coherent narrative produced by another.[b]

As he worked on his memories, Tolstoy often commented on his difficulties in his diary. On June 4, 1903: "Today I sat down to work: I wanted to continue with the 'Reminiscences,' but couldn't: it does not go" (54:177). A few months later he described a new strategy: recording his memories "out of order," or rather in the order in which "times, states, feelings" spontaneously came to mind, and in the same breath he noted his desire to give up editing any of his writings (August 17, 1904; 55:76). But nothing seemed to help. In

---

[b] In his biography, Biriukov cited Tolstoy's reminiscences at great length, identifying them, per the author's request, as the "uncorrected draft" of Tolstoy's memoir notes (*chernovye neispravlennye zapiski*). It should be noted that while Tolstoy indeed insisted that he would not "correct," that is, edit his reminiscences, his archive contains 259 pages of drafts (which I had the chance to examine). The State L.N. Tolstoy Museum (Gosudarstvennyi muzei L.N. Tolstogo, folder 104, 105, no. 90, 1–9).

the next three years, Tolstoy would note again and again that he had made abortive or failed attempts to recover and record his memories.[18]

One day, instead of writing his memoir, he mused about the general concepts of time and space that "delimit man on both sides" (June 4, 1904; 55:45). Switching into a theological key, he tried to rescue "life" from time: "Life, the true life, lies only in the present, that is, apart from time.... Always, in every moment of one's life, one can remember this, and transport one's life into the present moment, that is, into the consciousness of God. And the moment one does this, everything disturbing disappears: memories of the past, repentance, anticipation or fear of the future" (June 10, 1904; 55:48). In this passage Tolstoy redefines the very meaning of the word *to remember* (*vspominat'*), using it to mark those moments in which he recalls that life—the true being in communion with God—lies only in the present. This realization makes "remembering" in the conventional sense (recollection of concrete past experiences) obsolete. In the days that followed, he noted in his diaries the moments in which he did "remember" that time was no more (and consequently, that there was nothing to "remember" from his past).[19] At the time, his own past was very much on Tolstoy's mind: He was reluctantly reading the draft of the first volume of Biriukov's biography.[20]

"The Green Stick": "Où Suis-Je? Pourquoi Suis-Je? Que Suis-Je?"

We have seen how, after several attempts, beginning in 1878, Tolstoy remained uncertain what it meant "to write one's life." A profession of faith? A story of "my life" based solely on firsthand memories? A confessional memoir for the edification of others? When his "Reminiscences" came to a halt in 1904, he embarked on another project.

On December 1, 1904, he noted in his diary: "I started *Who am I*" (55:104). On a separate piece of paper, Tolstoy wrote a title: "Who am I?" He started by posing questions: "Where am I? Why am I? Who am I?" Then, he switched into French: "*Où suis-je? Pourquoi suis-je? que suis-je?*" (36:737). Yet another piece of paper from his archives reads: "~~Where am I? Why am I? Who am I?~~" (crossout Tolstoy's). It seems that here Tolstoy started again, crossed out the whole line, and again came to a stop. A few days later, on December 7, 1904, judging by his diary, Tolstoy started yet another project: "I started a statement of faith. . . ." (55:104). On December 11: "Stopped short in my statement of faith" (55:104). On March 9, 1905: "Wrote 'Who am I?' Neither good nor bad" (55:128). On April 6, 1905: "Yesterday I tried 'The Green Stick.' It didn't go. . . ." (55:133). After many trials and revisions, Tolstoy did produce a short essay, "The Green Stick" (*Zelenaia palochka*), whose title refers to the game from his childhood described in the "Reminiscences." He made no attempt to publish it.[21]

The essay starts with the image of a man awaking from sleep in a new, unfamiliar dwelling, having forgotten everything that had happened earlier. First, he would try to understand who had put him into this strange place and for what purpose (36:407). The next question he asked would be about the nature of his own origins:

> If I ask when did I begin, the real I, I will get a still less satisfactory answer. I am told that I came into being some years ago from my mother's womb. But that which came into being from my mother's womb is my body—that very body which for a long time did not know and does not know about its own existence and which very soon, maybe even tomorrow, will be buried in the earth. . . . That which I am conscious of as my *I* appeared apart from my body. That *I* began not in my mother's womb, and not upon emerging from it, when the umbilical cord was cut, and not when I was weaned from the breast, and not when I started to speak. . . . I have always been, but I have only forgotten my previous life. (36:407–8)

Tolstoy ends by admitting both his failure to define his own "I" and his firm belief that "I" is not the body alone: "I decisively cannot say what I am. I only know that I and my body are not one and the same" (36:408).

In 1878, in the unfinished memoir "My Life," which he attempted to write solely on the basis of his recollections, Tolstoy had also lamented—in similar terms—that he could not recall how he was fed, how he was weaned, how he began to speak (23:470). He intimated even then that his true "I" might be found beyond the temporary boundaries of this life. Now in 1904, in "The Green Stick," he attempted to create a narrative of the self not as a memoir but as a philosophical, or rather theological, self-definition. The answer to the question "Who am I?" could be obtained only, concluded Tolstoy, by making religion into the foundation of one's life: by living at one with God. From the perspective of autobiography, this question was unanswerable. In this essay, rather than speak about his life, Tolstoy reiterated the basic principles of his religious teaching.

With his "Green Stick," Tolstoy seems to have affirmed that the key to the mystery of the self did not lie in a narrative that started with "I was born on August 28, 1828, in Yasnaya Polyana. . . ." because it followed that his life narrative, and his self, would come to an end with death, and this was unacceptable. In the face of death, the limitations of autobiography were only too obvious. But, hard as he tried, he could not abandon the autobiographical mode. After all, the title of his latest attempt, "The Green Stick," was derived from the same memories of his childhood that were (almost concurrently) recorded in the "Reminiscences." Remarkably, Tolstoy did not use the phrase "the green stick" in the body of his essay and said not a word about the childhood game. But the title provided a personal code for an abstract philosophical-religious discourse.

(I will mention in passing that, in Tolstoy's "Reminiscences" too, "God" is present: The last full draft in his archive bears the word "God" [*Bog*] on the inside of the cover.)[22]

When Tolstoy died, in November 1910, his body was buried, in accordance with his instructions, where the green stick was supposed to have been buried; there was no stone, no inscription. Concluding the final volume of his biography, Pavel Biriukov (for whose benefit the "Reminiscences" were written) suggested an allegorical reading of the burial: "The procession extended toward the grave, dug in the ravine, in the forest, a mile away from the house, where, according to the family legend, brother Nikolai had buried the 'Green Stick': a magic talisman with the power to bring about mankind's resurrection. . . . The Love and Reason that lit this great life have been freed from the wrappings of individuality. And a new epoch of disseminating the great ideas has begun."[23] With these words, Tolstoy's biographer may have come close to defining what Tolstoy himself refrained from verbalizing: his paradoxical desire that, contrary to everything he had said about the unimportance of his biographical self, the secret of universal love and mankind's resurrection might be inscribed on his body.

Tolstoy and the Autobiographical Tradition

The autobiographical tradition has a long lineage, and Tolstoy was acutely aware of the precedents. He explicitly considered following Rousseau in giving an "absolutely truthful" account of everything vile and despicable in his life ("even more truthful than that of Rousseau") but discarded this idea because of the moral dangers it presented for the reader (73:279). Goethe's name also came up, and Tolstoy rejected *Dichtung und Wahrheit* as "insincere": The book was lacking in genuine descriptions of impressions and emotions. Goethe was mainly interested in providing the biography of a writer; Tolstoy, by contrast, shunned all "*Dichtung*" (the German word connotes both poetry and fiction), which, for him, meant artifice.[24]

While Tolstoy engaged with gusto in rejecting obvious sources, he did, of course, borrow from his predecessors. What is more, Tolstoy's efforts acquire meaning in the framework of the existing tradition.

Rousseau famously insisted that the truth of life-writing lay in following the history of one's feelings. In his *Confessions* and its sequels, he wanted to reveal "every impression that has left a trace" and to show how he came to be the person he was.[25] The famous affirmation of this principle appears in Book Seven of the *Confessions*:

> I have only one faithful guide on which I can count: the succession of feelings which have marked the development of my being, and thereby recall the events that have acted upon it as cause and effect. . . . I may omit or transpose facts, or make mistakes in dates, but I cannot go wrong about what I have felt, or about what my feelings have led me to do; and these are the chief subjects of my story. The true object of my confessions is to reveal my inner thoughts exactly in all the situations of my life. It is the history of my soul for which I have need of no other memories; it is enough if I enter again into myself, as I have done till now.[26]

Rousseau's unqualified belief in the inner truth of feelings, it has been amply shown by scholars, had a strong impact on both literary and emotional culture for many years to come.

The young Tolstoy, an ardent reader of Rousseau, had opened his first diary in 1847 by proclaiming his intention to "enter into himself" (46:3). Back then, at the age of eighteen, he had been unencumbered by the past. But when the older Tolstoy started probing his memories (in 1878 and 1903), he was no longer enchanted with himself. And, in light of his new religious ideals, preoccupation with the self became morally suspect. But Tolstoy still shared Rousseau's belief that he enjoyed unmediated access to exactly what he had felt in the remote past. Yet there was a substantial difference: Rousseau had spoken about the "succession of feelings" and hoped to recover the sequence of cause and effect: the influence of events upon his feelings. He had hoped to write the *history* of his soul. Unlike Rousseau, Tolstoy, a century later, realized that he did not remember the succession of his emotional states. In contrast to Rousseau, Tolstoy knew that he could not trace his present to a determining source in the past and that he could not order his reminiscences in time. To be true to himself, he had to resort to producing a series of disconnected memories.

For this strategy, too, there was a precedent: Stendhal's autobiography, *La Vie de Henry Brulard*, written in 1835–36. Working in the footsteps of

Rousseau, Stendhal (though he wrote in the third person) rested his "pretensions to truthfulness" on strict adherence to his memory of feelings: "trying to describe my feelings of the time *exactly as they were*. . . . Dare I add: *like the Confessions of Rousseau?*" (his emphasis; 263).[27] But he did know that Rousseau "told artful lies" (460). Stendhal deviated from Rousseau by embracing the principle of fragmentary recollection: "I can see mental images, I remember the effects on my emotions, but, as for causes and the physiognomy, nothing" (192). Writing in this way, Stendhal soon noticed that he was not writing a "history" but simply recording his memories (mostly memories of childhood). Yet he refrained from doing more "for fear of writing fiction" (481). Indeed, Stendhal (as he claimed) wrote spontaneously, from memory, without stylistic editing or revisions. He used the *aide-mémoire* technique of mentally walking through familiar rooms, supplying his narrative with maps and charts. And yet, Stendhal saw his memoir as an attempt to answer the questions that had preoccupied Rousseau: "What have I been? What am I?" (226–27). Unfinished (it barely extends beyond his adolescence), this abandoned narrative was intended to be published in the remote future: Remarkably, Stendhal kept addressing and imagining the reader of 1880, 1900, and beyond. Thus, rather than producing another *confession d'un enfant du siècle* (as did some of his contemporaries), Stendhal left a series of raw memoir vignettes that he knew did not adhere to the established autobiographical conventions of his time. But when Stendhal's autobiography first appeared in print in 1890, at the threshold of modernism, its fragmentation, impressionism, and avoidance of coherent plots and portraits felt remarkably pertinent.

Whether or not Tolstoy knew Stendhal's autobiography, in some respects his own efforts were similar.[28] First, Tolstoy could not put complete trust in his ability to "display a portrait in every way true to nature." After all, Tolstoy (like Stendhal) wrote *after* Rousseau. Rousseau's insistence on publicizing unsavory incidents from his life began to meet with criticism already from the Romantics.[29] In Russia, Dostoevsky, taking a cue from Heinrich Heine, bitterly ridiculed Rousseau's claim to confessional sincerity in his *Notes from Underground*. What is more, Tolstoy did not purport to produce a coherent history of his soul. Like Stendhal, Tolstoy sought the key to a new "truth" in the absence of artfulness and organization: To this end, he followed the psychological process of recollection based on mnemonic techniques and claimed that he refrained from editing. But Tolstoy differed from Stendhal in his insistence on a religious, rather than secular, approach to self. And whereas Stendhal, writing in the 1830s, confidently addressed his disordered memories to future readers, including the readers in the 1900s, Tolstoy did not have confidence in his raw product.

Tolstoy wrote his "Reminiscences" in 1903–06, that is, in the age of modernism, when fragmented narratives, retrogressive screen memories, and unstable identities were embraced as a viable alternative to realist life stories and, following Nietzsche, the concept of the self ("ego" or "subject") was questioned. (It may be indicative that one of the first to notice the remarkably innovative qualities of Tolstoy's early memories, in the 1930s, was the modernist Russian writer Ivan Bunin, who lived in France.)[30] But Tolstoy had no use for modernist experimentation, and he found his attempts inadequate.

It should be mentioned, too, that Tolstoy made a point of putting on record his rejection of Nietzsche. He was morally disgusted by the idea of human life rooted solely in this world and placed "beyond good and evil." As for Nietzsche's fragmented narratives, they seemed like the product of a deranged mind. But he was mostly put off by Nietzsche's popular appeal. In his youth, Tolstoy had detested the enormously popular Hegel, rejecting his idea of a unified, self-propelling, self-understanding subject; now, with the same vehemence, he rejected the current fad. As on other occasions, Tolstoy consciously turned his back on his own age. At the same time, Tolstoy eagerly appropriated Nietzsche's rejection of institutionalized Christianity and his critique of the family, and he once commented, with satisfaction, "Some of his formulations seem as if taken directly from me."[c]

Like his conversion narrative, the *Confession*, Tolstoy's autobiographical experiments have much in common, I would argue, with an ancient model: Augustine's *Confessions*. I will now revisit the place of Tolstoy in the tradition of self-writing that extends from Augustine to Rousseau and beyond (returning to issues discussed in chapter 3) to speak not about conversion but about the workings of memory and the uses of narrative.

---

[c] Tolstoy read *Also sprach Zarathustra* in 1900, noting in his diary that Nietzsche, with his incoherent narrative and his rejection of all "higher foundations of human life," was "insane": "not in the metaphorical, but in the direct sense" (54:77). Nevertheless he copied in his notebook a "wonderful" (his word) passage from *Zarathustra*, which critiques marriage and child rearing (54:34). He later read *Der Antichrist*, keeping the library copy borrowed from the librarian V. V. Stasov for two years, from 1902 to 1904 (73:336; 75:86). In 1904, Tolstoy published an excerpt from Nietzsche's critique of institutionalized Christianity in his anthology *A Circle of Reading* (*Krug chteniia*) (41:580–82; 42:622); in the same volume he called Nietzsche a "miserable madman" (42:320). Discussing this piece at the dinner table on May 24, 1905, Tolstoy said: "Someone wrote or told me that Nietzsche has read my works. Some of his formulations seem as if taken directly from me" (42:622). Indeed, the passage from Nietzsche that Tolstoy included in his *Circle of Reading* reads as if it had been written by Tolstoy: "Christianity is life. It teaches how to act. A person who would say 'I do not want to serve in the army,' 'I won't have anything to do with courts,' 'I have no need for police,' 'I do not want to do anything that will disturb my inner peace' . . . that man would be a true Christian" (41:582).

To recapitulate, Augustine distinguished between the questions "Who am I?" and "What am I?" To answer the question "Who am I?" is to tell the narrative of one's life, but the question "What am I?" asks about the nature of man, created in the image and likeness of God. It is a theological issue.[31] Augustine's *Confessions* is as much a book of memories as a study in theology of the self.[32] By contrast, Rousseau, in his *Confessions*, made an essentially modern move to reclaim the autonomy of the self: The inner self became the source of knowledge. In the end, Rousseau secularized the conception of the self.

I would argue that Tolstoy, in his memoiristic or autobiographical pieces, returned to the theological mode of self-exploration. If in the *Confession* he reproduced the generic pattern of the Augustinian conversion narrative, in "My Life" and the "Reminiscences" he tried to supplement the *Confession* with a psychological, philosophical, and theological exploration of self, memory, and time in the mode of Augustine's *Confessions*.

Indeed, as we have seen, in both "My Life" and the "Reminiscences," asking about his being before birth and after death, Tolstoy attempted to reach toward that which lay beyond his biographical self. The impulse to describe his inner life could have come from Rousseau, but the method was different: His concept of memory resembles Augustine's.

For Augustine, the "vast hall of my memory" is an inward space to which he withdraws to retrieve images he has been able to experience and things he knows from the stories of others (10.8.14). Augustine also allows for a type of memory that is not immediately accessible to recall ("memory retains forgetfulness"). But how can forgetfulness be remembered? This problem leads Augustine to an impasse: "Who can find a solution to this problem? . . . I at least, Lord, have difficulty at this point, and I find my own self hard to grasp" (10.16.24).[33] Continuing to probe the nature of his self, Augustine offers his famous self-definition: "It is I who remember, I who am soul [*ego sum, qui memini, ego animus*]" (10.16.25).[34] It is at this point in his narrative that Augustine replaces the question "Who am I?" with "What am I?" This question is addressed to God: "Great is the power of memory, an awe-inspiring mystery, my God, a power of profound and infinite multiplicity. And this is soul, this is I myself [*et hoc animus est, et hoc ego ipse sum*]. What then am I, my God? What is my nature?" (10.17.26). Augustine began his story with his infancy: "I threw my limbs about and uttered sounds, signs resembling my wishes. . . . When I did not get my way, either because I was not understood or lest it be harmful to me, I used to be indignant with my seniors for their disobedience, and with free people who were not slaves to my interests; and I would revenge myself upon them by weeping" (1.6.8).[35] Having no recollection of his "temporal origins," Augustine relies on what he has been told by others. From there, he passes to the question of a still earlier existence, and he asks God: "Tell me, God, . . . tell me whether there was some period of my life . . . which preceded my infancy? Or is this period that which I spent in my mother's womb? . . . What was going on before that, my sweetness, my God? Was I anywhere, or any sort of person? I have no one able to tell me that . . . neither the experience of others nor my own memory" (1.6.9). Thus, Augustine works with two different notions of memory. On the one hand, he connects the self with personal memories (as Locke would do in the modern age); on the other, he asks, albeit tentatively, about his being beyond the borders of his biographical life. In this case, Augustine's conception of memory echoes the Platonic and neo-Platonic doctrines of *anamnesis* (bringing to consciousness that which the soul knows from an earlier existence).[36] This was of tantamount importance for Augustine: The limitations of his memory cut him off not only from his infancy but also from eternity.[37]

I would argue that Tolstoy's memories of his infancy and his queries about his being before birth and after death in "My Life" (cited at the beginning of this chapter) sound like echoes of Augustine's ("I scream and cry . . . my cries affect them . . . but [they] do not unbind me as I want and I cry yet louder"; "When did I begin? When did I begin to live?"; 23:470). What is more, Tolstoy seems to have operated with a similar conception of memory and self.

While my argument is not limited to a claim of direct influence, Tolstoy did know Augustine. In his old age (no later than in 1884), as one scholar has recently demonstrated, Tolstoy carefully perused Augustine's *Confessions*.[38] He used a bilingual Latin-French edition that featured the seventeenth-century Jansenist translation of Arnauld D'Andilly (in a slightly modernized version).[39] Tolstoy's copy bears traces of his reading. Thus, Tolstoy marked chapters 15 through 18 of Book Ten, which discuss the mysteries of memory and identity. In Tolstoy's copy of Augustine, the key passage on memory and identity (the one Hannah Arendt would later highlight) is prominently marked: "Mon Dieu, cette puissance de la mémoire est prodigieuse, et je ne puis assez admirer sa profonde multiplicité, qui s'étend jusqu'à l'infini. O, cette mémoire n'est autre chose que l'esprit; et je suis moi-même cet esprit. Que suis-je donc, ô mon Dieu! que suis-je, moi qui vous parle."[40] (This passage, from 10.17.26, is cited above in the English translation.)

Tolstoy may have not read Augustine's *Confessions* before 1884.[41] It may well be that, when he read Augustine in 1884, he found ideas that echoed and confirmed what he had thought on his own when he had tried to recover his infantile memories in 1878.[42] But whether his reflections on the limitations of memory in "My Life" in 1878 or in the "Reminiscences" in 1902–06 were a product of reading Augustine is not the main point.

It is more important is to locate Tolstoy's autobiographical memories in a broader cultural context. In his attempts to produce a personal memoir or autobiography (as well as in his *Confession*), Tolstoy entered the tradition that rests on Augustine and Rousseau, but he refused to follow the well-worn path of modern authors who followed Rousseau in his secularization of self.

One scholar has recently revisited the contrast between Augustine's self and the modern self born in Rousseau, and I will follow him and use his remarkable formulations. The secularization of self implied a fundamental change in the understanding of the temporality of human life. The temporality of Augustine's *Confessions* (even in its autobiographical, or memoiristic, strand) is timeless eternity. In contrast, Rousseau and the modern authors operate with temporal biography and with history. "Augustine raised two essential complaints about the temporality of humans' earthly existence. First, and obviously, what was wrong with such existence was that it came to an end: mortality. Second, and less obviously, time causes us to relate to everything, even ourselves, in a mediated fashion: the present forever slips from our grasp because we can capture experience only in memory or expectation. Modernity gave up on such complaints and simply embraced the contingent and mediated character of human existence— finitude in the broadest sense of the term."[43]

To turn to Tolstoy: the old Tolstoy refused to embrace the modern condition first and foremost because he refused to embrace the finitude of human existence. In his attempts to write a memoir or autobiography, he turned back from Rousseau toward Augustine. Indeed, remarkably modern, even proto-modernist, in some respects (in his intuition on the nature of "screen memories" and his distrust of the linear order of narrative), Tolstoy's memoir was pointedly retrogressive in other respects—in his insistence that the true self lay beyond the confines of biological life, chronological time, and individual memory. From his first memoir, "My Life," to his later "Reminiscences" and "The Green Stick," the "I" of Tolstoy's self-definitions is the Augustinian "I": "I who am soul." He attempts to resacralize the self.[44]

So, how can we explain why Tolstoy, the accomplished novelist, the author of *Childhood*, *Boyhood*, and *Youth*, of *War and Peace* and *Anna Karenina*, proved unable, hard as he tried, to produce a memoir or autobiography? As Tolstoy himself made clear, there were moral, technical, and philosophical difficulties.

On the moral side, he feared that a completely truthful account of his life, written in the footsteps of Rousseau's *Confessions*, would be a seductive book and might lead the reader into temptation.

On the technical side, while he put his trust in the authenticity of mental images that had made imprints on his memory, he was unable to connect such memories, including what we may call screen memories, into a narrative sequence.

Finally, there were philosophical reasons for Tolstoy's failure as a memoirist: his refusal to accept that memories are limited to biological or biographical life.

His difficulties, I argue, derive from Tolstoy's location in intellectual history and in his personal history.

Approaching the end of the nineteenth century, he increasingly felt the pressure of the tradition in history, philosophy, and literature as well as in science, which accorded primacy to narratives of temporal sequence and teleological progression. From the Enlightenment to the late nineteenth century, narrative forms that rest on a sequence of events plotted from their origins to the present had been a dominant mode of representing and understanding human life. Autobiography, as well as historiography and the novel, followed this tradition.[45] Tolstoy felt an increasing distrust in narratives of progression not only because they promised deterministic explanation but also because they implied finitude. (In this, modernist fragmented narratives brought no relief.)

In a biographical perspective, at the time when he attempted to produce a story of his life, he was increasingly driven by an urge to define his "I" and his "life" in a way that would bypass the basic dimensions of human existence: in the body and in time. He was aware that memoirs and autobiographies were, as a rule, confined to the story of this life. But for the old Tolstoy (after the age of fifty), this seemed quite insufficient. In the face of impending death and destruction, he desperately tried to extend his self beyond the borders that delimit man on both sides.

Tolstoy, I claim, tried to write his life not like Rousseau and his modern successors but like Augustine: to produce an autobiography of the "soul." In this sense, I would say, his design was retrogressive: A modern man, he pushed back toward past, theological models. But a full return was, of course, impossible. Tolstoy put himself in the untenable position of trying to write like Augustine despite 1,500 years of intervening literature. In the end, Tolstoy's failure to produce a memoir or autobiography can be seen an achievement of literary honesty: He found out that the autobiography of the true self (the "soul") cannot be expressed in words and plots.

CHAPTER FIVE

"What Should We Do Then?":
Tolstoy on Self and Other

"Why Have You, a Man from a Different World, Stopped near Us? Who Are You?"

In early 1882, Tolstoy started working on an "article" inspired by his experience of living in the city (against his best judgment, the family had moved from their country estate to Moscow). It was eventually published (in 1889), under the suggestive title "What Should We Do Then?" The article opens with a statement that situates the first-person speaker within his "whole life": "I had spent my whole life away from the city, and when in 1881 I came to live in Moscow, the sight of city poverty surprised me. I knew country poverty, but city poverty was new and incomprehensible to me. In Moscow one cannot pass a street without meeting beggars, and beggars who are not like those in the country" (25:182).[1] The narrative starts with painstakingly detailed reports on the author's solitary walks through the city. One day, walking along Afanasiev Lane, he saw a policeman putting a beggar—a ragged peasant swollen with dropsy—into an open cab (throughout the essay, Tolstoy is specific and precise in identifying locations in the city). Tolstoy took another cab and followed them to the local police station. One such story follows another, until Tolstoy interrupts his narrative to address the moral ambiguity of his position: "'Why go to look at the sufferings of people I cannot help?' said one voice within me. 'No, if you live here and see all the allurements of town-life, come and see that also,' said another voice" (25:186). "Come and see" (*idi i smotri*) is a New Testament commandment (Revelation 6:1).

And so, one frosty windy day in December, Tolstoy went to the heart of the town's destitution—the Khitrov market. What he saw—hordes of displaced, homeless peasants, vagrants of all classes, teenage prostitutes, drunks of all ages, beggars, and policemen picking up those who "begged in the name of Christ"—impressed him as the true image of the new world in which he had come to live: the modern urban civilization.

Wanting to penetrate this world further, Tolstoy volunteered to participate in a population census, and he chose a neighborhood filled with slums and poorhouses (night shelters for the homeless) such as the Liapinsky and Rzhanov Houses. In his role as a census worker, he was no longer a flâneur, and he entered the living quarters of the poorest of the poor. Soon the ethnographic impulse gave way to a moral one. Writing about the urban poor preoccupied Tolstoy for four years, from 1882 to 1886. What was planned as a short article grew into a long and formless book, but Tolstoy continued to call it an "article" (stat'ia).

The work's final title—"What Should We Do Then?"—alludes to the words of John the Baptist from the Gospel of Luke: "And the people asked him, 'What, then, should we do?' He answered, 'Whoever has two shirts must share with the one who has none, and whoever has food must do the same'" (Luke 3:10–11). The phrase also echoes one of Kant's famous three questions, which (in his correspondence with Nikolai Strakhov) Tolstoy took as a starting point of his quest for faith in 1875. Now, ten years later, his focus shifted from "What may I hope?" to "What ought I to do?" (At that time he also said that all three questions amounted to a single one: "What is my life? What am I?") As on many other occasions, Tolstoy found posing a question to be easier than giving the answer. When Tolstoy first published his still-unfinished work in 1886, it appeared under the title "What Is My Life?" (Kakova moia zhizn'?). (The complete text was published in Geneva in 1889.)

Much of the work is written as a memoir. One of the fragments was even published under the title "From Memories of the Census" (Iz vospominanii o perepisi; 25:750). These were memoirs of a transformative experience, and, as Tolstoy's report took four years to complete, many episodes were written as reminiscences of the recent past, formed from the vantage point of the present moment, the shifting moment of writing. In later chapters, Tolstoy turned to generalizations about the problem of poverty and moral reflections on his own position in relation to the poor. As in many of Tolstoy's writings, the autobiographical, the theological, the ethical, and the philosophical are fused.

At the core of this treatise (I would argue) stands the philosophical problem of self and other. Tolstoy approaches it in a social key: The "others" are the poor who have been disenfranchised and displaced by the coming of modernity to Russia. But as he confronts the other face to face, the problem of his own self and his own life comes to the fore. Tolstoy describes himself standing in the crowd of homeless people in front of the doors of a free night shelter (the Liapinsky House), awaiting entry under their watchful eyes. On their faces he reads a question: "Why have you, a man from a different world, stopped near us? Who are you?" (25:187–88).

Throughout his past life Tolstoy has asked himself, "Who, what am I?" Now he feels that the other asks him, "Who are you?" Tolstoy becomes aware that he is an object of the other's gaze. He interprets this question in a social and moral light: " 'Who are you? A self-satisfied rich man who wishes to enjoy our misery to relieve his dullness . . . or are you what-does-not-and-cannot-exist—a man who pities us?' This question was on every face" (25:188). Tolstoy describes his face-to-face encounter with the other in minute detail, glance by glance, gesture by gesture, word by word: "Widely as life had separated us, after our glances had met twice or thrice, we felt that we were both human beings and ceased to fear one another. Nearest to me stood a peasant with a swollen face and a red beard, in a torn coat and with worn-out galoshes on his bare feet. There were eight degrees Celsius of frost. I met his glance three or four times, and felt so close to him that instead of being ashamed to speak to him, I should have been ashamed not to say something. I asked where he came from. He answered readily and began talking, while others drew near" (25:188). The "I" and the other have thus recognized their mutual humanity. But the difference in their situation does not allow the moment of mutual recognition to last. One man asks for money, and Tolstoy gives him some. Another asks, and a third, and then the crowd besieges him. He gives away all the money in his pockets, returns home, and sits down to a dinner of five courses.

At this point Tolstoy's story reaches a high emotional pitch. He recalls how thirty years earlier, in Paris, he watched, in the presence of thousands of spectators, as a man's head was cut off with a guillotine. (This episode is related in the *Confession* as a pivotal moment in Tolstoy's life.) On both occasions, "then" and "now," "here" and "there," he understood, not with his mind or his heart but with his whole being: "I approved this sin, by my presence and non-intervention, and shared in it" (25:190). But what could he do? "Here, I could have given not only . . . the trifling sum of money I had with me, but the overcoat I wore and all I had at home. But I had not done it, and I therefore felt, and feel, and shall not cease to feel that as long as I have any superfluous food and someone else has none, and I have two coats and someone else has none, I share in a constantly repeated crime" (25:190). Tolstoy accepts his moral complicity in the desperate situation of the other. He couches his judgment in terms of the Gospel commandment, but he takes it as a guide to practical action.

Thus, the article then describes, at great length, how Tolstoy attempted to organize and put into action a charity campaign among the Moscow rich, to arrange that people should no longer be cold and hungry; how his undertaking failed; and how he came to realize that it was impossible to help the other (chapters 3–16). For one, he soon found that some of those who accepted his charity returned, with extraordinary rapidity and resignation, to the same destitute condition. But what he felt about his own situation was something else: "I felt that I could not live like this any more."

In the course of his futile attempts to help the poor, it became clear to Tolstoy that the cause of their misery lay deeper: "The majority of the unfortunates I saw were unfortunate only because they had lost the capacity, the wish, and the habit of working for their bread." From this he makes an unexpected conclusion, reevaluating the relationship between the self and the other: "That is to say, their misfortune consisted in being like me" (25:224). When he encountered the destitute who came from the impoverished gentry and wanted nothing else but to return to their privileged lives, Tolstoy saw this clearly: "In them, as in a looking-glass, I saw myself" (25:207). The other turns out to be a mirror image of the self.

"Now" Tolstoy sees that the conclusion he reached "then" (when, ashamed of his easy life, he made plans to help the poor) was an error: "I then felt that my life was bad and that it would not do to live so. But from the fact that my life was bad and that one must not live so, I did not draw the clear and simple conclusion that I must improve my way of life and live better, but drew the strange conclusion that to enable myself to live better it was necessary to correct other people's lives; and so I began to correct the lives of others" (25:227). The dialectic of self and other takes a new turn: Rather than make efforts to improve other people's lives, Tolstoy decides to change his own.

At this point, he inquires into the nature of his own self, formulating this eternally returning question in terms of his position vis-à-vis the other: "Who am I who wishes to help people?" (25:245). He answers:

> I spend my whole life in this way: eat, talk, and listen; I eat, write, or read, then again talk and listen; I eat and play; I eat and again talk and listen; I eat and go to bed; and so it is every day. . . . And that I may do this it is necessary that from morning to evening the porter, the handyman, the male and female cook, the footman, the coachman and washerwoman, should work; to say nothing of those working people who are needed that these coachmen, cooks, footmen and the

rest should have utensils and the things with which and on which they work for me: axes, barrels, brushes, crockery, furniture, glass, wax, blacking, kerosene, hay, wood-fuel, meat. (25:246)

So, Tolstoy concludes, "And all these people work hard . . . so that I may be able to talk, eat, and sleep" (25:246).

Tolstoy's descriptions of the situation are concrete and detailed. And yet, I think, underlying all of this is a philosophical paradigm of the relationship between self and other: Hegel's famous master-and-slave dialectic. (But Tolstoy does not acknowledge Hegel.)

Master and Slave: Tolstoy Rewrites Hegel

To summarize it in popular terms, *Herr und Knecht*, master and slave (or master and servant) is a parable that illustrates the development of the self through a confrontation with the other. (In this, Hegel's model compliments Descartes', which deals solely with the single, self-reflecting self.) It appears in paragraphs 178–96 of *The Phenomenology of Spirit*, where it represents a stage in Hegel's overall model of the human spirit, or mind, involved in search of self-knowledge.[2] Hegel implies that what occurs within a human mind also occurs in the external, social world between two (or more) individuals.

The "I" sees the "other." In Hegel's words, "self-consciousness is faced by another self-consciousness." This is a moment fraught with conflict, and it has consequences. First, the self "sees in the other its own self." But a rise to true self-knowledge can only come from "mutually recognizing each other."[3] To turn to the social level of the paradigm, for the self, the existence of the other is a threat and a challenge. At the outset, the two are antagonists and might fight to the death. To avoid mutual annihilation, they enter into the relationship of master and slave: The one driven by a stronger fear of death surrenders to the other. But this does not bring complete resolution: If, within a human mind, the self, without mutual recognition of and by the other, cannot be fully self-conscious, then in the social world, neither a master nor a slave can be fully free in the absence of mutual recognition.

Elaborating the social plane of the allegory, Hegel appeals to a third element: nature, or material reality. The slave toils for the master, shaping nature into products for the master's consumption. As a result, the master emerges as the weaker member of the pair. Thus, through his mastery of the material world, the slave achieves a degree of independence. But the master remains wholly dependent on the material products and degrading services that the slave provides to satisfy his needs and desires; he is a "pure consumer."[4] The master relates to the very materiality of life only through the intermediary of the slave.[5] True, the slave lacks the capacity for contemplation or self-reflection: He merely produces. But in the end, the master is enslaved by the labor of his slave or servant. What is more, he depends on the slave for his very identity: Without slaves, he is no master. On the mental plane of the allegory, the mind of the master is locked in the circle of self-coincidence, where I = I. This is Hegel's model in a nutshell (his analysis is, of course, far more complex and nuanced).

It would be difficult to exaggerate the importance of the master-and-slave paradigm for European philosophical and social thought. Hegel's commentators have shown its deep roots and its far-reaching potential for interpretations and appropriations. We can find a similar treatment of the categories of domination and servitude already in Rousseau, who even used the phrase "*les maîtres et les esclaves*" to describe the core pattern of inequality in his "Discourse on the Origins and the Foundations of Inequality among Men."[6] (It may well be that Tolstoy, who, throughout his life, read Rousseau with the feeling that he had written some of his pages himself, accepted the master-and-slave paradigm precisely because, behind Hegel, he saw the shadow of Rousseau.) Later, Karl Marx made use of Hegel's take on domination and servitude to analyze the political economy of exploitation and to offer a program of liberation.[7] But, as Jean Hyppolite made clear, this paradigm "not only plays an essential role in social relations, in relations between people, but also serves to translate a certain conception of the relations between God and man."[8] What is more, relations between the master and the servant were a part of the very process by which Hegel developed his philosophy of subjectivity. As Alexandre Kojève has put it, it was the servant's work that produced and set the table on which Hegel wrote his *Phenomenology*, and this work was a part of the "I" that Hegel analyzed in answering the question "What am I?"[9] In a word, from its distant roots (going back to Aristotle) to its modern uses, master and slave has been seen as a universal paradigm that not only expresses the philosophical relations of self and other and the social relations of lord and bondsman but also models the dualism of mind and body, spirit and matter, contemplation and action, all of which exhibit the dialectic of ruling and subordination.[10]

Opinions differ about whether or not Hegel believed in resolving this situation, but if he did, the solution lies in overcoming the conflict between the master and the slave in an act of genuine mutual recognition. Tolstoy's solution, as I am about to show, is different.

But first, let us note that the master-and-slave dialectic had a special resonance for the Russians, long plagued by serfdom, as well as for Tolstoy personally. Until the Emancipation Act of 1861, a member of the class of hereditary landowners (the gentry) was almost certain to be a serf owner.[a] Tolstoy, who had lived much of his life as the owner of a considerable number of serfs, had expressed his feeling of guilt in his recent *Confession* ("I consumed the labor of the peasants, sentenced them to punishments. . . ."). At the time when he was writing "What Should We Do Then?" he was still surrounded by his former serfs, now the impoverished peasants who continued to rely on him for help and the house servants (who worked for wages). He was painfully aware that the emancipation of the serfs had not resolved the relationship of mutual bondage.

Before Tolstoy presents his solution, he describes, in considerable detail (chapters 17–22), the historical development of the relations between master and slave, couched in the discourse of political philosophy and political economy. He surveys social institutions involved in the progress of inequality: private ownership of land (for both Rousseau and Tolstoy, the root of all evil), division of labor, monetary economy (one of the main topic of Tolstoy's analysis is the evil of money), taxation, capital, ownership of means of industrial production, and so on, all advancing increasing "alienation of the land and the implements of labor from those who cultivate the land and use the implements" (25:254). He names institutions of state power, such as the government, the police, and the army, as forms of legitimized coercion or, indeed, violence (*nasilie*). In the course of history, Tolstoy concludes, all of this has contributed to the enslavement of one person by another under the threat of death (25:272). (Note that Tolstoy's argument, engaging as it does the threat of death, is very close to Hegel's.) But Tolstoy's immediate goal is to reveal the true nature of his own current situation. The point is that this is not only how things worked in "primitive times" but also how they remain in our own time: "Slavery," the condition that "I" enjoyed when "I owned serfs," exists to this day (though both Russians and Americans may believe that slavery has been abolished; 25:288).

---

[a] The Russian language is, moreover, exceptionally equipped to express the master-and-slave dialectic, *barin i rab*. (The Russian phrase reinforces the link through a palindrome: the two words, when combined in this phrase, are mirror images of each other.) The relationship of mutual dependency and the palindrome *barin-rab* (landlord-slave) are memorable to many a Russian reader from Goncharov's Oblomov and his servant Zakhar. The critic Nikolai Dobroliubov developed the sociological interpretation of their mutual dependency in his famous article "What is Oblomovism?" (*Chto takoe oblomovshchina?* 1859), where he highlights the phrases *barin* and *rab*, *barstvo* and *rabstvo*.

Tolstoy does not acknowledge his sources. I would argue that in Tolstoy, Rousseau meets not only Hegel but also Marx. Tolstoy reiterates his conclusions in terms still closer to Marxist ones in the 1900 article "The Slavery of Our Time" (*Rabstvo nashego vremeni*). We do know that by 1895, if not before, Tolstoy had "carefully read *Das Kapital* and felt ready to pass an exam on this book."[11] Tolstoy, like Marx, speaks about socioeconomic dependencies between people arising from the way they produce and reproduce their existence. Like Marx before him, Tolstoy clearly emphasizes labor, and he focuses on how the relationship between the master and the slave is mediated through the world of things. But he also, like Hegel, illustrates both the dialectic of the division of labor and the dialectic of the division of consciousness. Underlying the discourse of political economy is the Hegelian philosophy of subjectivity, focused on the issue of self and other. What is more (as I am about to show), in his later writings, Tolstoy revealed that underlying both the social and the philosophical issue is the problem of the relations between man and God.

His socioeconomic reflections lead (in chapter 23) to Tolstoy's attempt to confront, finally, the question "What should we do then?" In specific terms: What must we do to break the condition of slavery of all kinds that binds people to one another? Tolstoy has come, he says, to the following simple conclusion, one that concerns him personally: "[I]n order not to produce suffering and depravity, I must use as little as possible the work of others and must myself work as much as possible" (25:295). Tolstoy then switches into the language of the Gospel: "For him who sincerely suffers from the sufferings of those about him, there is a very clear, simple, and easy means . . . the same that John the Baptist gave in reply to the question: 'What then should we do?' and which Christ confirmed: not to have more than one piece of clothing and not to have money, that is, not to make use of other people's labor. And in order not to make use of other people's labor—to do all we can with our own hands" (25:295). (Note that "not to have more than one piece of clothing" is not actually what John the Baptist advised.)

As always, Tolstoy is very precise as to what such abstract principles involve: He goes on to specify that if you want to urinate and defecate inside the house, you should take the stinking waste out yourself. And you should try to make your own clothing.

We know that Tolstoy did try to translate this program into action. In 1884, much to the dismay of his family and servants, he started to clean his room and take out his chamber pot. He chopped wood, fetched water for the house, and made boots. And he meticulously recorded these occupations in his diary.[b] He also noted that the tension between himself and his wife, Sofia Andreevna, who had not followed him into his new life, grew and grew. In 1884, Tolstoy made his first attempt to leave home. There was still more to follow. In 1891, Tolstoy surrendered the ownership of his estates by distributing his property between his wife and his nine children as if he were dead. (He would have preferred to give all his land to the peasants.) Then he publicly renounced the copyright of his works published after 1881 (with the exception of "The Death of Ivan Ilyich," which he had given to Sofia Andreevna for her own edition of his works). He made every effort not to handle money. His wife did not approve of any of this; she was intensely miserable.[12]

But let us describe his solution in philosophical language. In "What Should We Do Then?" Tolstoy decides to dissolve the master-and-slave bondage *not* through mutual recognition between self and other but by denying the other. Indeed, in taking on the work of a slave in order to produce services and commodities for his own needs, he alone achieves self-mastery. To translate this into the phenomenology of mind: Tolstoy removes the self from the field of the other.

This is not what Hegel's master-and-slave dialectic entails. Tolstoy has used the Hegelian paradigm to advance his own solution to the problem of self and other, one rooted in his personal experience.

Tolstoy and the Washerwoman

Having reached his conclusions by way of lengthy theoretical reflections, Tolstoy shifts (in chapter 24) to a personal perspective. One day, he was told the following story:

> There lived a washerwoman of about thirty years old, a blond woman, quiet and well-conducted but sickly. . . . The washerwoman was in debt for her lodging and felt guilty, and so she tried to be quiet. She was less and less often able to go to work, her strength was failing, and so she could not pay the landlady; for the last week she had not been out to work at all, and with her cough only poisoned the life of all tenants. . . . [T]he landlady told the washerwoman to leave unless she

---

[b] Consider the following diary entry, from March 8, 1884: "Got up at 9, joyfully cleaned the room with the younger children. It's embarrassing to do what should be done—take out the chamber pot. . . . Worked long and pleasantly on the boots" (49:64).

could pay. . . . A policeman, with a sword and a pistol on a red cord, came to the lodging, and using only polite and proper words fetched the washerwoman out into the street.

It was a clear, sunny, cool March day. Water was running down the gutters, and the yard-porters were breaking up the ice on the pavements. The sledges of the cab-drivers bumped over the crusted snow and screeched as they scraped on bare stones. The washerwoman went up the sunny side of the slope, came to the church, and sat down on the sunny side of its porch. But when the sun began to sink behind the house and the puddles began again to coat with ice, she felt cold and frightened. She got up and dragged herself along. . . . Where to? Home, to the only home she had had of late. Before she got there, resting on her way, it was growing dark. She came to the gates, turned in at them, slipped, uttered a cry, and fell.

One man passed, and then another. "Must be drunk." Yet another man passed, stumbled over the washerwoman, and said to the yard-porter: "Some drunken woman is lying in your gateway, I nearly broke my head tumbling over her. Get her moved away, can't you!"

The yard-porter went to see about it. The washerwoman was dead. (25:299–300)

Having heard this story (from a destitute drunk who had shared the washerwoman's lodgings), Tolstoy went to see her body. The weather was good, he reports, the sun was shining, the church bells were ringing, and the sound of the bells mingled with that of practice shooting in the military barracks: the whistle of bullets and their smack against a target. He then describes the dead body of the washerwoman: "her face clean and pale, with prominent closed eyes, sunken cheeks, and soft flaxen hair above the high brow" (25:301).

Addressing the reader, Tolstoy insists on the absolute authenticity of his account: This actually happened, in the course of his work on this article, on one fine day in March 1884 (he does not remember the exact date). Indeed, the story is mentioned in his diary, on March 27, 1884 (49:74), and it also appears in Tolstoy's letter to Vladimir Chertkov of the same day (85:42–43).

Tolstoy then extends his initial question: "What, then, must we do? It's not us, after all, who have done this? But if not we, then who?" (25:307). The "we" refers to a community of which Tolstoy had once been a member, but he now objects to those who continue to maintain, "We didn't do it."

Indeed, long before his confrontation with the dead washerwoman, when he reported on his initial discovery of the city poor, Tolstoy formulated his heartfelt conviction: "What came to me from the first at the sight of the hungry and cold people at the Liapinsky House: namely, that I was to blame for it, and that one could not, could not, could not go on living as I was living—that was the one thing that was true!" (25:243). While Hegel (as his interpreters insist) shows that the master is enslaved by the labor of his servant, Tolstoy (I would argue) emphasizes the master's moral responsibility for the subjugation and suffering of the slave.

And having told the story of the washerwoman, Tolstoy proceeds to translate his moral principle of personal responsibility and his refusal to maintain the status quo into practical conclusions: They concern his shirt. His love of cleanliness (*chistota*; the same word is used in Russian for "purity") was, Tolstoy concludes, a direct cause of the death of the washerwoman: "I like cleanliness, and give my money only on condition that a washerwoman washes the shirt I change twice a day, and this shirt has drained her last strength, and she has died" (25:306). It follows that "I" am to blame. So, what is to be done? To Tolstoy, the answer seems clear: "I" must stop giving my shirts to another to wash.

It is significant, I think, that Tolstoy uses a story that involves his "shirt" to formulate his answer to the question "What should we do then?" Indeed, this story represents his own translation and adaptation of Luke 3:10–11 ("Share your shirt with the other, who has none"). But Tolstoy's commandment is different from Luke's: Rather than sharing his shirt with the other, he would rather have none himself, thus removing himself from the relationship with the other.

Reasoning from familiar premises, Tolstoy comes to a conclusion that goes against the spirit of both the Gospel commandment, "Share your shirt with the other," and the Hegelian master-and-slave paradigm, in its appeal for mutual recognition. In rejecting any engagement with the other, Tolstoy may have departed from Hegel to return to Rousseau (whose analysis of domination and servitude was among the sources that informed Hegel). Indeed, Rousseau's social ideal (articulated in the "Social Contract" as well as in *Émile*) was self-sufficiency (Émile's model was Robinson Crusoe).[13] But Tolstoy does not acknowledge the revolutionary character of his own solution.

The Order of Things: The Church, the State, the Arts and Sciences

If things are so arranged. . . . Once this has been started and injury has been done, why should not I share in it too? What difference will it make if I wear a dirty shirt . . . ? Would anyone be the better for it—ask those who wish to justify themselves. . . . What difference will it make if I wear a shirt for a week and not for a day? (25:306)

Tolstoy is vehemently opposed to this line of reasoning, and he evokes it with heavy irony. For his part, he wants to remove himself, once and for all, from the existing order of things.

But how has it happened, he asks, that the majority of the educated people of our time not only consume other people's labors but also "consider such a life the most natural and reasonable? (25:316). Strange as it may seem, he suggests, the invention of such justifications has been the chief occupation and purpose of the "sciences" and the "arts." In the chapters that follow the story of the washerwoman, Tolstoy surveys and refutes, one by one, theories (including Darwin, Comte, Malthus, and Herbert Spencer) and classes of people (government and church officials; men of industry, finance, and commerce; scientists and artists) that justify a society in which some consume the labor, and thus the lives, of others.

Throughout his critique, Tolstoy singles out "Hegel's theory that so long prevailed, with its assertion that what exists is reasonable and that the State is a form necessary for the perfecting of personality" (25:317). Tolstoy evokes here the famous slogan from Hegel's *Philosophy of Right*, "What is rational is actual and what is actual is rational" ("*Was vernünftig ist, das ist wirklich; und was wirklich ist, das ist vernünftig*"), relying on its well-known Russian interpretation. Like his older contemporaries before him, he chooses, to misunderstand or at least to oversimplify this proposition. Like Russian thinkers before him, in the 1840s, Tolstoy reads Hegel's formula as a call to accept the social order and the state based on domination and servitude, a *carte blanche* of sorts for inequality and coercion.[14]

A comment on Tolstoy and Hegel is due. On many occasions, Tolstoy made a point of putting on record his profound distaste for Hegel.[c] Yet it would be a mistake to take him at his word.[15] As we have seen, in "What Should We Do Then?" Tolstoy heavily relies, without naming Hegel, on the master-and-slave dialectic, even as he explicitly attacks (more than once) Hegel's thesis on the rationality of the real and his philosophy of the state.

To return to Tolstoy's explanation of the terrible delusion that some people can consume the labor of others (offered in chapter 28). This injustice has been legitimized by the authority of what amounts to "religious doctrines"

---

[c] Derogatory comments abound not only in essays, but also in diaries and letters: "A weak thinker" (48:345; diary February 14, 1870); "I don't understand a single word" (61:348; letter to Strakhov, November–December 1872). Tolstoy's wife believed him. On February 14, 1870, she wrote in her diary that all the previous summer Tolstoy had read philosophy; he admired Schopenhauer, who quite enthralled him; he read Hegel, too, but said of him that "it was just an empty set of phrases." S. A. Tolstaia, *Dnevniki* (Moscow: Khudozhestvennaia literatura, 1978), 1:495.

(*veroucheniia*), not one but three, which over the ages have built up one upon the other and solidified into "one monstrous deception, or humbug, as the English say" (25:326).

The first and oldest is institutionalized Christianity, according to which some men are appointed by God to rule over all the rest.

The second "justificatory doctrine" is the "sacred philosophy of the state" (25:327). Once again (in chapter 29), Tolstoy attacks and parodies Hegel: "all that exists is reasonable, that there is no evil and no good, and man need not struggle with evil, but need only manifest the spirit: one man in military service, another in the law-courts, and a third on a fiddle. . . . no one is to blame for anything" (25:331–32). These "beliefs," he mentions, were predominant in Russia "when I started life" (25:332) (Indeed, men of the 1840s had described the status of Hegelian philosophy among Russian intellectuals as that of a religion: a "mystery evoking fear and faith.")[16]

Finally, Tolstoy comes to the third, currently dominant "creed" (*verouchenie*) that justifies master-slave relations: It is upheld by scientists and artists (25:327; 330). He speaks about the recent appearance in Europe of a "large class of rich and idle people who serve neither church nor state." This "new estate," headed by scientists and artists, attacks the servants of the church, the state, and the army, considering their activity harmful, but its members believe that they themselves serve "civilization" and "progress" and are thus fully justified in their parasitic existence. Tolstoy wants, I think, to point an accusing finger at a new social class, known in Russia as the "intelligentsia" (he does not use the term).

Their own justification of inequality rests mainly on the principle of the division of labor—some people in society perform physical work, others intellectual work. This, Tolstoy says (in chapter 31), is "humbug." (An issue with roots in Plato and, in modern times, Adam Smith, the division of labor had risen to new prominence after Darwin, inspiring Marx in his 1867 *Capital* and Émile Durkheim in his 1893 *The Division of Labor in Society*.)

Today, Tolstoy argues, it is those who purport to do mental and spiritual labor (mainly scientists and artists) who form the dominant master class. It is their "creed" that provides us with the most powerful justification of master-slave relations. They are the clergy of today: In publishing newspapers and books, organizing picture galleries and musical societies, kindergartens and schools (the list is Tolstoy's), members of this new estate fulfill functions that were formerly performed by ecclesiastics.

Tolstoy returns here to a theme posed in his *Confession*: the sacralization of art (now wrapped together with science and education), which elevates modern scholars and artists to a form of priesthood. Then, in his *Confession*, he lamented that, as a writer, he himself had been a priest of this false religion; now, equipped with concepts borrowed from political theories, he subjects this cult to analysis. He exposes (in chapter 32) the justifications of his own cohort: " 'Thou, or rather you' (for it always takes many to feed one), 'you feed me, clothe me, and do all that rough work for me which I demand . . . and I will do for you the mental work. . . . You give me bodily food and I will give you spiritual food' " (25:349). Such a demand would be justified only if this exchange of services were voluntary and reciprocal. Tolstoy makes this point clear by voicing the hypothetical demand of the laborer: " [B]efore I serve you with bodily food, I need spiritual food, and unless I receive it, I cannot work" (25:350). (Much of the narrative in this section is a dialogue between "scholars and artists," on the one side, and "laborers," on the other. The narrative "I" shifts, standing now for one, now for the other position.)

This hypothetical dialogue is then replaced with a reality test: "What will happen if the laborer says that? And if he does, it will not be a joke, but only the simplest justice" (25:350). After that, the narrative shifts to the first person plural: "What shall we, mental workers, reply if such simple and legitimate demands are presented to us? How will we satisfy them?" (25:350).

Tolstoy, the author and narrator, includes himself in the ranks of those "scholars and artists" who prey on the labor of others, and he treats his class to a battery of heavy irony. "How shall we satisfy a laborer's demands? With Filaret's Catechism . . . and with leaflets issued by various monasteries to satisfy his spiritual needs? with the Code of Laws . . . and the statutes of various Committees and Commissions to satisfy his demands for social justice? with spectral analysis, measurements of the Milky Way, abstract geometry, microscopic investigations . . . and the proceedings of the Academy of Sciences to satisfy his demands for knowledge?" (25:350). The question reaches a high pitch when it comes to the laborer's aesthetic needs: "With Pushkin, Dostoevsky, Turgenev, L. Tolstoy, with pictures from the French Salon and from our own artists, representing naked women, satin, and velvet, with landscapes and genre pictures, with Wagner's music . . . ? None of these things suit him, and they could not possibly suit him" (25:350). These statements reflect Tolstoy's current views on art.[17] But there is more. At this point, it becomes clear that "L. Tolstoy," the popular Russian fiction writer, is not the person to whom the author of "What Should We Do Then?" refers when he says "I."

Tolstoy then tries to wrap up his argument. He poses (in chapter 33) a historical succession of powers—the church, the state, and, in our days, the arts and sciences—which all purported to guide the people, and all betrayed their vocation when they stipulated their right to use other people's labor. He then extends Rousseau's argument to modern days (without naming him) and painstakingly refutes (in chapters 35–37) the views of those of his contemporaries who claim that the activities of science and art have helped humanity's progress. (Tolstoy obviously finds it difficult to bring his argument to a conclusion.)

At the end of chapter 38, he has finally found the answer to his question "What should we do?" at least inasmuch as it concerns himself. It is necessary, he finds, to reject my belief in my own rights and the privileges that distinguish me from others, to acknowledge myself as being to blame, and to fulfill the "eternal, indubitable law of man": with the labor of my whole being to work for the maintenance of my own and other people's lives (25:392).

"I have finished, having said all that relates to myself," Tolstoy says (in chapter 39), but he adds that he "could not restrain his desire to also speak about things that concern everybody" (25:392). The article finally comes to an end (in chapter 40) with Tolstoy telling the women of this world what they have to do: Bear children and bring them up to free mankind of the evils of our time. In this lies the salvation of the world. Tolstoy (as he knows) generalizes his personal solution into a commandment addressed to all humankind.

"Master and Man"

In the mid-1880s (as his work on "What Should We Do Then?" was coming to a close), Tolstoy actually turned his personal efforts to meeting the spiritual needs of those working people who (as he said in his article) could not be satisfied by the fiction of "Pushkin, Dostoevsky, Turgenev, [or] L. Tolstoy."

In 1884, Tolstoy and his disciples launched (with the participation of a commercial publisher, I. D. Sytin) a publishing house, Posrednik (The Intermediary), whose mission was to supply peasant readers with morally edifying literature, as near as possible to the teachings of Christ.[18] Over the years, Tolstoy produced a number of "folk stories" (narodnye rasskazy) for Posrednik, mostly fables and parables with a clear moral message and religious underpinnings, aimed for distribution (at a minimal cost) among barely educated readers.

One of these stories, I think, represents yet another revision of Hegel's master-and-slave paradigm: the famous "Khoziain i rabotnik" (Master and Laborer, usually translated into English as "Master and Man" and into German as "Herr und Knecht"; 1894–95). Written in Tolstoy's distinct post-conversion style, "Master and Man" is a short narrative drawing on characters, situations, and language from peasant life and complete with a clear moral-religious message. One of the most successful of Tolstoy's folk stories, it was instantly reprinted by most Russian newspapers. It was received with ecstatic admiration by Tolstoy's close associates (such as Nikolai Strakhov), but socially minded populist critics considered it psychologically unconvincing.

The main heroes of the story are the exploitative merchant Vasily, driven by his unbridled ambition to accumulate money, and the poor peasant laborer Nikita, who lives a life of endless toil and loyal service, at peace with nature and domestic animals. Convinced that he is the man's benefactor, the master cheats his laborer out of his earnings, virtually enslaving him, and the servant, aware that he is being cheated, accepts this condition as his destiny. It is winter, the day after the St. Nicholas feast. The master, intent on beating his competitors in the sale of a tree grove, decides to brave the deadly weather, and his man, though he does not want to go, has long been accustomed to having no will of his own and serving others, so he runs off to harness the horse, Mukhorty, who also does not want to go, and he explains his actions to the horse. (The healthy relationship between laborer and horse is clearly contrasted to the twisted link between master and man.) The master and man set off in a sledge drawn by an intelligent horse. Thrown together by the master's will for accumulation, the man's subservience, and the horse's obedience, the three are soon lost in a blizzard.

After hours of wandering in the snowstorm (and pages of exquisite prose worthy of the author of *War and Peace*), the master abandons his servant, mounts the horse, and rides off alone, in an attempt to save his own life. The servant calmly lies down "in the master's place in the sledge to die": " 'Lord, heavenly Father!' he muttered, and the consciousness that he was not alone, but that the One who heard him would not abandon him, comforted him" (29:37). He does not know whether he is dying or falling asleep, but feels as well prepared for the one as for the other. In the meantime, in the darkness, the master rides the horse through an apocalyptic snowstorm. When the clever horse brings the master back to the sledge, they find the servant nearly frozen to death. "Forgive me for Christ's sake," the dying servant asks his master, as he prepares to face his heavenly Master (29:41). In this moment the master experiences a sudden epiphany: He lies down on top of his servant, covering him not only with his fur coat but with the whole of his body, which glows with warmth. Feeling the warming body of his servant beneath his, he now feels not the terror of death but rapturous joy. Not conscious of the passage of time, the master is carried away by dreams and visions, until "he who called him and told him to lie down on Nikita" comes for him. " 'I'm coming!' the master cries joyfully." He wakes up in the other life, not at all the same person he was when he fell asleep (29:44). So the master dies, giving his own life to save the life of his servant. (The horse also dies, frozen solid on his feet.) The narrative then shifts into the present to describe the death of the servant some twenty years later, and to draw the author and reader into the story: "Is he better or worse off there where he awoke after this actual death? . . .—We shall all soon learn" (29:46).[19]

Critics saw in this story an autobiographical projection of the author's own religious conversion. What is more, Pavel Biriukov believed that Tolstoy conceived it when, during a famine in the cold and miserable winter of 1892–93, he lived in a village (Begichevka) organizing soup kitchens for the starving peasants. There, one day, Tolstoy became lost in a snowstorm and was saved by one of his helpers.[20] But this is not all. As a fable, the story lends itself to allegorical readings.

The story's setting, the snowstorm, reads as an allegory of man's search for the salvation of the soul. The snowstorm is a common topos in Russian literature, from Pushkin's *The Captain's Daughter* (which made a brief appearance in a dream in Tolstoy's "History of Yesterday"), to Tolstoy's own early story "Snowstorm" (*Metel'*). Tolstoy used the image of the man lost in a snowdrift in his *What I Believe?* (1883–84), where it served as an allegory for his religious quest for the meaning of his personal life in relation to the lives of others (23:400).

But let us turn to the story's central image: master and man. If, as I believe, this fable dramatizes the Hegelian master-and-slave dialectic, what does it mean?

First, in this fable, a specific part of Hegel's master-and-slave dialectic comes to the fore: the fear of death. Tied by the bondage of mutual dependency and delusion (played out in specific economic and psychological terms applicable to post-reform Russia), the master and his servant are tested when they face death together. Unlike Hegel's slave, whose excessive fear of death initially drives him into servitude, Tolstoy's laborer, true to his naive peasant faith, is free from the fear of death. Not so his master, in spite of his position as a village church elder. The master attempts to save himself by dissolving his bond with the slave. He abandons the slave, but in the end he returns to him (in large measure through the agency of the horse, who is faithful to *its* master, the servant). It is the act of making master and slave literally (physically) one that brings about mutual salvation. The slave is saved for earthly life, while the master saves his soul for life everlasting. Tolstoy's response to Hegel, then, is to suggest Christian self-abnegation for the sake of the other or to advocate merging with the other rather than struggling for dominance: not a struggle for survival to the death but self-abnegation to the death. (It should be noted that this does not entail relating to the other.)

This story is somewhat different from the fable of Tolstoy and the washerwoman in "What Should We Do Then?" In "Master and Man," Tolstoy rethought and again re-wrote, I think, the master-and-slave dialectic.

Indeed, overshadowing the relationship between master and man is the relationship established by both the slave and the master with their heavenly Lord. The servant, Nikita, from the start puts his life into the hands of "Lord, heavenly Father," who will not abandon him, while his master, Vasily, hears Him only in his last hours. In the end, sooner or later, both the master and the slave die, but death has lost its sting: Both wake up to a new life.

This is not Hegel; this is Christian ethics according to the Tolstoy of the 1890s. And yet Hegel is transparently present. For one, as Kojève has noted, "[I]n a general way, Hegelian anthropology is a secularized Christian theology."[21] What Tolstoy does is to reverse the tide of secularization, revealing the underlying Christian subtext. In Tolstoy's second rewriting, the main purpose of the parable of master and slave is to remind Christians that God is not dead.

Tolstoy's diaries show that not only in his writings, but also in his daily life, he was preoccupied with the dialectic of self and other as it appeared in the light of Christian ethics. One day, a possible solution came to him in a dream: "March 2, 1889. . . . I dreamt that the purpose of every man's life lies in improving the world and people: oneself and others. This is what I saw in my dream, but this is not true. The purpose of my life, as of any life, is improving life; there is only one means for this: improving oneself. (Can't figure this out—later.) This is very important" (50:44). Here, Tolstoy is debating with himself, in dreaming and in waking, about the meaning of life. He does so in terms of the dialectics of self and other (to better oneself *and* others or to better oneself as the only means to a better life), and he feels confused. Later in the day, while taking a walk, he returns to this problem: He replaces the opposition "self and other" with the opposition "I and God," and he strives to overcome it by claiming identity: "I thought about this as I took a walk and I came to what satisfied me: that one really should be perfect, like the Father. One should be like the Father. . . . I and the Father are one. . . . This is what I thought during my walk. Yes, express this in the following way: you are the Father's missionary, to do His deeds" (50:44). With the formula of identity, Tolstoy, of course, follows Christ: "I and the Father are one" (John 10:30). Underlying this famous formula is Christ's sense of his mission, as the one sent by his heavenly Father to fulfill His will. This is how Tolstoy explained this principle in a letter to Chertkov written (on January 30–February 3, 1885) when he was still working on "What Should We Do Then?": "The Father has sent me, I have been sent, I fulfill the will of the one who has sent me" (85:136). According to Tolstoy's authorized biographer Pavel Biriukov, for the rest of his life Tolstoy saw himself primarily in these terms: the one who has been "sent," a missionary of God, sent to do the deeds [*delo*] of the Father.[22]

On another day, April 14, 1889, in his diary, Tolstoy tried to express this idea in a form that presaged the allegory of master and man. He pictures people as "laborers from whom the result of their work is hidden. What is given is an opportunity to participate in work, the merging of one's interests with those of the master." He admires Jesus' parables that express this last conclusion. "This is not even a comparison," he decides, "but the essence of the matter." He continues: "All life is work: work for the master (factory work and other), the work of ploughing and sowing, harvesting and sowing again, improving the soil and the animal breeds, building, intellectual creations—none of this for oneself." When Tolstoy unfolds the metaphor "all life is work," listing different kinds of labor, he seems to be thinking not allegorically but literally. He then elaborates on the idea that, working for the master, we are given "the opportunity to transfer one's own interest into the interest of the other . . . the interest of the master or of the cause [*delo*]." In the end, Tolstoy came up with a self-definition that he wanted to write on his fingernail: "Remember that you are a laborer in God's enterprise [*delo*]" (50:67).

In yet another entry, on September 10, 1889, Tolstoy tried to develop his metaphor of master and slave in terms that suggested the New Testament parables of Jesus: "I got up at 10. Felt much better. Thought with particular clarity: the Master (this is God) entrusted his estate to his slaves (these are people). . . . The master entrusted his vineyard. . . . A deal with the debtors . . . (a double analogy) . . ." (50:139). He recalls Jesus' parables—the Two Debtors, the Unjust Steward, the Talents—and tries out his own. On September 14, 1889, he tries again: "One laborer cannot understand the whole business. However miserable and small is this comparison . . . this very disparity shows all the more man's inability to understand all God's will." Then he shifts the allegory to another level: "The horse knows that it moves in accordance with the master's will . . . but it doesn't know the master's will" (50:142–43). On March 24, 1891, Tolstoy again juxtaposes the image of God and man to that of master and horse (52:22). He has built his chain of being.

There are reasons to believe that Tolstoy was thinking of Hegel when he worked with the allegorical image of master and man in his diary. On May 29, 1893, he recorded, side by side, two thoughts that occurred to him during a walk: "Without a doubt, the purpose of life is in fulfilling the will of the one who sent you," and "They say that the actual is reasonable; on the contrary, everything that exists is always unreasonable" (52:80–81). As in "What Should We Do Then?" he thought in terms of the Hegelian master-and-slave paradigm while rejecting Hegel's later justification of "reality."

To sum up: for years, in his daily life and in his diary, Tolstoy used the "master and man" allegory, with its Hegelian roots, to think through the vexed issue of his relations to the other and to God, until, on September 6, 1894, he decided to turn it into a piece of fiction: "In the morning, in bed, after a bad night, I thought up a lively story about a master and man" (52:137). His parable, "Master and Man," presented a solution to a problem that had long preoccupied him. True, this was a piece of fiction, but fiction of a very special kind: In both message and form, this story was as near as possible to the teachings of Christ.

In the 1880s, in the article entitled "What Should We Do Then?" Tolstoy turned his first-person writing to the problem of self and other. Addressing it as a social problem with immediate relevance to himself, he focused on his relationship with the new class of the urban poor and disenfranchised. He spoke about the things that he, Leo Tolstoy, now residing on Khamovnichesky Lane in Moscow, had seen. True, he could not resist his urge to apply the heartfelt conclusions drawn from his own experiences on the city streets to "everybody," but, first and foremost, he was concerned with developing a personal program of social action. He did this from a position that separated his present writings from the image of "L. Tolstoy," the famous fiction writer. After his conversion, Tolstoy thought of all action in a religious key, and he used the Gospel commandments—in his own translation and interpretation—as a guide to everyday life. In the end, this was both a social program and a continuing religious-philosophical quest. Reflecting on the question "What ought I to do?" Tolstoy kept coming back to the question "Who, what am I?" The Gospel was overlaid with a philosophical paradigm: Hegel's master-and-slave dialectic. I claim that, in "What Should We Do Then?" as well as in other writings, Tolstoy attempted to work through the problem of self and other by modifying the Hegelian paradigm. Like many others who were influenced by Hegel, he understood that neither the slave nor the master could be fully free, but unlike Hegel and his followers, he did not strive for a synthesis and did not aim at a reconciliation of the self with the world. Tolstoy's initial impulse in "What Should We Do Then?" was to break the connection, removing himself from the relationship with the other (if not from the world). This impulse, I argue, underlies Tolstoy's desire to consume less of the labor of others. Over the years that followed "What Should We Do Then?" Tolstoy worked through the problem in his diary, replacing master and slave with God and man. In the story "Master and Man," Tolstoy shifted the issue of self and other from the socioeconomic into the religious domain. He resacralized Hegel's anthropology, returning it to its source in Christian theology. The very act of substitution seemed to bring a resolution. Indeed, in accordance with the allegorical logic of Tolstoy's story, the fatal bind between the self and the other, master and man, dissolves as each shifts his allegiances from a fellow man to God. In the end, Tolstoy could contemplate either (as in "What Should We Do Then?") dissolving his bond with the other or (as in "Master and Man") merging with the other, but not relating to the other; in the end, he was hoping to forge another bond: between "I" and God.

Coda: Nonparticipation in Evil

As an ethical thinker, Tolstoy has made a lasting contribution with his teaching of nonparticipation in evil/nonresistance to evil. It is better known for its latter part—the commandment "Do not resist evil by violence," explicitly stated in Tolstoy's major religious-ethical writings, *What I Believe?* (*V chem moia vera?* 1884) and *The Kingdom of God Inside Us* (*Tsarstvo Bozhie vnutri nas*, 1890–93). And yet the first part, "do not participate in evil," is arguably an essential element of this social strategy. I would further argue that the move to withdraw himself from the field of the other, initially formulated in "What Should We Do Then?" on the basis of the master-and-slave dialectic, underwrites Tolstoy's famous ethical teaching.

The roots of Tolstoy's ethics lie in his religious conversion. In *What I Believe?* he explains why Christianity as preached by the official church has failed to satisfy him: "To the question: What am I? What shall I do? . . . they answer: Obey the authorities and have faith in the Church. But why is there so much suffering in the world? Why is there so much evil? Can I not refuse to take part in it? Can evil not be mitigated? They answer: no" (23:412). He then decided to reinterpret the whole Christian doctrine.

Tolstoy (as he repeatedly claimed) derived his version of Christian ethics from the Sermon on the Mount. Christ said, "You have heard that it has been said, 'An eye for an eye, and a tooth for a tooth.' And I say to you, do not resist evil." One day (Tolstoy tells the reader of *What I Believe?*) he suddenly understood what this means: "Christ says, 'You have been taught to consider it right and rational to protect yourselves against evil by violence, to pluck out an eye for an eye, to institute courts of law for the punishment of criminals, and to have police and an army to defend you against the attacks of an enemy; but I say to you, do no violence to any man, take no part in violence, never do evil to any man, not even to those whom you call your enemies'" (23:328). Note that what Tolstoy hears Christ say (you have been taught to consider violence "right and rational") is remarkably close, even in its diction, to Hegel's dictum in *The Philosophy of Right.*

Tolstoy's next move is to replace this outdated political philosophy based on the justification of the status quo with his own commandment: Do not participate in violence or coercion (*nasilie*).

A simple example is his turn to vegetarianism (in 1885), which he considered the first step toward a righteous life. As he argued in the article "The First Step" (*Pervaia stupen'*, 1891), those who eat meat participate in the taking of animal life. One individual's giving up meat would not bring this practice to an end, but it would remove this individual from the chain of evil.

To explain how the principle of nonparticipation in evil works, I will provide one extensive example: Tolstoy's famous invective on the death penalty (a measure widely used in Russia after 1905 for rebels and revolutionaries). Written in 1908 (the year he turned eighty), it is suggestively entitled "I Cannot Be Silent" (*Ne mogu molchat'*).

Tolstoy starts with a concrete experience: today, on May 9, he opened a newspaper to learn that twenty (as he later found out, twelve) rebellious peasants had been put to death by hanging. These crimes were committed by "you" (the government), he says, against "them" (the revolutionaries), but "they are doing just the same as you": Both sides practice violence. Tolstoy is not oblivious to the fact that, from the perspective of his principle of nonresistance to evil, his own decision to speak out against capital punishment is fraught with paradox, but he feels an emotional compulsion to speak—hence the title. What is more, he realizes that by keeping silent, he participates in the government's actions: "Everything now being done in Russia is done . . . in the name of the protection and tranquility of the people of Russia. And if this is so, then it is also done for me, since I live in Russia." Step by step, Tolstoy lists each evil that is perpetuated on his behalf: "For me, therefore, the destitution of the people, deprived of the first and most natural right of man: the right to use the land on which they were born. For me those half-million men are torn away from wholesome peasant life, dressed in uniforms, and taught to kill. For me that false so-called priesthood, which is mainly responsible for the perversion and concealment of true Christianity. . . . For me these hundreds of thousands of hungry workmen wandering throughout Russia. . . . For me these dozens and hundreds of men have been interned and shot, for me the horrible work goes on for these . . . hangmen" (37:94–95). This chain of evil was first outlined in "What Should We Do Then?" more than twenty years earlier. So was Tolstoy's heartfelt conviction that his privileged position in society in itself constitutes an act of participation in evil: "As strange as it seems to say that all this is done for me, and I am a participant in these terrible deeds, I cannot but feel that there is an interdependence between my spacious room, my dinner, my clothing, my leisure, and these terrible crimes" (37:95).

It is his other privilege as a member of the educated classes—self-consciousness or self-awareness—that binds him to action: "And being conscious of this, I can no longer endure this, but must free myself from this intolerable position." This is not a matter of abstract principle but an emotional imperative: "It is impossible to live so. I, at any rate, cannot live in this way, I cannot and will not" (37:95). Step by step, Tolstoy outlines a practical course of action:

> That is why I write this and will circulate it by all means in my power, both in Russia and abroad. I hope that one of two things may happen: either that these inhuman deeds may be stopped, or that my connection with them may be terminated by my imprisonment, whereby I would be clearly conscious that these horrors are not committed on my behalf. Or still better (so good that I dare not even dream of such happiness), I hope that they may put on me, as on those twelve or twenty peasants, a shroud and a cap and may push me also off a bench, so that by my own weight I may tighten the well-soaped noose round my old throat. (37:95)

Extended to its logical end, the ethical position of nonparticipation leads to what Tolstoy feels as his ultimate desire: his own death by execution. (Note that in describing this fantasy, Tolstoy, his aversion to literature notwithstanding, uses his remarkable rhetorical power and his trademark literary devices to the utmost.)

The ethical position of nonparticipation led to a paradoxical result: After 1881, Tolstoy spoke out against social evil, actually believing that his teaching might have immediate practical applications to the intolerable social situation in Russia.

On March 1, 1881, Alexander II was assassinated by members of the revolutionary organization "The People's Will." No friend of the government, Tolstoy was sickened at heart by the violence. But the prospect that the terrorists would be sentenced to death also pained him to the extreme. A few days after the assassination, after a heated discussion of the situation at the dinner table, he dreamed of the execution, and in his dream, he himself faced execution, and he himself (and not, as he put it, "officials carrying out the sentence of the court") was the executioner. Tolstoy woke up in horror and wrote a letter to the new emperor, Alexander III, in which he suggested that, true to the law of Christ, the emperor should forgive his father's assassins: "Give them some money and send them to America." The terrorists were executed on April 3, 1881.[23]

In the wake of the 1905 Revolution, Tolstoy appealed to all sides to refrain from violence in "Address to the Russian People: to the Government, to the Revolutionists, and to the People" (*Obrashchenie k russkim liudiam. K pravitel'stvu, revoliutsioneram, i narodu*, 1906). When he wrote to Nicholas II in 1901, he admonished him to abolish the root of all social evil, private ownership of land. This text is called "To the Tsar and his Assistants" (*Tsariu i ego pomoshchnikam*, 1901).

After "What Should We Do Then?" Tolstoy penned a large number of admonishments and exhortations on the occasions of social disasters, horrors, and injustices. He wrote about the famines that were ignored by the government in the essays "On Famine" (*O golode*, 1891) and "Famine or No Famine (*Golod ili ne golod*, 1898); he also personally participated in the organization of soup kitchens in the countryside. He directed public attention to the corporal punishment of peasants in "Shame on You" (*Stydno*, 1895); to the catastrophic situation of industrial workers in "The Slavery of Our Time" (*Rabstvo nashego vremeni*, 1900); to the dangers of patriotism in "Christianity and Patriotism" (*Khristianstvo i patriotizm*, 1894), "Patriotism or Peace?" (*Patriotizm ili mir?* 1895), and "Patriotism and the Government" (*Patriotizm i pravitel'stvo*, 1900); to the carnage of the Russo-Japanese War in "Come to Your Senses!" (*Odumaites'!* 1904); to the death penalty, not only in "I Cannot Be Silent" (*Ne mogu molchat'*, 1908) but also in "Do Not Kill" (*Ne ubii*, 1910), and much more.

Many of his moral missives took the form of letters, public and private: "To the Young People Who Do Not Work" (*K molodym liudiam, zhivushchim nerabochei zhizn'iu*, 1901), "To the Working People" (*K rabochemu narodu*, 1902), "To the Clergy" (*K dukhovenstvu*, 1902), "A Letter about Education" (*Pis'mo o vospitanii*, 1901–04), "A Letter to a Peasant about Land" (*Pis'mo k krest'ianinu o zemle*, 1905), "A Letter to a Chinese" (*Pis'mo kitaitsu*, 1906), "A Letter to an Indian" (*Pis'mo indusu*, 1908), "A Letter to a Student about Law" (*Pis'mo studentu o prave*, 1909), "A Letter to a Revolutionary" (*Pis'mo revoliutsioneru*, 1909), "On Science. Response to a Peasant" (*O nauke (otvet krest'ianinu)*, 1909), "Again about Science" (*Eshche o nauke*, 1909), and many others.

In the 1890s and 1900s, Tolstoy was a "moral celebrity" of unprecedented proportions whose appeals were heard around the world, inspiring a range of emotions, from veneration, religious devotion, and active support to appre-hension, derision, and rage.[24]

Tolstoy's moral exhortations were many and varied, but there are com-monalities: the use of the personal "I" and the appeals to his personal ex-perience, direct address to the reader (a real or imaginary "you"), a didactic tone, and occasional moments of masterful description worthy of the author of *War and Peace* (an animal killed in a slaughterhouse in "The First Step," a hungry three-year-old in "On Famine," a condemned man on the scaffold in "I Cannot Be Silent"). Whether or not Tolstoy wanted it, the writer in him worked side by side with the religious teacher and moralist. And yet things were different than when he wrote fiction: In his writings on religion and morality, Tolstoy made every effort to close the distance between the con-ventional narrative "I" of the writer and the "I" that referred to a living and acting person ("I, Leo Tolstoy").

CHAPTER SIX

"I Felt a Completely New Liberation from Personality": Tolstoy's Late Diaries

Tolstoy Resumes His Diary

In 1884, after several abortive attempts, Tolstoy resumed his diary, and he continued to write, with remarkable consistency, until his death in 1910.[1] For a long time, he had doubts: to write or not to write? how? for whom? One day, in 1889, he decided that he should "write with the idea of not showing his writings, including this diary, within one's lifetime." Then, he contemplated, with "horror," not writing. He asked himself: "Would I have the strength to write for God?" (February 20, 1889; 50:39). It seems that, like Rousseau, Tolstoy imagined himself appearing before the Sovereign Judge with his writing in his hand.[2] His late diaries are a text with religious and philosophical significance.[3]

In his lifetime, Tolstoy's late diaries were accessible to his wife and to various members of his household (some of whom made copies and took notes). In 1910, in addition to the regular diary, there was a "secret diary," which Tolstoy, whose relationship with his wife was becoming more and more strained, kept for himself alone.[4] In his last years, the diaries became a point of contention between Tolstoy's wife and his disciple Vladimir Chertkov. Tolstoy's last secretary Valentin Bulgakov believed that a confrontation between S. A. Tolstaya and Chertkov over the diaries in summer 1910 had precipitated Tolstoy's final departure from home.[5]

The Temporal Order of Narrative: The Last Day

The diaries of Tolstoy's late years are written with an eye toward approaching death: For some twenty years, Tolstoy expected death daily. Scholars have long noted the centrality of death in Tolstoy's art and thought; his diaries document his personal preoccupation with death, day by day.[6]

His existential situation called for a special time scheme. When, in the evening, Tolstoy described his day and made a plan for tomorrow, under tomorrow's date (as had been his habit since his youth), he was aware that tomorrow might not come. Accordingly, the account of a day usually ends not with a plan for tomorrow but with the formula "*esli budu zhiv*" ("if I live," usually abbreviated "*e.b.zh.*"), which follows tomorrow's date. An account of tomorrow often starts with the affirmation "alive."[7] The formula may have its origin in the New Testament, in James's admonishment to those who boast about tomorrow.[a] In his diary, Tolstoy puts this commandment to practical use.

The following entry, from 1897, clearly demonstrates the workings of this pattern. (The first line, under the date February 25, was written on February 24 (Tolstoy also marks the place); the last, under February 26, on February 25.)

> 25 Feb. 1897. N[ikol'skoe]. E.b.zh.
> 25 February [1897]. Alive. Did not write much, not as easily as yesterday. Went for a walk, twice. Read Aristotle. Today received letters with Seryozha who came here. Unpleasant letter from S[onia]. Or rather I am in a bad mood. Yesterday, during a walk, prayed, and experienced a wonderful feeling. It was probably like the feeling that mystics evoke by the Jesus prayer: I felt solely my spiritual self, free, tied down by an illusion of the body.
> 26 F. 97. *E.b.zh.* (53:141)

Recall that in his early diaries Tolstoy conceived of a narrative utopia: to capture the present moment and to render life in its entirety. (This plan received its clearest realization in "A History of Yesterday" in 1851.) Such a project

---

[a] "Now listen, you who say, 'Today or tomorrow we will go to this or that city, spend a year there, carry on business and make gain.' You, who do not even know what will happen tomorrow. What is your life? You are a mist that appears for a little while and then vanishes. Instead, you ought to say, 'If, Lord willing, we will live, we will do this or that.'" (James 4:13–15) I thank Denis Zhernokleyev for this reference.

involves writing one's life to its end. In his late diaries, the formula "*e.b.zh.*" (under tomorrow's date) not only questions but also posits a tomorrow—a point from which today appears as yesterday. It would seem that the late Tolstoy aspired to produce a diary in which the account of each day— including the last day in his life—would be written as the history of yesterday. His diary would thus be a total history of the evolving present.

The same diary entry that creates a grid fit to capture time in its entirety reveals an alternative, and competing, aspiration: to achieve a narrative-free and timeless consciousness of self—a different self—through an act akin to the mystical Jesus prayer. (Originating in the Hesychast tradition, the Jesus prayer, or "internal prayer," is practiced in Eastern Orthodoxy.)[8] The power of this prayer (performed by repeating the name "Jesus") relies on the non-verbal. As one enters into a mystical state, the word loses its linguistic encasement; in silence, man attains direct knowledge of God. Tolstoy, it would seem, faced a dilemma: total articulation of self or total silence? It is no exaggeration to say that throughout his late diaries, he fluctuated between these two impulses.

The old Tolstoy often claimed that he was no longer a writer. Once, when he had made such a remark, he added, somewhat incongruously: "I feel sad because it seems as though, even while I am dying, I will continue to write, and even after death, too" (December 22, 1893; 52:105). This astounding remark seems to indicate that, hard as he might try not to be a writer, he could not imagine a condition in which he would not be writing.

Tolstoy had taken to heart the Stoic precept to live each day as if it were the last. But he also wanted to leave an account of his last day. Tolstoy may have been prompted by Victor Hugo's *Le dernier jour d'un condamné* (1829), which produced a strong impression on his contemporaries. The fictive diary of a man condemned to death, Hugo's story records its hero's feelings and thoughts on the last day of his life. In *The Idiot* (1868), Dostoevsky extended Hugo's image into a metaphor of the human condition in the nineteenth century, afflicted as it was with nonbelief: a whole life, when lived in full awareness of one's finitude, becomes the last day of a *condamné*.[9] In his diary, Tolstoy used Hugo's image to describe his personal situation: "In one's old age, one can and even should do this, although this is possible already in one's youth, namely, assume the condition not only of a man sentenced to death, but of a man transported to the place of execution" (January 3, 1909; 57:4). For Tolstoy (as for Dostoevsky), the situation of a condemned man provided a unique narrative potential: to give a transcription of completely authentic experience—the Heideggerian being-toward-death *avant la lettre*.[10] In his late diaries he attempted to provide such an account. It could be that he aimed to do even more. Hugo's *Le dernier jour*—unlike Alfred Maury's famous dream account of his own execution—stopped at the moment when the hero was about to climb the scaffold and face the guillotine. (Maury described his head separating from his body under the guillotine.) But, as we are about to see, Tolstoy may have hoped to take his record further. In his youth (in "A History of Yesterday"), he had provided an account of a dream text from the point of view of the sleeping person.[11] If self-consciousness were to pursue the writer even into death, what kind of text would he produce?

Mikhail Bakhtin once commented that "Tolstoy depicts death not only from the outside looking in but also from the inside looking out, that is, from the very consciousness of the dying person, *almost* as a fact of consciousness." Bakhtin speaks here about Tolstoy's fiction (about the death of Tolstoy's characters), and he adds that "in order to depict death from within, Tolstoy does not hesitate to violate sharply the real-life verisimilitude of the narrator's position (precisely as if the deceased himself had told him the story of his own death). . . . By contrast, Dostoevsky *never* depicts death from within."[12] Having dealt not with fiction but with Tolstoy's diaries, I would remove the word "almost": in his personal writings Tolstoy speaks of death as a fact of *his*, Tolstoy's, consciousness.

"On Life and Death"

Before we turn to the diaries, a comment is necessary on the essay "On Life" (published in 1888), which contains Tolstoy's theoretical formulations on life and death.[13] In the summer of 1886, during a serious illness, Tolstoy decided to formulate his views on his impending death in the language of professional philosophy. He even presented his ongoing essay, under the title "On Life and Death," to the Moscow Psychological Society, chaired by Professor Nikolai Grot (whose own work on the concept of the soul may have inspired Tolstoy's project).[14] About a year later, Tolstoy's wife recorded in her diary that the manuscript was now complete: "he crossed out the word death from the title. By the time he had finished the essay, he had decided that *there was no death*" (August 4, 1887; 26:767).

The crucial chapter, suggestively entitled "Bodily Death Destroys Spatial and Temporal Consciousness, But Cannot Destroy That Which Makes the Foundation of Life," advances this conclusion through a set of seemingly consistent propositions. Why, then, do we fear death? The fear (Tolstoy suggests) stems from mistakes in conceptualizing the self, from our inability to conceive a proper answer to the questions "What am I? What is my life?": "I have lived 59 years, and for all this time I have been conscious of myself in my body, and this consciousness of myself, it seems to me, has been my life" (26:402). This, he has decided, is an absolutely arbitrary conclusion.

For one thing, mistakes about self result from relying on bodily images. But the body—muscles, bones, brain cells—changes on a daily basis. For this reason alone, we have every reason to believe that our "I" resides outside our bodies. So, what is "my life"? And what is "I"? Tolstoy poses this question as a key to the problem of death.

He reasons logically, on the basis of philosophical ideas about the consciousness of self and identity over time: "What if, at any moment of my life, I put the question to myself, to my consciousness, what am I?" He answers: "My consciousness says to me only: I am. . . ." ;"of my birth, my childhood, of many periods of my youth . . . I often remember nothing." What is more (he adds), we "lose consciousness every day when we fall asleep": "Every day, during deep sleep, consciousness completely ceases and then is restored again" (26:404). Tolstoy concludes (contrary to Locke) that continuity of self-consciousness cannot serve as a firm foundation for the sense of self.

To define the "I," then, one must go beyond the biological limits of human life. Man's true "I" unites "all remembered states of consciousness and the states of consciousness that precede the remembered life, as Plato says and as we all ourselves feel it" (26:407). (Note that Tolstoy appeals, in one breath, to the authority of classical philosophy and to direct experience.) Tolstoy also goes beyond the limits of the individual "I": He speaks of a shared reason, "reasonable consciousness" (*razumnoe soznanie*), a "Logos, Wisdom, Word" that unites all living people into one single whole. (Tolstoy seems to be working with the idea of Logos, or "a universal reason," as developed in classical antiquity and extended by the early Christians.) This is the "non-I" that will not die. In the end, by reconceptualizing the self, Tolstoy seems to have philosophized death away.

Tolstoy's ideas about self and death, of course, have precedents. He names Plato, but Tolstoy's immediate source was Schopenhauer, the famous chapter 41 of *The World as Will and Representation* (*Die Welt als Wille und Vorstellung*), entitled "On Death and Its Relation to the Indestructibility of Our Inner Nature," and the essay from *Parerga and Paralipomena*, "On the Teaching about the Indestructibility of Our Essential Essence by Death."

Tolstoy became acquainted with Schopenhauer in 1868 and soon realized that he had found a kindred spirit. In a letter to the poet-philosopher Afanasy Fet (a close friend), he described the summer of 1869 as "a continuous ecstasy over Schopenhauer and a series of mental pleasures such as I've never before experienced." He added: "I ordered all his works and have read and am reading them (I also read Kant)" (62: 219). This was a difficult time for Tolstoy: Another crisis had followed the completion of *War and Peace*. In his ecstatic letter to Fet, Tolstoy made a point of noting that in Schopenhauer, he found a confirmation of his own thoughts: Schopenhauer in his treatise says the same thing (albeit from a different perspective) that he, Tolstoy, had just written in the epilogue to *War and Peace* (61:217). In fact, in the drafts of the Epilogue, Tolstoy calls Schopenhauer "the greatest thinker of this century and the only direct follower of Descartes, Spinoza, Locke and Kant" (15:246). Tolstoy started translating *Die Welt als Wille und Vorstellung*, and he asked Fet to join him in the project. In 1881, when the book finally appeared in Russian (translated by Fet alone), Tolstoy read it again, making copious marginal notes. In a word, he made Schopenhauer's thought his own. (He could have said—as he had said earlier about Rousseau—that he might have written many of Schopenhauer's pages himself.) Soon after *Anna Karenina*, where Schopenhauer is transparently present, Tolstoy rejected his favorite philosopher on account of his pessimism—his idea that privation, misery, and suffering, crowned by death, are the aim and object of our life. In "On Life," Tolstoy explicitly recalls Schopenhauer in order to call his negativism morally unsound. And yet, without any acknowledgment, he operates with Schopenhauer's concepts. Indeed, Schopenhauer had a hold on Tolstoy to the end of his life.[15]

In "On Life," Tolstoy echoes Schopenhauer's words that "nonexistence after death cannot be different from nonexistence before birth, and is therefore no more deplorable" (This idea has Platonic origins, but Schopenhauer also refers to Hindu and Buddhist thought, as does Tolstoy.) He follows Schopenhauer's extension of Kantian epistemology, his assertion that, since concepts of destruction or continued existence belong to the phenomenal realm of time, space, and causality, death too is only phenomenal.[16] Tolstoy's analogy between death and sleep sounds like a paraphrase of Schopenhauer's aphorism: Consciousness is extinguished by death—as it is by sleep or by any form of fainting.[17] Finally, Tolstoy followed Schopenhauer's famous sophism: Since life is a constant dying, death and life are one; consequently, there is no death.

Schopenhauer, in turn, started the famous chapter "On Death" by evoking Plato's dialogue *Phaedo*, the paradigmatic source on death in Western thought, and he followed Socrates' understanding of philosophy as *melete thanatou*: an exercise in dying. But Schopenhauer, in the nineteenth century, translated Platonic concepts for the modern era. Thus, he rejected both the materialistic view of death as a mere cessation of bodily existence (which was raised to dominance with the advances of science) and evaded the Christian idea of death as a transitional step to resurrection in the flesh (which, for many, seemed incompatible with the modern outlook). After Schopenhauer, overcoming death implied a philosophical revision of the notion of the self: The "I" had to be reconceptualized, separated from the contingency of human individuality and from the contents of an individual life. Tolstoy joined Schopenhauer in this historical task. (Other thinkers, such as Georg Simmel, also followed this path.)[18]

Tolstoy, like Plato's Socrates, not only conceptualized but also experienced his own life in these terms. And in contrast to Schopenhauer, he responded to the presence of death not with pessimism but with joy. Tolstoy's late diaries are a document of this experience.

The Diary as a Spiritual Exercise

As his diaries show, Tolstoy awaited death cheerfully, making records of his expectations in the context of routine daily occupations:

> 31 October 89. Y[asnaya] P[olyana]. . . . Apathy, sorrow, despondency. But it does not trouble me. Ahead lies death, that is, life—how can one not rejoice? (50:170)
> 23 January 90. If I live.
> And so, presently, it's the 27th. Got up late. I had an excellent conversation with Chertkov about art and death and went for a walk. . . . What one must never forget about death is that life is a constant process of dying. And by saying "I am constantly dying," one might just as well say "I live." (51:15)

In these entries, Tolstoy makes it clear that his joy rests on a philosophical premise. In another such entry, he even names Schopenhauer (among details of his daily life): "29 June 1894. Y[asnaya] P[olyana]. Morning. . . .—I have somehow lost my watch. Still more and more often and more and more vividly, I think about death, only about physical death. The death that used to terrify me, now I don't see it anymore. . . . What is better in this regard is simply readiness. Reading Schopenhauer's Parerga. . . ." (52:124). Tolstoy's philosophy of death was not a theory but a life-practice. Indeed, long after Tolstoy published his essay "On Life," he repeated his philosophical reflections, on the basis of his everyday experience, in his diary.

In his diary, I suggest, Tolstoy engaged in "spiritual exercises": personal practices meant to bring about an actual transformation of the self. Beginning with Socrates, many authors, from antiquity to modern times, have practiced philosophy in this way. "Philosophy" appears not as a sum of abstract propositions written with the intention of creating a system but as an experience that involves one's whole being. It has been argued that Plato's Socratic dialogues, the *Meditations* of Marcus Aurelius, Seneca's *Epistles,* Montaigne's essays, Pascal's *Pensées*, and, in the nineteenth century, Henri Amiel's *journal intime* and Schopenhauer's aphorisms in *Parerga und Paralipomena*, among other texts, can be viewed as such spiritual exercises (acts as well as texts).[19] (These books happen to have been among Tolstoy's favorite books to read, especially in the last decades of his life.) In his turn, Tolstoy found in his diaries a medium for such a practical philosophy of life and death. This is why he writes poorly; this is why he repeats, again and again.[20] In his diary, year after year, day in and day out, Tolstoy performed written exercises of death.

"I, the Body, Is Such a Disgusting Chamber Pot"

Starting his diary for 1908, during which he turned eighty, Tolstoy defined what he should do in his "last day" in Socrates' terms: "liberate one's soul" (56:88). For Tolstoy, as for Socrates, this implied separating oneself from the body (and from the selfish conduct it entails). He commented that now, at eighty, he should do what he had done at a young age, that is, work for self-perfection, but that his ideals of perfection had changed (December 3, 1908; 56:160). The old Tolstoy echoed his young self by noting deplorable moments of moral weakness, especially vanity, vexation, and, last but not least, sexual desire—but this was not all. To liberate one's soul implied no longer projecting oneself into the future. This meant cultivating something other than self as a basis for living one's life. Much was at stake: As Tolstoy once put it, "It's precisely what is not 'I' that is immortal" (June 19, 1886; 49:129). Tolstoy's late diaries, the accounts of his "last day" (which lasted some twenty years), reflect his daily struggle with his mortal self: body, emotions, desires, satisfactions, habits, and consciousness itself.

In his eightieth year, Tolstoy was especially attentive to the changes in his body and soul. Thus, on January 1, 1908, he noted that in the morning, for the first time, he became clearly conscious of his own spirituality: He woke up feeling ill, weak in body, and clearly imagined what his future transition would feel like: "not death, but liberation from the body." He became aware that "that which is my true 'I'" was indestructible. He wondered: "Is this new state of mind a step towards liberation?" (56:89). On another day, he noted: "I want to live in God, not in my bodily self, Leo T[olstoy]. What does this mean? It means that I want to replace the consciousness of Leo T[olstoy] with the consciousness of all humankind" (April 21, 1908; 56:123).

But daily life kept interfering with his spiritual progress: For one thing, his health improved; moreover, the public celebrations of his eightieth anniversary, affecting his vanity, posed a threat for his "higher soul." And yet Tolstoy kept struggling, and he used his diary to record his progress. On September 14, he "took up this notebook to record" that, in the morning, he felt "complete indifference towards everything bodily" and "continuous interest in his spiritual growth, or spiritual life" (56:150). But it proved difficult to account for his inner, spiritual life in the diary.

In one remarkable entry (from March 1908) Tolstoy addressed this problem directly: "I haven't written anything all month. . . . My internal labor, thank God, goes without stopping, better and still better. I want to write about what happens inside me and how it happens; about things I have never told anyone and about which no one knows." He proceeded, however, to give a summary account of his external life—his daily routine:

> This is how I live: I get up, my head is clear, good thoughts occur to me, and, as I sit on the pot, I write them down. I get dressed and I empty the contents of the pot with an effort but with pleasure. I go for a walk. On my walk I wait for the post from force of habit, although I don't need it. I often guess to myself how many steps it will take to get to such and such a place, and I count them, dividing each into four, six, and eight breaths: one and *a* and *a* and *a*; and *two* and *a* and *a* and *a*. . . . Sometimes, from force of habit, I want to guess that if there are as many steps as I suppose, all will be well. But then I ask myself: what is "well"? and I know that everything is very well as it is, and there's no need to try and guess. Then, when I meet someone, I try to remember—though for the most part I forget that I wanted to remember—that He and I are one. It's particularly difficult to remember this during a conversation. (56:109–10)

This account reflects the ambivalence in Tolstoy's situation. Striving to free his soul for communion with God, he feels how his old self asserts its habitual power (the habit of projecting oneself into the future intrudes into the game of guessing how many steps it will take to get to a place).

His body provided evidence of man's perishable nature on a daily basis: "Yes, I, the body, is such a disgusting chamber pot—just remove or open the lid of spirituality, and there's stench and abomination. Today I will try to live for the soul" (July 7, 1908; 56:173). This metaphor is likely to have been prompted by experience: As Tolstoy mentioned in the inventory of his daily routine, he used to record his thoughts while sitting on the chamber pot. Such moments in the diary achieve a rare effect: the experiential and the philosophical converged.

"I Am Conscious of Myself Being Conscious of Myself Being Conscious of Myself. . . ."

There was hope for liberation from the body, which gave obvious signs of deterioration (such as failures of the digestive system), and Tolstoy faithfully, joyfully, marked these signs in his diary. But one thing seemed inescapable: consciousness.

Tolstoy claimed to know from personal experience that the inescapable "I" was not the body, but rather consciousness, forever locked in the apprehension of itself: "I remember how in childhood I was surprised at the appearance of my distinctive trait, which still did not know how to find realization for itself. I remember, I was always surprised that I could, being conscious of myself, be conscious of the self being conscious of itself, and, asking myself again, I was conscious that I was conscious of myself being conscious of myself. And from there: I am conscious of myself being conscious of myself being conscious of myself, and so on to infinity" (56:128).[b] If we are to believe the old Tolstoy, as a child he had discovered a concept from post-Kantian philosophy, Fichte's *Ich-an-sich* or Schelling's *Ich ist Ich*—the "I" understood solely as the act of thinking of the "I."

Since Descartes, philosophers have struggled with the concept of the self as a subject that thinks and thus continually relates to itself. After Kant (Fichte pointed out), it was clear that all mental representations had to be accompanied by "I think." For his part, Tolstoy noticed (as did other thinkers before him) that such an understanding of the subject allowed for two responses. One was to see human consciousness as a prison house for the "I," forever locked in the apprehension of itself. In Fichte's formulation: "Throughout every moment of our entire lives we are constantly thinking 'I,' 'I,' 'I,' and never anything except 'I' [*Ich, Ich, Ich, und nie etwas als Ich*]. Or it may be viewed from the philosopher's standpoint, in which case it means the

---

[b] A similar formula appears in chapter 19 of Tolstoy's *Boyhood* (*Otrochestvo*; 1854): "I asked myself: what am I thinking?—And I answered: I am thinking what I am thinking. And now, what am I thinking? I am thinking that I am thinking what I am thinking, and so on."

following: Whatever we may think of as occurring within consciousness, we must also think of the 'I' as well. In explaining the various determinations of our mind, we may never abstract from the 'I.'"[21] Another response was to attempt to break out of the reflexive circle. For his part, Fichte posited another type of consciousness, subject-less knowing, a knowledge that can only be accomplished in an action but cannot be grasped conceptually.[22] Schelling, in his turn, spoke about not an individual but an "absolute" ego; not a thing but an infinite freedom, given in intuition. Tolstoy's musings on "I is I" often sound like paraphrases of Fichte or Schelling.

In his late diaries and notebooks Tolstoy returned to this topic again and again: "What is consciousness? I will ask myself: what, who am I?—And I will answer: I am I. And then I will ask myself: but who is this second I?—And there is only one answer: again, I; no matter how many times you ask, it is always: I am I. Clearly, there is an I that is beyond space, beyond time" (April 29, 1910; 58:42). Tolstoy, like Fichte, attempted to break out of the self-reflexive circle by positing a distinction between two different types of consciousness. In Tolstoy's words, the first one is the consciousness of man as an individual; the second is the consciousness of one's participation in the universal. The first (lower) consciousness "gives the notion of the body, matter, space and time." The second consciousness knows "neither the body, nor movement, nor space, nor time." The task of life lies in transferring one's "I" from the individual into the universal, spiritual consciousness (June 18, 1903; 54:179–80). But such philosophical solutions did not relieve Tolstoy's feeling of imprisonment within individual consciousness.

It would seem that Tolstoy relied on his personal experience:

August 6 [1892.] . . . I remember: I am sitting in the bathhouse, and a shepherd boy walked in. I asked: Who is there?—I am.—Who is I?—It's I.—Who are you?—But it's I. . . . It is the same with everybody.
    August 7, 1892. If I live. (52:69)

And yet Fichte had used this very situation: "Suppose you call out to someone in the dark, 'Who is there?' [*Wer ist da?*] And suppose too that, acting on the assumption that you will recognize his voice, he replies, 'It is I' [*Ich bin es*]."[23] Even though Tolstoy may indeed have acquired his sense of inescapable consciousness through personal experience rather than philosophical reading, there is no doubt that he knew Fichte and Schelling.[24]

Fascination with theories of subjectivity derived from Kant, Fichte, and Schelling had been a starting point for the philosophical education of a whole generation of Russian thinkers, beginning with Nikolai Stankevich and his famous "circle." For the members of Stankevich's generation, in the 1830s and 1840s, and for the one that followed in the 1850s, much of this education was gained informally, through intense personal exchanges in a circle of friends, and much of it has become known to us from their private documents. It struck Stankevich, who shared his discovery in a letter to a friend in 1835, that the principle "I = I" (which he learned from Schelling) served as a foundation of all philosophy or, in his terms, "*razumenie*" (roughly, "reasoning"); he suggested that one should start with Kant (he added that he had not yet turned to Hegel).[25] To another friend he recommended Fichte: "I haven't read Fichte, but I've heard that his 'I' is a human one, and Schelling's is absolute."[26] The emotional intensity, intimacy, and naivete of these philosophical exercises contributed (as historians of Russian thought like to argue) to their appeal and efficacy. Tolstoy, in his turn, read Stankevich's letters in 1858, when they appeared in published form and (as he wrote to a friend) was moved to tears (60:272). There are reasons to believe that in his philosophical education, Tolstoy retraced their steps.[27]

To sum up: following in the steps of subject-centered thinkers (the line that runs from Descartes to Kant and culminates in Fichte), Tolstoy, in his diary, repeatedly came to the impasse of "I = I," the inescapable reflexive circle of consciousness. Even if one could liberate the soul from the body, was it possible to shed consciousness itself?

"I Have Lost the Memory of Everything, Almost Everything. . . . How Can One Not Rejoice at the Loss of Memory?"

In his eightieth year, Tolstoy discovered that it was indeed possible: He was now subject to fainting spells—a temporary loss of consciousness (*poteria soznaniia*) followed by a temporary loss of memory. He interpreted this experience as a prefiguration of the complete oblivion to be gained in death.

About his first fainting spell, which occurred on March 2, 1908, he wrote, with joy, in the March 10 entry: "About a week ago I got ill. I had a fainting fit. And it made me feel very good. But the people around me make a *fuss*[c] over it" (56:109).[28] During the next two such episodes (in April), of which he made no record, Tolstoy felt the presence of his long-dead brother Dmitry.[29]

On several occasions, he experienced a loss of memory upon awakening from sleep: "Today, on May 13, upon awakening, I experience a strange state

---

[c] Tolstoy wrote the word "fuss" in English.

of mind: it's as if I have forgotten everything. . . . I cannot remember: what is the date? what am I writing?—And meanwhile, my dreams, not so much representations as emotions from today's dreams, seem especially vivid" (May 28, 1907; 56:35).[d] On this occasion, his dreams seemed more real to Tolstoy than the impressions of his waking life.

On another occasion, he experienced such an awakening as a liberation from self: "I now more and more [begin] to forget. Just now I slept long and, having awakened, I felt a completely new liberation from personality: it is so wonderful! If only I could be liberated altogether." From this, he made a most important methodological conclusion: "Awakening from sleep, from dreaming, this is the model of such a liberation" (January 31, 1908; 56:98). (He put this model to good use—a matter for later comment.)

Even apart from episodes of complete oblivion, the old Tolstoy noticed that his memory was diminishing. Taking this as an advance in the process of liberation, he joyfully marked the progress of memory loss in his diary. He claimed that he had not regretted it once ("I can regret, and do regret, the loss of hair, but not the loss of memory . . ."; 56:161).

Among the other things Tolstoy forgot were his writings. He once told a visitor (Il'ia Mechnikov, a distinguished biologist who shared his preoccupation with aging and death) that he had forgotten the content of *Anna Karenina*.[30] His wife reminded him of the plot, but Tolstoy listened without interest. This fact got into the newspapers, and Tolstoy was touched to tears by the article, entitled "I don't remember . . . I have forgotten" (*Ne pomniu . . . Zabyl . . .*), which interpreted this fact in a religious key: Tolstoy wanted to forget all of his past, all of his former works, everything except the commandment "Love thy neighbor."[31]

Tolstoy indeed had a tendency to translate observations on his daily life into general principles imbued with moral or metaphysical significance, applicable to other people: "I have lost the memory of everything almost everything that has been, of all my writings, of everything that has brought me to the consciousness in which I now live. . . . How can one not rejoice at the loss of memory? Everything that I worked out in the past (through my internal labors, in my writings), I live by all this now, I benefit from it, but the labors themselves—I don't remember. It's amazing. And I think that this joyful change happens to all old men: life concentrates itself in the present. How wonderful!" (October 23, 1910; 58:122). On this (as on several other occasions), Tolstoy focused on the consequences that memory loss entailed for

---

[d] The dates in this entry show a discrepancy.

his experience of time. The past disappeared: Tolstoy no longer remembered his history. In view of his imminent death, the future was no longer there. It seemed that time had come to a standstill. He had achieved what, in his early diaries, remained beyond his grasp: Tolstoy was finally living "a timeless life in the present" (58:122). But (as in his early diaries), it was still far from easy to make an account of the present. For one thing, he now frequently forgot what had happened during the day. Occasionally, all he recorded was the fact that he did not remember: "22, 23, 24 Feb. [1910.] I poorly remember what happened in these two days" (58:19).

Sleeping, Dreaming, and Awakening

In his last years Tolstoy spent more and more time sleeping. He used the experience of sleeping, dreaming, and awakening as a "model" for investigating what might happen after death. He reasoned by analogy, trying to align several elements—going to sleep, dreaming, waking from a dream—into a pattern that brought clarity or comfort. He tried different variants: "Dreams [*snovideniia*] are a complete analogy of life" (January 13, 1907; 57:91). (Here he relies on a metaphor, life is a dream, which Plato, Descartes, Pascal, Schopenhauer, and yet others used to philosophize about how to distinguish real life from illusion.) "Sleeping-and-dreaming [*son*]ᵉ is a complete analogy of death" (May 28, 1907; 56:34). (This idea also has a cultural lineage, including the memorable lines from Shakespeare, "To die, to sleep; to sleep, perchance to dream.") He tried again: "I told myself that death is like dreaming, like falling asleep: you are tired and you fall asleep—and this is true; but death is still more like awakening" (September 15, 1904; 55:89). In his diary, Tolstoy went through these three options again and again. It seems that on many days, as he went to sleep, dreamed, and woke up again, he tested what happens in the transition between life and death. One day, when he woke up, while lying in bed, he thought of a complex analogy that linked the cycle of sleeping and waking, as well as life and death, into a circle: "Today is February 5, 1892. Begichevka. Have just got up. In bed I thought: One wakes from a dream into what we call life. . . . But isn't this life also a dream? And don't we wake up, in death, into what we call future life, what both precedes and follows the dreams of this life?" (52:62). In the years to come, Tolstoy continued to connect and reconnect the elements of

---

ᵉ In Russian, one word, *son*, means both sleep and dream.

the analogy into different patterns, but the idea that death is *both* falling asleep *and* awakening to a new life, and a new consciousness, had a special hold over him.

It should be noted that this was not the first time Tolstoy had thought—and dreamed—that death was an awakening. The following record appears in his notebook on April 11, 1858:

> I saw in a dream that a door in my dark room suddenly opened, then closed again. I was frightened but tried to believe that this was the wind. Someone told me: go open the door, I wanted to open it, but someone held the door from the other side. I wanted to run, but my legs would not move, and I was overwhelmed with horror. I woke up, I was happy to wake up. What made me happy? I have gained consciousness, and I have lost the consciousness that I had in my dream. Couldn't a man be happy also when he dies? They say, he loses the consciousness of his "I." But don't I lose it when I fall asleep, and still, I continue to live. What is lost is personality, the individual. (48:75)

On the same day that Tolstoy recorded this dream in his notebook, he made a note in his diary: "a nightmare and a philosophical theory of unconsciousness" (52:12). The thirty-year-old Tolstoy understood that he had made a whole theory of consciousness, or rather unconsciousness, from his dream.

And he did not stop at that: This dream (as scholars have noticed) informed the famous scene in *War and Peace* that features Andrei's revelation, reached in a dream, about the illusory nature of death: "I died—I woke up. Yes, death is an awakening!"[32] Liberated by his vision, the hero of Tolstoy's novel dies without fear or regret. But Tolstoy, unlike his character, had not found the final consolation in this symbolic dream. In his late diaries, as we have seen, dreams of death and awakening continued to haunt him, both as actual nightmares and as philosophical theories of consciousness.

Tolstoy's Dreams

Since his youth, Tolstoy had viewed dreaming and awakening as a significant experience, and he recorded noteworthy dreams in his diary or in his notebook (kept at his bedside). In his late years, he did this with increasing frequency. I will pause to make a general comment on Tolstoy's dreams. The following examples have been selected to demonstrate recurrent patterns.

A number of the dreams Tolstoy chose to record deal with emotions and morals. On May 5, 1884, he recorded a happy dream: "I dreamt that my wife loves me. How easy, clear everything has become! Nothing like that in waking life" (49:90). On May 25, 1889, he dreamed that he was drafted to be a soldier and complied with orders; he felt that, when asked to swear an oath of allegiance, he would refuse, but immediately thought that perhaps instead he should give up his convictions; there was an inner struggle, and his conscience prevailed (50:85). On June 29, 1889, he dreamed, with horror, of a frog the size of a man; he felt that this was the horror of death. Upon awakening, he decided, "no, it was just fear as such" (50:101). On September 29, 1895, he dreamed that he was hit in the face but refused to challenge his offender to a duel; he felt ashamed, but then thought that he could actually refrain from challenging his offender because this proved his adherence to the doctrine of nonresistance. When he awoke, he was disgusted with the "base" feelings of this dream (53:59). On January 22, 1897, he dreamed of the same insult and woke under the impact, feeling ill (53:132).

Throughout his life, Tolstoy also dreamed of elaborate philosophical or social conceptions; upon awakening, he would sometimes outline thoughts and whole theories that came to him in his dreams. For example, on March 23, 1890, he dreamed that matter changed form but did not disappear; and he saw a proof of immortality: "some powder on a plate." It was new and clear; but when he woke up, this clarity was lost (51:31). On June 20, 1909, after reading Engels's discussion of Marx, he woke up with a vision of a clear, simple, obvious rebuttal of materialism. In his waking state, he did not find it as clear, but some of his dream thoughts, he decided, still stood (57:86).

In one remarkable dream he saw himself as Christ. He saw himself, simultaneously, as a subject (rather, two antagonistic subjects) of the action and author of the text: "This night I saw in my dream that I, in part, write or compose, and in part, experience the drama of Christ. I am both Christ and a warrior. I remember how I put on my sword. It's very vivid" (November 29, 1908; 56:158). When Tolstoy makes these records, he stands outside his dreams, observing and analyzing his own feelings and thoughts.

This effect is well known to students of dreams. Indeed, dreaming creates a special relationship to self. Who is the "I" of dreams?[33] A dream, though a product of our own psychic activity, "strikes us as something alien to us."[34] After waking, the dreamer, who in some ways is the author of the dream, does not fully understand his creation.[35] Thus, there is a unique relationship to self that resides in observing oneself dream and in recording one's dreams. For one thing, there is a disjunction between "I" as the protagonist and "I" as the author of the dream. What is more, potentially, there is a disjunction between "I" and "my text." Thus dreaming becomes an experience of confronting one's hidden depths and one's potentials. Dreaming includes the splitting of the subject and the ambivalence of feeling and knowledge. There is also a temporal dimension: Dreams try out possibilities, playing a crucial part in imagining and preparing for the future. (In this way, dreams can be taken as prophecies.) In a word, dreaming stages an encounter between the subject and object and between the knowing and the nonknowing self, amplified when the dream is recounted.

This complex relationship to self played out clearly when Tolstoy produced written work on the basis of his dreams.[36] On October 22, 1909, Tolstoy had a vivid dream featuring a protagonist who eloquently spoke to assembled guests about the injustice of private ownership of land (57:158). On the next day, Tolstoy recorded his dream. (It was in part informed by Henry George's *Progress and Poverty*, which Tolstoy knew and admired.) Over the next two months, this dream record turned into an essay, "Dream" (*Son*). This dream-based essay (published in 1911) remains one of Tolstoy's most eloquent statements on the situation of the peasants in post-reform Russia, an issue that had preoccupied him since "What Should We Do Then?" (38:23–29). When he had finished his essay, Tolstoy made a point of putting on record that it was based on an authentic dream experience. He wrote in his notebook: "Everything that I have written down I have, indeed, seen, heard in my dream. True, in a waking state, too, I often think of the agrarian question, but what I have heard in this dream, I have not thought through in a waking state, but have only heard in a dream" (57:264). A complex relationship between the knowing and the nonknowing self also played out when Tolstoy used his own dreams for philosophical purposes in his diaries. In the section that follows, I will provide some examples.

Dreams: The World beyond Time and Representation

In his late diaries, Tolstoy often used his own dreams to make generalizations about the mechanisms of consciousness and means of representation.

One day he recorded a significant dream: "Had a dream. I am talking with Grot and know that he's dead, but carry on all the same, showing no surprise.

And in the conversation I want to remember somebody's judgment on Spencer, or Spencer's own—in the dream, this didn't make a difference. And I knew and had spoken of this argument before. So this argument existed both before and after." At this point, Tolstoy paused to validate his incongruous vision:

> The conversation with Grot, despite the fact that he had died, and the fact that the argument about Spencer existed both before and after and belonged both to Spencer and to somebody else—all of this is no less true than what exists in real life, distributed in time.
> 8 March 1904. If I live. (55:19–20)

This dream draws its content from Tolstoy's past experience. It features Tolstoy speaking with the philosopher who hosted the public presentation of Tolstoy's essay "On Life and Death," Nikolai Grot. Grot, in his early work, had been a follower of Herbert Spencer and, like Spencer, a proponent of evolution and a committed agnostic, but when he invited Tolstoy to speak on life and death at the Psychological Society in 1887, he was more taken with Plato; he was working on Plato's dialogue on the death of Socrates, *Phaedo*. At the end of his life, he hoped for a synthesis of empirical science and metaphysics. Grot died in 1899, before he could offer an empirical proof of the immortality of the soul.

Two days later, Tolstoy returned to his dream to formulate his conclusions in philosophical (Kant's or Schopenhauer's) terms: "I had a dream that explained a lot, namely, that dreams unite as one what in real life was broken into time, space, and causality" (March 10, 1904; 55:19–20). Still later, also in the diary, he returned to his observations to formulate a general philosophical principle about life as represented within dreams: "Life within a dream takes place outside of time and space and independently of personalities: in dreams, one deals with the dead as if they were living, even though one knows they are dead. The same is true of space—both in Moscow and in the country; and of time—both in the past and in the present" (July 12, 1904; 55:64). Many of Tolstoy's actual dreams (some of them trivial in content) furnished him with evidence of the illusory nature of time, space, and selfhood.

I will pause to note that the idea of the illusory nature of time, space, and other categories, of course, comes from Kant and, still more, from Schopenhauer's extensions of Kantian epistemology. Tolstoy had also expressed similar ideas much earlier and without reference to his dreams.

One of Tolstoy's notebooks (even in the years when he did not keep regular diaries, Tolstoy jotted down his thoughts and dreams in a notebook) contains a remarkable entry, made on July 21, 1870:

> I went for a swim. My horse, tied up [to a tree], looks at me when I emerge from the water. Does it know that this is the same I who rode it [to the pond]?
>
> Kant says that space and time are forms of *our* thinking. But in addition to space and time, there is yet another form of our thinking: *the individuality*. For me, a horse, I, and a bug are all individuals . . . but does the horse think in the same way? (48:126).

While Tolstoy mentions only Kant, he may also have been inspired by Schopenhauer's insistence that the individual is only a phenomenon and that the animal species do not exhibit individuality.

Yet, as we have seen, it was important for Tolstoy to claim these ideas as his own. This is how Tolstoy once described his relationship to the thought of his predecessors: "I have read Kant, Schopenhauer, and it is to them that I owe my views on space and time as forms of cognition. But, you know, a thought becomes dear to you only when, at the bottom of your soul, you were already aware of it, when, as you read, you feel that you have already had it yourself, that you knew all of this; when it's as if you only recall it."[37] In matters of intellectual history, he seems to have adhered to the Platonic idea of knowledge as recollection. And he held dear those ideas that were rooted in his daily experience (riding a horse, having a dream).[38]

In his last years, dreams furnished Tolstoy with empirical evidence that humans, like horses, may be in possession of a type of consciousness to which the categories of time, space, causality, and self do not apply. What is more, such dreams gave him an actual foretaste of a condition in which consciousness operates apart from time, space, causality, and selfhood. This was a domain where the distinction between "before" and "after," as well as "here" and "there," disappeared, where thoughts belonged equally to everybody, and where one could hold philosophical discussions with the dead.

After much observation and reflection, Tolstoy came up with a theory on the origin of dreams: Dream narratives, he decided, "are formed at the moment of awakening"; it is at this point that our dreams are "ordered sequentially in time." From this perspective, he returned to the analogy between life, or death, and dreams. Reasoning by analogy, he concluded that our whole life may only seem to be ordered in time (from the past to the future). What if (he wondered), upon awakening to a different life, we lose this illusion and gain, as after a long sleep, a new, fresh consciousness? (He tried to reason along these lines more than once.)[39]

In this context, Tolstoy's attention again turned to the so-called retrospective dreams he had described in "A History of Yesterday" sixty years earlier—dreams that end in waking from some external impression (a sound, touch, or fall), which, within the dream, figures as a conclusion to a long sequence of events.

In the diaries of his last years, Tolstoy discussed such dreams on several occasions. One such discussion appears in the diary on March 25, 1908 (on the same day, the feast of the Annunciation, which, in 1851, Tolstoy had chosen for his "History of Yesterday").

On March 24, he wrote that "[one] cannot help thinking about falling asleep and waking up as an analogy of death and birth" (56:114). He reasoned that, if, on falling asleep, one loses consciousness and gains another type of consciousness, the same thing happens in death . . . (Tolstoy noted that he could not quite get hold of the idea, 56:114.) On the next day, March 25, he returned to his idea by way of a retrospective dream:

> The main analogy was with respect to time: in sleep, as in awakening, there is no time, but we imagine, we cannot not imagine, time. I remember a long, coherent dream, which ends with a shot, and I awake. The sound of the shot was the knock of a window slammed shut by the wind. I require time in remembering a dream, I need it, while awake, to place all my impressions from a dream in an order. It's the same thing in remembrances of the waking state: all my life is in the present, but in remembering it, or rather in being conscious of it, I cannot fail to arrange it in time. I—the child, the man, the old man—it's all one and the same, all present. I just cannot be conscious of it outside of time. (56:114)

Concluding his discussion of the March 25 dream, Tolstoy expresses the hope that death will correct the corrupt text, or misrepresentation, of our earthly life: "Just as, awakened by the knock of a window slamming shut, I know that dreaming was an illusion, so too, upon my death, will I learn the same about all the earthly events which seem to me so real" (56:115). On another occasion Tolstoy was still more explicit in his far-reaching philosophical conclusions. On September 15, 1909, after a night full of vivid dreams, he woke up with a remarkably clear head. He felt acutely conscious that he had a being outside of time and space. And a clear thought about the significance of retrospective dreams came to him. He gives an example of such a dream:

> I come to see my brother and find him at the porch with a rifle and a dog. He invites me to go hunting with him, and I tell him that I do not have a rifle. He tells me that one could take a clarinet instead. I am not surprised, and follow him along a familiar route, but, walking along this familiar route, we come to the seaside (which does not surprise me either). There are ships on the sea, and they are also swans. My brother tells me to shoot. I fulfill his wish, put the clarinet into my mouth, but nothing happens. He says that he, then, will shoot, and he shoots. . . . I wake up. (57:139–40)

He proceeded to provide a philosophical interpretation. (Tolstoy may or may not have been aware of the erotic potential of this dream. In fact, he reminded himself that he should be aware of himself as a part of God, and not of his bodily self, "Leo Tolstoy.") The shot, Tolstoy explains, was the sound of a screen being knocked down by the wind. We all know such dreams, and we all wonder about the temporal discrepancy. Indeed (he concludes), the dream narrative has been created instantly, at the moment of awakening, and in retrospect, which shows the illusory nature of time. Tolstoy sums up: "there is no time, and we imagine things in time only because such is the quality of our mind" (57:140).

In his late diaries the old Tolstoy addressed, point-blank, the problem of time, which had troubled him already in his youth: "At night, I thought: what is time?" (January 27, 1904; 55:10). His dreams furnished him with an answer: There is no time. In his conclusions, Tolstoy went much further than professional philosophers. Thus, extending the metaphor of life as a dream, he posited the existence of another life, in which Kantian epistemology does not apply. Dreams, he argued, show that time is an illusion. From this it follows: " The same illusion takes place in what we call real life. The only difference is that we do wake up from such dreams, but we will wake up from the dream of life only in death. Only then will we know" (57:140). Tolstoy comes very close to saying that after death we may be in possession of a type of consciousness that would be free from time.

It was not long before Tolstoy noticed a fatal contradiction in his reasoning: There could be no such consciousness and no opportunity to correct the narrative misrepresentation of the world—because thought and its forms are a property of this world. On October 29, 1909, Tolstoy reminded himself of the ultimate limitation of speech and thought. Dreaming, he reiterated, is "a complete analogy of life," inasmuch as it ends with death, or "complete awakening." He continued:

> I would like to say that life before birth was perhaps just the same, that the character that I carry into life is the fruit of previous awakenings, and that future life will be the same; I would like to say this, but I don't have the right, because I cannot think outside time. In true life there is no time, life merely presents itself to me in time. I can only say one thing—that this future life exists, and death does not destroy life, it only opens life still further. To speak of what *was* before life and what *will be* after life would be to use a mode of thought peculiar only to this life to explain other forms of life, still unknown to me. (57:142)

The old, philosophically educated Tolstoy was aware of this paradox: Our knowledge is limited to what is representable; therefore, true life and the true self—life and the self outside time, space, causality, personhood—are unknowable. Yet he kept trying.

It should be noted that in the far-reaching conclusions Tolstoy extracted from the properties of dreams and in his interest in retrospective dreams, Tolstoy was not alone. Retrospective dreams figure prominently in contemporary studies of dreams by well-known authors, such as Adolphe Garnier (1852), Alfred Maury (1861), d'Hervey de Saint-Denis (1867), and F. W. Hildebrandt (1875).[40] Like Tolstoy, they made observations on the basis of their own dreams. In 1885, the German philosopher Carl Du Prel, in his *Die Philosophie der Mystik*, offered an interpretation that accords with Tolstoy's. (There is no evidence, as far as I could ascertain, that Tolstoy knew Du Prel.) In the "dream-life," Du Prel suggested, a different "measure of time" was in operation. Dream images are evoked according to the laws of association, and we "turn over the leaves of half-forgotten memories in the book of our life without regard to date."[f] In dreams of the retrospective type (he noted), the effect precedes the cause, and the beginning and the end coincide. (Du Prel mentioned Maury's famous guillotine dream, but

---

[f] Du Prel and Tolstoy had a common source. Thus, Du Prel must have borrowed this metaphor from Schopenhauer: "Life and dreams are leaves of one and the same book. The systematic reading is real life, but when the actual reading hour (the day) has come to an end, and we have the period of recreation, we often continue idly to thumb over the leaves, and turn to a page here and there without a method or connection. We sometimes turn a page we have already read, at others one still unknown to us, but always from the same book." Paragraph 5 of *The World as Will and Representation*.

he also reported a dozen of his own dreams of this type.) Like Tolstoy after him, Du Prel viewed such dreams in the context of post-Kantian thought and in opposition to the positivistic trends of his day. (Du Prel followed Schopenhauer and Eduard von Hartmann, the author of *The Philosophy of the Unconscious*.) For him, the "seeming duration" of time not only provided empirical evidence of Kant's idea of the purely subjective nature of time but also opened access to a side of human consciousness in which the laws of causality and the "physiological measure of time" do not operate, giving way to the "transcendental measure of time." This made Du Prel recall the words of Luther: God sees time not in its length but in its breadth. It seems that for Du Prel, such dreams opened a window on God's perspective on time. What is more, this "dream-world" formed an empirical evidence for the doctrine of the soul.[41]

Tolstoy, thinking along similar lines, went even further—all on the back of his analogy between "life" and "dreams." Retrospective dreams prefigured for Tolstoy what would happen after death. He returned to this idea again and again, even after (on October 29, 1909) he had realized, and wrote, that he had no "right" to say "what *will be* after life."

A year later, on October 26, 1910 (two days before Tolstoy's flight from home, which led to his death), he had another such dream, which he described in a letter to his disciple Vladimir Chertkov:

Today I had several thought-feelings. One is that tonight I have experienced a heart tremor, which woke me up, and, waking up, I remembered a long dream: I walked downhill, grabbing onto tree branches, but I still slipped and fell—that is, I woke up. The whole dream, which seemed to be in the past, has formed instantly, so one of my thoughts is that at the moment of death, there will be an extratemporal moment, like a heart tremor during sleep, and all of life will become such a retrospective dream. But now, you are in the midst of this retrospective dream.—Sometimes this seems true to me, and sometimes, it seems like nonsense. (89:230)

This remarkable dream realizes the metaphor of the journey of life (which Tolstoy had used prominently in his *Confession*). The "I" is a protagonist involved in a perilous journey, which is on its last, downward, stretch. The journey is interrupted by awakening (occasioned by the sleeping subject's heart failure). But upon awakening, Tolstoy—now not as the protagonist, but as the author of the dream—understands that this whole vision of life was an illusion.

Writing to another, Tolstoy expressed his doubts about his theory, which sometimes seemed to him utter nonsense. Yet sometimes, Tolstoy did hope that, in death, one might wake up to realize that life was only a dream. (If this were the case, his dream of October 26, 1910 would gain a prophetic quality.)

Chertkov took this missive very seriously: He reported this dream in his account of Tolstoy's last days, published in 1911.[42] This is Tolstoy's last recorded dream.[g]

The Book of Life: "It Is Written on Time"

Let us recall the young Tolstoy, who, in his first diaries, wanted to turn himself into a book ("so that I could easily read myself and others could read me as I do"; 1:279).[43] Despair gripped the young diarist when he tried to capture his life "by tracing characters on paper" (46:65). We have seen that this despair remained with Tolstoy for life. In his late diaries, confronted with the limitations not only of narrative but of the self, Tolstoy also worked with the age-old metaphor of the book of life.[44]

In 1888 (soon after he turned sixty), Tolstoy imagined a book that told the story not of his life but of the life of the whole world in the light of a renewed Christianity (his own version), and he also thought of another volume of the book of life:

> I thought: life, not my life, but the life of the whole world, which, with the renewal of Christianity, comes as spring comes, from all sides, in trees, in grass, and in waters, becomes incredibly interesting. In this alone lies the interest of my life, too, and, at the same time, my earthly life is over. It's as if you kept reading a book, which became more and more interesting, and suddenly, at the most interesting moment, the book comes to an end, and it turns out that this is only the first volume of a many-volume edition, and that one cannot get hold of the sequel. One could only read it abroad, in a foreign language. But one would certainly read it.—(November 24, 1888; 50:4)

---

[g] There was a second dream Tolstoy wanted to share with Chertkov (but did not describe in his letter): an "aesthetic dream" (*khudozhestvennoe snovidinie*) and a "marvelous one." This dream is mentioned in his diary, on October 26: "Had a dream. Grushenka, a novel by N.N. Strakhov. A marvelous plot" (58:123). In the preceding weeks Tolstoy had read *The Brothers Karamazov* (which features a character named Grushenka), and he wrote to Strakhov about the novel (89:229). After his flight from home, in Optina pustyn', on October 28, Tolstoy made a plan to record the plot of the second dream, but this record remained unfinished (58:123, 235).

Now, when (he thinks) he has read the book of his life almost to the end, he tries to envision the book of life-after-death, but he knows that there is no such book. In this image, Tolstoy gives a new twist to the metaphor: His reader is a traveler who crosses the border between life and death, obtaining the sequel to the book of his life from a foreign publisher, in a foreign language.

In 1909, Tolstoy reworked the book of life metaphor in the context of his end-of-life reflections on the illusory nature of time. The resulting image is remarkably suggestive: "There is no time. There is my life. Only it's written on time. There is a composition, but not characters, lines. It's only written by means of characters and lines. And the fact that a good composition is written with characters and lines does not prove that further lines and characters in the book will continue the same composition or will make a similar composition" (February 2, 1909; 57:19). He thinks that time is like paper and that his life is written on the paper of time. If the young Tolstoy, the diarist, deplored the messy act of conveying his impressions by scribbling characters and phrases on a piece of paper, the old Tolstoy, the retired novelist, doubted that the other life—life after awakening—would be a book at all.

The Circle of Reading: "To Replace the Consciousness of Leo Tolstoy with the Consciousness of All Humankind"

But was he writing or reading the book of life? Unsure, Tolstoy tried to do both. Thus, in his last years, in addition to writing the diary, he compiled almanacs for reading. Intended for publication, these almanacs contained both aphorisms drawn from various authors and Tolstoy's own thoughts. Arranged according to the calendar, the almanacs contained readings for every day of the year. Tolstoy conceived this idea in 1902, when, gravely ill and confined to bed, he tore the pages off a wall calendar which hung above his bed and read the sayings of various thinkers printed on them.[45] After he had plucked all the leaves from this tree of life, Tolstoy decided to plant his own. From 1902 until the end of his life, working on his almanacs was a central task of each day. This work went on ceaselessly: having hardly completed the first such edition, *Thoughts of Wise People for Every Day* (*Mysli mudrykh liudei na kazhdyi den'*; 1903), he started an improved variant, *The Circle of Reading* (*Krug chteniia*; 1906–07), then reworked it into yet another, *The New Circle of Reading, or For Every Day* (*Novyi krug chteniia, ili Na kazhdyi den'*; 1909–10). (There was also *The Path of Life* [*Put' zhizni*], a book from 1910, which appeared after Tolstoy's death; it was organized thematically, independently of chronology.)[46]

Tolstoy selected thoughts from a wide range of authors, those whom he saw as kindred spirits. On different occasions, speaking of his project in his diary and letters, he highlighted the following: Marcus Aurelius, Epictetus, Xenophon, Socrates, Seneca, Plutarch, Cicero, Confucius, Lao-Tzu, Buddha, the Gospel, Pascal, Montesquieu, Rousseau, Voltaire, Lessing, Kant, Georg Christoph Lichtenberg, Schopenhauer, Henri-Frédéric Amiel, Emerson, William Ellery Channing, Theodore Parker, John Ruskin, Matthew Arnold (49:68, 64:152, 75:169). Tolstoy's list is eclectic and all-embracing: He reached beyond Europe (to China, India, and America) and beyond the canon. Yet there is consistency: He chose his authors for their advice on "how to live," for their rejections of society, and for the aphoristic quality of their writing. (He preferred Lichtenberg's *Sudelbücher* to Kant, Schopenhauer's *Parerga and Paralipomena* to his *The World as Will and Representation*.) Tolstoy left his stamp on the thoughts of these wise men: Many aphorisms appear in his own free translations; many are heavily edited. Interspersed with the thoughts of others are Tolstoy's own: Tolstoy no longer distinguishes his own words from those of others; the self and other have become one.

Some of the thoughts in Tolstoy's almanacs have previously appeared in his notebooks, diaries, letters, or essays. Thus, the vignette about a peasant boy in the bathhouse ("Who is there?"—"I am") appears in *The New Circle of Reading* as reading for July 1. Under July 30, one finds an analogy between a man's life, from birth to death, and a day, from awakening to falling asleep. Kant's three questions (which had figured in Tolstoy's correspondence with Strakhov) figure, without Kant's name, under August 1. Tolstoy's principle of nonresistance to evil is summarized in the August 15 and October 15 entries. Pascal's aphorism on the similarity between life and a dream appears under November 29.

In these books, coauthored by Tolstoy and the wise men of the world, the consciousness of "Tolstoy" (as he put it in another context) was replaced with "the consciousness of all humankind" (56:123). He seems to have viewed these almanacs as an incarnation of the divine logos of sorts. In a conversation recorded by his secretary (Gusev), Tolstoy explained his idea of a collective soul, which came to him in a dream: "In my dreams, I keep thinking about *The Circle of Reading*. Today, in a dream, I saw an inscription on a piece of paper: 'You have a soul, but you should form another, cultural soul in yourself.' Signed: Kant. And I thought: 'It's Kant, and I should pay attention.'"[47] On another day, taken by Pascal's thoughts on self-abnegation, Tolstoy told another secretary (Bulgakov) that, "though Pascal had died two hundred years ago," he felt: "My soul merged with Pascal's soul, Pascal's thought were my own. . . . Pascal was alive . . . in the same way as Christ."[48] This meant that his (Tolstoy's) soul, too, was not subject to death.

Furthermore, *The Circle of Reading* provided a "diary" that did not depend on the "if I live" clause—each entry was guaranteed to make a complete circle. Reading such a diary turned the world around Tolstoy into a friendly and predictable place in which the lives of many people (along with his own) ran, day by day, in accordance with a prescribed pattern: a preprinted diary of sorts. Tolstoy himself used his almanacs in this way: He was not only the *Circle*'s author but also its dutiful reader, perusing it daily, usually at bedtime.

"The Death of Socrates"

Tolstoy actually placed his peculiar vision of the immortality of the soul within *The Circle of Reading*: in his rendition of "The Death of Socrates." His own free translation from Plato's *Phaedo*, it appears under September 22 (42:625). Reading it brought Tolstoy comfort. (Thus, on September 24, 1910, Tolstoy said to his secretary, Bulgakov, who recorded this conversation in his diary, that he knew nothing stronger than the description of Socrates' last hours in *Phaedo*.) Tolstoy's Socrates banishes his loud wife, Xanthippe, and tells his disciples that "the soul, with its ability for knowledge and memory, cannot die with the body; as ideas are not subject to death, in the same way our soul is not subject to death" (42:67).

I want to pause to suggest that Tolstoy strongly identified with the dying Socrates of Plato's *Phaedo*.

It should be mentioned that Tolstoy not only read but actually wrote, or rewrote, Plato's *Phaedo*, or "The Death of Socrates," more than once.[49] In 1886 (the same year Tolstoy started working on his essay "On Life"), a certain A. M. Kalmykova sent him the manuscript of her popular book *Socrates, a Greek Teacher*. Tolstoy decided to bring out an edition at his publishing house for the people, Posrednik (The Intermediary). He rewrote whole pages and even added a chapter of his own, "How to Live in the Family?" For the old Tolstoy, as for Socrates, this was a problem. As Tolstoy presented the situation, when Socrates began to neglect his craft, going instead to the marketplace to teach, his wife Xanthippe was annoyed, fearing that he would earn less. She nagged her husband for refusing to take money for his teaching. Xanthippe was a woman with a high temper; in anger she would break and smash anything that came to hand.[50]

On August 5, 1909, Tolstoy recalled Xanthippe in his diary. On this day (as on many other days), he recorded his thoughts about death: "They say: do not think of death, and there will be no death. The opposite is the truth: always remember death—and you will live a life that knows no death" (57:111).

From this, he turns to Socrates' ill-tempered wife, Xanthippe, and to the generalized image of "the Xanthippes" (plural):

> Why are the Xanthippes so malicious? Because it is always pleasant, almost essential for a wife to disapprove of her husband. And when a husband is Socrates, or someone approaching Socrates, then, his wife, not finding what is clearly evil in him, disapproves of the good. And disapproving of what is good, she loses *la notion du bien et du mal* [the notion of good and evil], and she becomes more and more—Xanthippean.
>
> Sofia Andreevna is preparing for [my trip to] Stockholm,[h] and every time she speaks about this, she becomes desperate. She pays no attention to my promises not to go. Salvation lies in living in the present and in silence. (57:111)

It seems that Tolstoy actually hoped to die like Socrates, away from his nagging wife and at one with the logos.

Tolstoy's Death

After his final escape from home, stopping at the monastic retreat of his sister Maria (near Optina pustyn'), Tolstoy found a copy of his *Circle of Reading*. He felt that the entry for the day (October 28) contained an answer to the question that was tormenting him at the time (58:125).

Several days later, on November 4, when Tolstoy lay dying at the railroad station Astapovo (where illness had interrupted his flight), he was intent on continuing to write down his thoughts. Delirious with fever, he kept asking his daughter Alexandra and his disciple Vladimir Chertkov to take dictation and then asking them to read back to him what he had dictated. But they found themselves in a difficulty: Tolstoy was not dictating anything. He kept insisting. Chertkov stared uneasily at his blank notebook. Tolstoy implored: "How strange! Why won't you read it to me?" This painful scene continued for some time. Alexandra suggested that Chertkov read from *The Circle of Reading*, which, as always, was at Tolstoy's bedside. Chertkov read the passages for the day, November 5 (it was 2 a.m.). Tolstoy listened with rapt attention. From time to time he asked: "Whose thought is this?" But as soon

---

[h] Tolstoy was planning to attend the Universal Peace Congress in Stockholm; in the end, this trip did not take place.

as Chertkov stopped, the delirious Tolstoy again tried to dictate his thoughts. This repeated several times. At last, Tolstoy was quiet.[51]

Some fifteen years earlier, Tolstoy felt that, when death came, he might continue to write, and after death, too (52:105). But now he could finally stop writing the book of life and turn into a reader. The ideal of silence, for which he had striven so many times, was at last within reach. Another writer, Andrei Bely, understood this well: "*The Circle of Reading*," he wrote, "is Tolstoy's silence."[52]

After Tolstoy died, on November 7, 1910, journalists reporting his death noted that the entry for that day in *The Circle of Reading* was a perfect fit: "One could view life as a dream and death as an awakening." And in conclusion: "We can only guess what will be after death, the future is hidden from us. Not only is it hidden, but it does not exist, inasmuch as the future implies time, but in dying we leave time."[53] Through his almanac, which merged his thoughts with the universal logos, Tolstoy succeeded in bringing the narrative of life to its ultimate conclusion—asserting, on the last day, that the possibilities of representation stopped there.

From his early years, Tolstoy knew that his narrative utopia—to turn himself into a book—would remain unfulfilled. In his "History of Yesterday," the young Tolstoy, unaware of the essential limitations of human consciousness, had attempted to create a text in which the categories of time and space and the antithesis of subject and object dissolved. In his late diaries, he seems to have accepted the impossibility of such knowledge. In the epistemological skepticism of his later years, Tolstoy was influenced, among other factors, by Kant and Schopenhauer. The older (and better educated) Tolstoy was a wiser man: He did not solve the problems which had tormented him since his youth but, learning from personal experience and the wisdom of others, came closer to accepting that they were unsolvable. He knew that the true self—or rather the non-self of true being—is precisely that which thought cannot grasp and language cannot formulate. And yet, as long as he lived, he could not stop trying. He left the gigantic text of his diaries—his own "critique of pure reason" and his own comment on the "world as representation"—as a monument to his failure. It was in death that Tolstoy hoped finally to experience authentic being—a timeless, selfless existence in the present, and in silence: that something which language cannot formulate. For years, he prepared himself, marking in his diary the process of shedding expectations, memories of the past, even consciousness itself. Sometimes, he knew that to leave a record of this kind of ultimate experience was impossible. As he once put it, "I don't have the right, because I cannot think outside time" (57:162). But on another occasion Tolstoy, who in his youth had attempted to transcribe his dream as it occurred, felt that he might continue to write even after death. If only the author could share the experience of his heroine: "The candle, by the light of which she had been reading that book filled with anxieties, deceptions, grief, and evil, flared up with a brighter light than before, lit up for her all that had before been dark, flickered, began to grow dim, and went out for ever."[54] Tolstoy had famously used these words to describe the final moment of Anna Karenina. The following aphorism (unsigned) appears in Tolstoy's *New Circle of Reading* for one of the last days of the calendar year, December 29: "At the moment of a man's death, the candle, by the light of which he has been reading the book filled with deceptions, grief and evil, flares up with a brighter light than before, lights up for him all that had before been dark, flickers, begins to grow dim, and goes out for ever." This dictum ascribes the experience of Tolstoy's character to every man, and the author could share in it as well. (In this sense, he stopped being the author of a work of fiction.)

In death, Tolstoy may have hoped to take leave of his vocation as a writer. He would stop both writing the book of his life and reading a preprinted one and, for just a moment, see a light open onto the unrepresentable.

Appendix: Russian Quotations

Listed below are the original Russian texts of quotations found in the book in the English translation. Appendix entries are keyed to the first words of quotations.

Introduction

"God only knows how many diverse, captivating impressions . . ."

Бог один знает, сколько разнообразных, занимательных впечатлений и мыслей, которые возбуждают эти впечатления [. . .] проходит в один день. Ежели бы можно было рассказать их так, чтобы сам бы легко читал себя и другие могли читать меня, как и я сам, вышла бы очень поучительная и занимательная книга (1:279).

"there is not enough ink in the world . . ."

не достало бы чернил на свете написать ее и типографчиков напечатать (1:279).

"a history of my life . . ."

такую историю жизни . . . будет полезнее, чем вся та художественная болтовня, которой наполнены мои 12 томов сочинений (34:348).

"to imagine myself back then . . . when I will again enter that state of death . . ."

представлять себя тогда, когда я опять вступлю в то состояние смерти, от которого не будет воспоминаний, выразимых словами (23:470).

"[i]t's precisely what is not 'I' that is immortal"
Бессмертно только то, что не я (49:129).

Chapter 1

"But how can one write this?"
Но как написать это. Надо пойти, сесть за запачканный чернилами стол, взять серую бумагу, чернила, пачкать пальцы и чертить по бумаге буквы. Буквы составят слова, слова—фразы, но разве можно передать чувство (46:65).

"Rules for Developing Will"
«Правила для развития воли», «Правила в жизни», «Правила», «Правила вообще» (46: 262–76).

24. Arose somewhat late and read . . .
24 [марта 1851 г.]. Встал немного поздно и читал, но писать не успел. Приехал Пуаре, стал фехтовать, его не отправил (*лень и трусость*). Пришел Иванов, с ним слишком долго разговаривал (*трусость*). Колошин (Сергей) пришел пить водку, его не спровадил (*трусость*). У Озерова спорил о глупости (*привычка спорить*) и не говорил о том, что нужно, *трусость*. У Беклемишева не был (*слабость энергии*). На гимнастике не прошел по переплету (*трусость*), и не сделал одной штуки от того, что больно (*нежничество*). У Горчакова солгал (*ложь*). В Новотроицком трактире (*мало fierté*). Дома не занимался Английск[им] яз[ыком] (*недост[аток] твердости*). У Волконских был неестественен и рассеян, и засиделся до часу (*рассеянность, желан[ие] выказать и слабость характера*). 25. С 10 до 11 дневник вчерашн[его] дня и читать. С 11 до 12 гимнастика. С 12 до 1 Английский язык. Беклемишев и Беер с 1 до 2. С 2 до 4 верхом. С 4 до 6 обед. С 6 до 8 читать. С 8 до 10 писать. Переводить что-нибудь с иностр[анного] языка на Русский для развития памяти и слога. Написать нынешний день со всеми впечатлениями и мыслями, к[оторые] он породит.
25. Встал поздно от *лени*. Дневник писал и делал гимнастику, *торопясь*. Английск[им] яз[ыком] не занимался от *лени*. С Бегичевым и с Иславиным был тщеславен. У Беклемишева *струсил и мало fierté*. На Тверском бульваре хотел выказать. До калымажского двора не дошел пешком, *нежничество*. Ездил с *желанием выказ[ать]*. Для того же заезжал к Озерову. Не воротился на калымажный, *необдуманность*. У Горчаковых скрывал и не называл вещи по имени, *обман себя*. К Львову пошел от *недостатка энергии и привычки ничего не делать*. Дома засиделся от *рассеянности* и без внимания читал Вертера, *торопливость*. (46:55)

"not because yesterday was extraordinary in any way . . ."
не потому, чтобы вчерашний день был чем-нибудь замечателен [. . .] а потому, что давно хотелось мне рассказать задушевную сторону жизни одного дня.—Бог один знает, сколько разнообразных [. . .] впечатлений и мыслей, [. . .] проходит в один день. Ежели бы можно было рассказать их так, чтобы сам бы легко читал себя и другие могли читать меня, как и я сам. . . (1:279).

"(It has long been my rule . . ."
(Я дал себе давно правило не ложиться позже 12 и все-таки в неделю раза 3 это со мною случается).

"involuntarily I passed from today to 1825."
невольно от настоящего перешел к 1825 году.

"I once again discarded what I had begun . . ."
я другой раз бросил начатое и стал писать со времени 1812 года [. . .] Но и в третий раз я оставил начатое (13:54).

I looked at my watch and got up . . .
Я посмотрел на часы и встал [. . .] Хотелось ли ей кончить этот милый для меня разговор, или посмотреть, как я откажусь, и знать, откажусь ли я, или просто еще играть, [но] она посмотрела на цифры, написанные на столе, провела мелком по столу, нарисов[ала] какую-то, не определенную ни математи[кой], ни живописью фигуру, посмотрела на мужа, потом между им и мной. «Давайте еще играть 3 роберта». Я так был погружен в рассматривание не этих движений, но всего, что называется charme, который описать нельзя, что мое воображение было очень далеко и [неразборчиво] не поспело, чтобы облечь слова мои в форму удачную; я просто сказал «нет, не могу». Не успел я сказать этого, как уже стал раскаиваться, т. с. не весь я, а одна какая-то частица меня.—Нет ни одного поступка, который не осудила бы какая нибудь частица души; зато найдется такая, которая скажет и в пользу: что за беда, что ты ляжешь после 12, а знаешь ли ты, что будет у тебя другой такой удачный вечер?—Должно быть, эта частица говорила очень красноречиво и убедительно (хотя я не умею передать), потому что я испугался и стал искать доводов.—Во-первых, удовольствия большого нет, сказал я [себе]: тебе она вовсе не нравится и ты в неловком положении; потом, ты уже сказал, что не можешь, и ты потерял во мнении . . .

"Comme il est aimable, ce jeune homme."
Эта фраза, кот[орая] последовала сейчас за моей, прервала мои размышления. Я стал извиняться, что не могу, но так [как] для

этого не нужно думать, я продолжал рассужд[ать] сам с собой: Как я люблю, что она называет меня в 3-м лице. По-немецки это грубость, но я любил бы и по-немецки. Отчего она не находит мне приличного названия? Замет[но], как ей неловко меня звать по имени, по фамилии, и по титулу. Неужели это от того, что я. . . . «Останься ужинать», сказал муж. — Так как я был занят рассуждением о формулах 3-го лица, я не заметил, как тело мое, извинившись очень прилично, что не может оставаться, положило опять шляпу и село преспокойно на кресло. Видно было, что умственная сторона моя не участвовала в этой нелепости (1:282–83).

"Morpheus, enfold me in your embrace."

Морфей, прими меня в свои объятия. Это Божество, которого я охотно бы сделался жрецом. А помнишь, как обиделась барыня, когда ей сказали: «Quand je suis passé chez vous, vous étiez encore dans les bras de Morphée. ». Она думала, что Морфей — Андрей, Малафей. Какое смешное имя! . . . А славное выражение: dans les bras; я себе так ясно и изящно предста[вляю] положение dans les bras — особенно же ясно самые bras — до плеч голые руки с ямочками, складочками и белую, открытую нескромную рубашку — Как хороши руки вообще, особенно ямочка одна есть! Я потянулся. Помнишь, Saint Thomas не велел вытягиваться. Он похож на Дидерих[са]. Верхом с ним ездили. Славная была травля, как подле станового Гельке атукнул и Налет ловил из-за всех, да еще по колот[и?]. Как Сережа злился. — Он у сестры. — Что за прелесть Маша — вот бы такую жену! Морфей на охоте хорош бы был, только нужно голому ездить, то можно найти и жену. — Пфу, как катит Saint Thomas и за всех на угонках уже барыня пошла; напрасно только вытягивается, а впрочем это хорошо dans les bras. Тут должно быть я совсем заснул. — Видел я, как хотел я догонять барыню, вдруг — гора, я ее руками толкал, толкал, — свалилась; (подушку сбросил) и приехал домой обедать. Не готово; отчего? — Василий куражится (это за перегородкой хозяйка спрашивает, что за шу[м], и ей отвеча[ет] горнич[ная] девка, я это слушал, потому и это приснилось). Василий пришел, только что хотели все у него спросить, отчего не готово? видят — Василий в камзоле и лента через плечо; я испугался, стал на колени, плакал и целовал у него руки; мне было так же приятно, ежели бы я целовал руки у нее, — еще больше. Василий не обращал на меня внимания и спросил: Заряжено? Кондитер Тульский Дидрихс говорит: готово! — Ну, стреляй! — Дали залп. (Ставня стукнула) — и пошли Польской, я с Василием, который уже не Василий, а она. Вдруг о ужас! я замечаю, что у меня панталоны так коротки, что видны голые колени. Нельзя описать, как я страдал (раскрылись гол[ые] [колени?]; я их во сне долго не мог закрыть, наконец закрыл). Но тем не кончилось; идем мы Польской и— Королева Виртем[бергская] тут; вдруг я пляшу казачка. Зачем? Не могу удержаться. Наконец принесли мне шинель, сапоги; еще хуже: панталон вовсе нет. Не может быть, чтобы это было наяву; верно я сплю. Проснулся.— Я засыпал— думал, потом не мог более, стал воображать, но воображал связно, картинно, потом воображение заснуло, остались темные представления; потом и тело заснуло. Сон составляется из первого и последнего впечатления (1:291–92).

"You have a long dream . . ."
вы видите длинный сон, который кончается тем обстоятельством, которое вас разбудило: вы видите, что идете на охоту, заряжаете ружье, подымаете дичь, прицеливаетесь, стреляете и шум, к[оторый] вы приняли за выстрел, это графин, который вы уронили на пол во сне (1:293).

"continuity and to the form of time . . ."
к последовательности и к той форме времени, в которой проявляется жизнь (1:293).

"the necessity to lie . . ."
о необходимости лжи, вытекающей из потребности в нескольких словах описывать действия тысячей людей, раскинутых на нескольких верстах (16:10).

"infinitely diverse and vague impressions."
бесконечно разнообразное и туманное впечатление [. . .] на жливое, но ясное [. . .] представление (16:10–11).

"the ability of man . . ."
способност[ь] человека ретроспективно подделывать мгновенно под совершившийся факт целый ряд мнимо свободных умозаключсний (16:15).

7 July [1854] . . .
7-го июля [1854]. [. . .]
Что я такое? Один из четырех сыновей отставного Подполковника, оставшийся с 7 летнего возраста без родителей под опекой женщин и посторонних, не получивший ни светского, ни ученого образования и вышедший на волю 17-ти лет; без большого состояния, без всякого общественного положения и, главное, без правил, человек, расстроивший свои дела до последней крайности,

без цели и наслаждения проведший лучшие годы своей жизни; наконец, изгнавший себя на Кавказ, чтобы бежать от долгов, а главное— привычек, а оттуда, придравшийся к каким-то связям, существовавшим между его отцом и командующим армией, перешедший в Дунайскую армию 26-ти лет прапорщиком почти без средств, кроме жалованья (потому что те средства, которые у него есть, он должен употреблять на уплату оставшихся долгов), без покровителей, без умения жить в свете, без знания службы, без практических способностей; но с огромным самолюбием! Да, вот мое общественное положение.

Посмотрим, что такое моя личность.

Я дурен собой, неловок, нечистоплотен и светски необразован.— Я раздражителен, скучен для других, нескромен, нетерпим (intolerant) и стыдлив, как ребенок. Я почти невежда. Что я знаю, тому я выучился кое-как, сам, урывками, без связи, без толку и то так мало.— Я невоздержан, нерешителен, непостоянен, глупо тщеславен и пылок, как все бесхарактерные люди. Я не храбр. Я не аккуратен в жизни и так ленив, что праздность сделалась для меня почти неодолимой привычкой.— Я умен, но ум мой еще ни на чем никогда не был основательно испытан. У меня нет ни ума практического, ни ума светского, ни ума делового.— Я честен, то есть я люблю добро, сделал привычку любить его; и когда отклоняюсь от него, бываю недоволен собой и возвращаюсь к нему с удовольствием; но есть вещи, которые я люблю больше добра—славу. Я так честолюбив и так мало чувство это было удовлетворено, что часто, боюсь, я могу выбрать между славой и добродетелью—первую, ежели бы мне пришлось выбирать из них.

—Да, я нескромен; оттого-то я горд в самом себе, а стыдлив и робок в свете. —(47:8)

"[I]t penetrates gradually . . ."

она понемногу и незаметно вкрадывается и потом развивается во всем организме [. . .]—она как венерическая (46:94)

"founding a new religion . . ."

основание новой религии, соответствующей развитию человечества, религии Христа, но очищенной от веры и таинственности, религии практической, не обещающей будущее блаженство, но дающей блаженство на земле (47:37).

Interlude

"Read Hume, wrote Ch[ildhood], read Rousseau."

Читал Hume, писал Д[етство], читал Rousseau.

"Who cares about the history of my childhood?"

Кому какое дело до истории *моего* детства? (59:214)

"the autobiographical form and the obligatory link between preceding and succeeding parts."

принятая мной форма автобиографии и принужденная связь последующих частей с предыдущей, так стесняют меня (59:202).

"I can write about him because he is distant from me."

Я могу писать про него, потому что он далек от меня (46:150–51).

"A person's convictions— ..."

Убеждения человека, — не те, которые он рассказывает, а те, которые из всей жизни выжиты им, — трудно понять другому, и вы не знаете моих ... Попробую, однако, сделать мою profession de foi ...

"that there is immortality ..."

что есть бессмертие, что есть любовь и что жить надо для другого.

"This occurred to me yesterday ..."

Жить незачем. Вчера пришли эти мысли с такой силой ... Кому я делаю добро? кого люблю? Никого! [. . .] Я пишу вам это не для того, чтобы вы мне сказали, что это? что делать ... Еще горе у меня. Моя Анна, как я приехал в деревню и перечел ее, оказалось такая постыдная гадость, что я не могу опомниться от сраму, и, кажется, больше никогда писать не буду. А она уж напечатана. . . (60:293–95).

"Vasily Petrovich! Vasily Petrovich!"

Василий Петрович! Василий Петрович! Что я наделал с своим «Семейным счастьем». Только теперь здесь, на просторе, опомнившись и прочтя присланные корректуры [. . .] я увидал, какое постыдное гавно, пятно, не только авторское, но человеческое—это мерзкое сочинение (60:296).

"Literature, or belles-lettres ..."

Изящной литературе, положительно, нет места теперь для публики (60:247).

"This is what it's all about."

Дело вот в чем. Мудрость во всех житейских делах [. . .] состоит не в том, чтобы знать, что нужно делать, а в том—чтобы делать прежде, а что после. В деле прогресса России, мне кажется, что, как ни полезны телеграфы, дороги, пароходы [. . .] литература (со всем своим фондом), театры, Академия художеств и т. д., а все это преждевременно и напрасно до тех пор, пока в России [. . .] учится 1/100 доля всего народонаселения. . . (60:328–29).

"Art is a lie . . ."
Искусство есть ложь, а я уже не могу любить прекрасную ложь (60:358).

"It seemed to me that I had corrupted . . ."
мне казалось, что я развратил чистую, первобытную душу крестьянского ребенка. Я смутно чувствовал в себе раскаяние в каком-то святотатстве. Мне вспоминались дети, которых праздные и развратные старики заставляют ломаться и представлять сладострастные картины для разжигания своего усталого, истасканного воображения. . . (8:307).

"Thank God, this summer I feel stupid as a horse . . ."
Я, благодаря Бога, нынешнее лето глуп, как лошадь. Работаю, рублю, копаю, копаю, кошу, о проклятой лит-т-тературе и лит-т-тераторах, слава Богу не думаю (61:236–37).
я не пишу и писать дребедени многословной вроде Войны я больше никогда не стану (61:247).

"I'm at work at the moment on that dreary, vulgar A[nna] Karen[ina] . . ."
Берусь теперь за скучную, пошлую А[нну] Карен[ину] и молю Бога только о том, чтобы Он мне дал силы спихнуть ее как можно скорее с рук, чтобы опростать место-досуг мне очень нужный [. . .] для других, более забирающих меня занятий (1:215).

"The rank of writer is loathsome; it's depraving."
Мерзкая наша писательская должность—развращающая (1: 259).

Chapter 2

"Your spiritual condition has been revealed to me . . ."
Немножко мне открылось Ваше душевное состояние, но тем более мне хочется в него проникнуть дальше (1:211).

"elucidate and define one's religious worldview."
уяснить и изложить [наше] религиозное мировоззрение (1:222).

"help those who are in the same miserable lonely condition."
помочь тем, которые в том же бедственном одиночном состоянии (1:222).

"I rejoice at your plan and challenge you to a correspondence."
радуюсь вашему плану и вызываю на переписку (1:226).

"My God, if only somebody would finish A. Karenina for me!"
Боже мой, если бы кто-нибудь за меня кончил А. Каренину! (1:226).

"translated into Christian language, how to save one's soul."
в переводе на христианский язык: как спасти свою душу (1:228).

"What is my life? What am I?"
что такое моя жизнь, что я такое? (1:230).

"I am one of the four sons of a retired Lieutenant Colonel ..."
Один из четырех сыновей отставного Подполковника, оставшийся
с 7 летнего возраста без родителей. [...] Я дурен собой, неловок,
нечистоплотен и светски необразован... (47:9).

"on two sheets of note-paper"
на двух почтов[ых] листиках бумаги [...] И сделал бы это, если бы
я писал не письмо вам, близкому человеку, но если бы я писал свою
profession de foi, зная, что меня слушают все человечество (1:290).

"I'm forty-seven years old ..."
Мне 47 лет. [...] я чувствую, что для меня наступила старость.
Я называю старостью то внутреннее, душевное состояние, при
котором все внешние явления мира потеряли для меня свой интерес
[...] Если бы пришла волшебница и спросила у меня, чего я хочу, я
бы не мог выразить ни одного желания (1:236).

"to tell how it was that I passed from a state of hopelessness and despair ..."
Рассказать о том, каким образом из состояния безнадежности и
отчаянья я перешел к уяснению для себя смысла жизни... (1:237).

"with the knowledge we possess ..."
как нам невозможно с нашими знаниями верить в положения
религий... (1:237).

"I exist ..."
Я существую. (17:340).

"I don't know to what extent Descartes' formulation is accurate ..."
Не знаю, в какой степени точно выражение Декарта: я мыслю, потому
я живу; но знаю, что, если я скажу: *я знаю [несомненно одно] прежде
всего себя: то, что я живу,* — то это не может быть не точно (17: 351).

"Your letter is an attempt to tread the same path as Descartes . . ."
Ваше письмо есть новая попытка пойти по тому же пути, по которому
шли Декарт, Фихте, Шеллинг, Гегель, Шопенгауэр. Они точно также
начинали из себя, от Cogito, ergo sum, от я, от сознания воли, — и
отсюда выводили понятие об остальном существующем. . . (1: 256).

"Your attempts both tempt and frighten me . . ."
Ваши попытки меня и прельщают и пугают. Если Вы потерпите
неудачи, если почувствуете сомнения, то для меня они будут страшнее
собственных неудач и сомнений. Потому что в Вас я верю; я жду от
Вас откровений, как те откровения, которые нашел у Вас в такой
силе и множестве в Ваших поэтических произведениях (1:257).

"You are trying to contain your views . . ."
Вы пытаетесь [. . .] привести Ваши взгляды в формулы обыкновенного
знания. Я заранее уверен, что результаты, которые Вы получите,
будут в сто раз беднее содержания Ваших поэтических созерцаний.
Посудите, например, могу ли я взгляд на жизнь, разлитый в Ваших
произведениях, не ставить бесконечно выше того, что толкует о
жизни Шопенгауэр, или Гегель, или кто Вам угодно? (1:257).

"Anna Karenina is arousing . . ."
Анна Каренина возбуждает такое восхищение и такое ожесточение,
какого я не помню в литературе. . . (1:258).

"I am afraid that I cannot say what I want to . . ."
боюсь, что не сумею сказать, как хочу; но вы избаловали меня
вниманием, и потому надеюсь, что вы поймете и дурно выраженное
(1:261).

"the living God and the God of love."
Бог живой и Бог любовь (1:261).

"You see in the world the living God and feel his love . . ."
Вы видите в мире Бога живого и чувствуете его любовь. Теперь мне
ясна Ваша мысль, и сказать Вам прямо, я чувствую, что ее можно
развить логически в такие же строгие формы, какие имеют другие
философские системы. Это будет пантеизм, основным понятием
которого будет любовь, как у Шопенгауэра воля, как у Гегеля
мышление (1:263).

"paying tribute to Petersburg and to littérature"
Тут вы платите дань [. . .] дань Петербургу и *литтературе* (1:244).

"You are losing your usual calm . . ."
Вы теряете Ваше обыкновенное хладнокровие, и, кажется, желаете от меня совета—прекратить печатанье Анны Карениной и оставить в самом жестоком недоумении тысячи читателей, которые все ждут и все спрашивают, чем же это кончится? [. . .] Вы меня привели в такое волнение, как будто мне самому приходится писать конец романа (1: 264).

"[Y]our opinion of my novel holds true . . ."
ваше суждение о моем романе верно, но не все—т.е. все верно, но то, что высказали, выражает не все, что я хотел сказать. (1:266).

But if I were to try to say in words everything that I intended to express . . .
Если же бы я хотел сказать словами все то, что я имел в виду выразить романом, то я должен был бы написать роман тот самый кот[орый] я написал, сначала. [. . .] Во всем, почти во всем, что я писал мною руководила потребность собрания мыслей, сцепленных между собой, для выражения себя, но каждая мысль выраженная словами особо, теряет свой смысл, страшно понижается, когда берется одна из того сцепления, в котором она находится. Само же сцепление составлено не мыслью (я думаю), а чем то другим и выразить основу этого сцепления непосредственно словами никак нельзя; а можно только посредственно—словами описывая образы, действия, положения.

"completely unexpectedly"
совершенно для меня неожиданно, но несомненно, Вронский стал стреляться (1:267).

"And if critics now already understand . . ."
И если критики теперь уже понимают и в фельетоне могут выразить то, что я хочу сказать, то я их поздравляю и смело могу уверить qu'ils en savent plus long que moi (1:268).

"Give up literature altogether . . ."
Бросьте литературу совсем и пишите философские книги. Кому же писать? Кто же скажет, что мы думаем? (1:293).

"I wish that you, instead of reading Anna Kar[enina] . . ."
Чтобы вам, вместо того, чтобы читать Анну Кар[енину], кончить ее и избавить меня от этого Дамоклова меча (1:276).

"to express, in the form of catechism . . ."
изложить в катехизической форме то, во что я верю (1:374).

"I believe in the one true holy church . . ."
Верую во единую истинную святую церковь, живущую в сердцах всех людей и на всей земле. . . (17:363).

"What is necessary for the soul's salvation?."
Что нужно для спасения души? [. . .] Ясное определение того, во что мы верим. . . (17:364).

"the word religion-faith is the word . . ."
слово религия-вера есть слово. . . (17:357).

"I wanted to express the thought that had come to me directly in the form of a dialogue . . ."
Хотел прямо в форме беседы высказать пришедшую мне нынче мысль и запутался (17:373).

"who definitely worked up a sweat and went to the loo."
непременно потел и ходил на час (1:430).

"I have a friend, Strakhov, a scholar . . ."
У меня есть приятель, ученый, Страхов, и один из лучших людей, которых я знаю. Мы с ним очень похожи друг на друга нашими религиозными взглядами; мы оба убеждены, что философия ничего не дает, что без религии жить нельзя, а верить не можем. И нынешний год летом мы собираемся в Оптину пустынь. Там я монахам расскажу все причины, по которым не могу верить. — (62:311)

"meaningless simply by virtue . . ."
Бессмысленны даже по тому одному, что они выражены словом. [. . .] Как выражение, как форма, они бессмыслены, но как содержание они одни истины (1:399).

"not by words, the instrument of reason . . ."
не словом, орудием разума [. . .] а всею жизнью, действиями, из которых слово есть одна только часть (1:399).

"I see that my way is not your way."
вижу, что мой путь — не ваш путь (1:405).

"Yes, such am I . . ."
Да, таков я . . .

"You've lived through two thirds of your life . . ."

Вы прожили 2/3 жизни. Чем вы руководились, почему знали, что хорошо, что дурно. Ну вот это-то, не спрашивая о том, как и что говорили другие, скажите сами себе и скажите нам (1:429).

"You ask me: how have I lived up to this point? . . ."

Вы спрашиваете меня: как же я прожил до сих пор? . . . А вот как: я никогда не жил как следует. В эпоху наибольшего развития сил (1857–1867) я не то что жил, а поддался жизни, подчинился искушениям; но я так измучился, что потом навсегда отказался от жизни. [. . .] я служил, работал, писал, все лишь настолько, чтобы не зависеть от других, чтобы не было стыдно перед товарищами и знакомыми. [. . .] Так что все время я не жил, а только принимал жизнь. . . Вот вам моя исповедь. . . (1:432–33).

"I hope that we shall be able to discuss the subject of our correspondence . . ."

О предмете нашей переписки надеюсь, что переговорим. Коротко сказать, что мне странно, почему вы неверующий. И это самое я говорил, но, верно, неясно и нескладно (1:434).

"I keep on at you about something that's tricky . . ."

Я пристаю к вам с нелегким: дайте мне ясный ответ, откуда вы знаете то, чем руководились и руководитесь в жизни? (1:439).

Your merit lies in the fact that you have proved . . .

Заслуга ваша в том, что вы доказали, что философия—мысль—не может дать никакого определения этим основам духовной жизни, но ошибка ваша в том, что вы не признаете того, что основы (если они—основы) необходимо существуют [. . .] и такие, которых мы— по вашему же определению—разумом, вообще своей природой, ниоткуда взять не можем, и которые поэтому даны нам. В этом то смысле я спрашивал вас: чем вы живете,—и вы неправильно, шутя о важнейшем, говорите: я не живу (1:447).

"I will write Instead of a Confession *. . ."*

Напишу *Вместо исповеди* и посвящу Вам (1:458).

But what value, what meaning does my life *have? . . .*

А какую цену, какое значение имеет *моя жизнь*? [. . .] Мне трудно говорить об этом предмете, и вот почему я не могу писать автобиографии. Каким тоном ее писать? Кажется, я бы всего сильнее выразил чувство отвращения.

"I am prepared to write this for you . . ."
Но для Вас я готов бы это написать, а для других—не вижу цели. . .
(1:463).

"not in himself"
я не находился сам в себе . . .

"Write your life story; I still want to do the same thing . . ."
Напишите свою жизнь; я все хочу то же сделать. Но только надо
поставить—возбудить к своей жизни отвращение всех читателей (2:
540).

"It's very hard for me to judge my life . . ."
О жизни своей мне судить очень трудно, не только о ближайших,
но и о самых далеких событиях. Иногда жизнь моя представляется
мне пошлою, иногда героическою, иногда трогательною, иногда
отвратительною, иногда несчастною до отчаянья, иногда радостною.
[. . .] Эти колебания составляют для меня самого немалое огорчение:
я сам от себя не могу добиться правды! И это бывает со мною не
только в воспоминаниях, но и каждый день во всяких делах. Я
ничего не чувствую просто и прямо, а все у меня двоится. . . (2:541).

"You write as if to challenge me . . ."
Вы пишите мне, как бы вызывая меня. Да я и знаю, что вы дорожите
моим мнением, как я вашим, и потому скажу все, что думаю. [. . .]
Чужое виднее. И вы мне ясны. Письмо ваше очень огорчило меня.
Я много перечувствовал и передумал о нем. По-моему, вы больны
духовно. [. . .] И вам писать свою жизнь нельзя. Вы не знаете, что
хорошо, что дурно было в ней. А надо знать. [. . .] Должно быть не
пошлю это. Я очень занят работою для себя, кот[орой] никогда не
напечатаю. Простите (2:545–46).

"I was glad to look into your soul . . ."
Я рад был заглянуть вам в душу, так как вы открыли; но меня
огорчило то, что вы так несчастливы, неспокойны. Я не ожидал этого.
[. . .] Вы не умели сказать то, что в вас, и вышло что-то непонятное.
Нам виднее—нам, тем, кот[орые] знают и любят вас. Но писать свою
жизнь вам нельзя. Вы не сумеете (2:550).

Something has as if suddenly dawned on me . . .
Меня как будто что-то вдруг озарило, и я все больше и больше радуюсь
и все вглядываюсь в этот новый свет. Скажу Вам откровенно, что
меня прежде смущало и отчего для меня так нова Ваша теперяшняя

мысль. Мне всегда казалось непонятным и диким личное бессмертие в той форме, в которой его обыкновенно представляют; точно так же мне был всегда противен мистический восторг, до которого старались доходить большинство религиозных людей, говоривших почти так, как Вы. Но Вы избежали и того и другого; как ни горячи движения Вашей души, но Вы ищете спасения не в самозабвении и замирании, а в ясном и живом сознании. Боже мой, как это хорошо! Когда я вспоминаю Вас, все ваши вкусы, привычки, занятия, когда вспоминаю то всегдашнее сильнейшее отвращение от форм фальшивой жизни, которое слышится во всех Ваших писаниях и отражается во всей Вашей жизни, то мне становится понятным, как Вы могли наконец достигнуть Вашей теперешней точки зрения. До нее можно было дойти только силою души, только тою долгою и упорною работою, которой Вы предавались. Пожалуйста, не браните меня, что я все хвалю Вас; мне нужно в Вас верить, эта вера моя опора. Я давно называл Вас самым цельным и последовательным писателем; но Вы сверх того самый цельный и последовательный человек. Я в этом убежден умом, убежден моею любовью к Вам; я буду за вас держаться и надеюсь, что спасусь (2:552).

"I usually say that you are writing a story of your relations to religion . . ."
Я говорю обыкновенно [. . .] что Вы пишите историю этих Ваших отношений к религии, историю, которая не может явиться печатно (2:553).

"I will speak as if at confession."
буду говорить как на исповеди. . . (2:624).

"I need to address God . . ."
нужно обратиться к Богу. И вот, хочу исповедаться перед Вами: мне становится страшно от этой мысли [. . .] не могу приступить к делу. Так со мною было всю жизнь. . . (2:994).

"Everything Tolstoy writes . . ."
Толстой *очень плохо* пишет все, что у него касается отвлеченного изложения христианства; но его *чувства*, которых он вовсе не умеет выразить и которые я знаю прямо по лицу, по тону, по разговорам, — имеют необыкновенную красоту. В нем много всего, но я поражен и навсегда остаюсь пораженным его *натурою*, хритианскими чертами его натуры.

"You told your faith only because you said what the church says."
Вы сказали только потому, что повторяли то, что говорит церковь (63:8).

"To tell one's faith is impossible . . ."
сказать свою веру нельзя [. . .] Как сказать то, чем я живу. [. . .] Я все-таки скажу—(63:8).

Endnotes

"Levin in Anna Karenina is not, after all, Tolstoy . . ."
Левин в «Анне Карениной» все-таки не Толстой,—между ними одно различие, всего одно, но какое! Левин делает и думает совсем то же, что делал и думал Толстой, кроме одного: он не написал «Войны и мира».

Chapter 3

I was baptized and brought up in the Orthodox Christian faith . . .
Я был крещен и воспитан в православной христианской вере. Меня учили ей и с детства и во все время моего отрочества и юности. Но когда я 18-ти лет вышел со второго курса университета, я не верил уже ни во что из того, чему меня учили (23:1).

"I killed men in war and challenged men to duels . . ."
Я убивал людей на войне, вызывал на дуэли, чтоб убить, проигрывал в карты, проедал труды мужиков, казнил их, блудил, обманывал (23:5).

"Lying, robbery, sexual sins of all kinds . . ."
Ложь, воровство, любодеяния всех родов, пьянство, насилие, убийство. . . (23:5).

ᵃ*"I still have the diaries from that time . . ."*
ᵃУ меня еще сохранились дневники всего того времени, ни для кого не интересные, с Франклиновскими таблицами, с правилами, как достигать совершенства (23:488–511).

"During that time I began to write . . ."
В это время я стал писать из тщеславия, корыстолюбия и гордости (23:5).

"Someday I will narrate the touching and instructive history of my life . . ."
Когда-нибудь я расскажу историю моей жизни—и трогательную и поучительную в эти десять лет моей молодости (23:4).

"Life in general goes on developing . . ."
[что] жизнь вообще идёт развиваясь и что в этом развитии главное участие принимаем мы, люди мысли, а из людей мысли главное

влияние имеем мы—художники, поэты. Наше призвание—учить людей (23:5).

"This faith in the meaning of poetry . . ."
Вера эта в значение поэзии и в развитие жизни была вера, и я был одним из жрецов её (23:6).

"But strange to say, though I understood this fraud . . ."
Но странно то, что хотя всю эту ложь веры я понял скоро и отрёкся от неё, но от чина, данного мне этим людьми, — от чина художника, поэта, учителя, — я не отрёкся (23:6).

"All that exists is reasonable . . ."
всё, что существует, то разумно. Всё же, что существует, всё развивается. Развивается же всё посредством просвещения. Просвещение же измеряется распространением книг, газет. [. . .] мы пишем книги и газеты, и потому мы—самые полезные и хорошие люди (23:7).

"When I saw the head part from the body . . ."
Когда я увидал, как голова отделилась от тела, и то, и другое врозь застучало в ящике, я понял—не умом, а всем существом, — что никакие теории разумности существующего и прогресса не могут оправдать этого поступка. . . (23:8).

"He fell ill while still young . . ."
он заболел молодым, страдал более года и мучительно умер, не понимая, зачем он жил, и ещё менее понимая, зачем он умирает. Никакие теории ничего не могли ответить на эти вопросы ни мне, ни ему во время его медленного и мучительного умирания. [. . .] Но это были только редкие случаи сомнения, в сущности же я продолжал жить, исповедуя только веру в прогресс (23:8).

"This work was [more] to my taste . . ."
Занятие это было мне особенно по сердцу, потому что в нём не было той, ставшей для меня очевидною, лжи, которая мне уже резала глаза в деятельности литературного учительства. [. . .] В сущности же я вертелся всё около одной и той же неразрешимой задачи, состоящей в том, чтоб учить, не зная чему (23:9).

"What for? And what comes next?"
Зачем? Ну, а потом? (23:10).

"My life came to a stop."
Жизнь моя остановилась (23:11).

"This is no fable . . ."
И это не басня, а это истинная, неоспоримая и всякому понятная правда (23:14).

"What am I? . . ."
«что я такое» или: «зачем я живу», или: «что мне делать» (23:19).

"wandering between the clearings of experimental knowledge . . ."
Так я блуждал в этом лесу знаний человеческих между просветами знаний математических и опытных. . . (23:21).

"Vanity of vanities, says Solomon . . ."
Суета сует, — говорит Соломон, — суета сует — все суета! (23:23).

"thankfully, there are means for that . . ."
благо есть средства: петля на шею, вода, нож, чтоб им проткнуть сердце, поезды на железных дорогах (23:28).

"What am I?"
Что я такое? . . . часть бесконечного (23:36).

"the likes of me, Solomon, and Schopenhauer."
мы с Соломоном и Шопенгауэром.

"So I went on for about two years . . ."
Я жил так года два, и со мной случился переворот, который давно готовился во мне и задатки которого всегда были во мне (23:40).

"I came to love good people . . ."
Я полюбил хороших людей, возненавидел себя, и я признал истину. Теперь мне все стало ясно (23:41).

" 'Well,' I said to myself, 'granted there is no God . . .' "
Хорошо, нет никакого Бога, — говорил я себе, — нет такого, который бы был не моё представление. . . (23:45).

"Why do I look farther? a voice within me asked . . ."
Так чего же я ищу ещё? — вскрикнул во мне голос. — Так вот Он. Он — то, без чего нельзя жить. [. . .] И сильнее чем когда-нибудь всё осветилось во мне и вокруг меня, и свет этот уже не покидал меня. [. . .] Когда и как совершился во мне этот переворот, я не мог бы сказать (23:46).

"the same faith that had borne me along in my earliest days."
та самая, которая влекла меня на первых порах моей жизни (23:46).

"and I again began to live."
и я опять начал жить (23:47).

"to avoid all arguments and contradictions . . ."
избегать всяких рассуждений, противоречий и пытался объяснить, сколько возможно разумно, те положения церковные, с которыми я сталкивался (23:49).

"fables illustrating thoughts."
как на фабулу, выражающую мысль (23:52).

"How often I envied the peasants their illiteracy and lack of learning!"
Сколько раз я завидовал мужикам за их безграмотность и неученость (23:52).

"in the situation of a catechumen."
как оглашенный (23:53).

Now a few days ago . . .
Это было написано мною три года тому назад. Теперь, пересматривая эту печатаемую часть и возвращаясь к тому ходу мысли и к тем чувствам, которые были во мне, когда я переживал ее, я на днях увидал сон.

I dreamt that I lay on a bed . . .
Вижу я, что лежу на постели. [. . .] И наблюдая свою постель, я вижу, что лежу на плетёных верёвочных помочах, прикреплённых к бочинам кровати. Ступни мои лежат на одной такой помочи, голени—на другой, ногам неловко. . . (23:57).

It is a dream. Wake up! . . .
Это сон. Проснись. Я пытаюсь проснуться и не могу. Что же делать, что же делать? —спрашиваю я себя и взглядываю вверх. Вверху тоже бездна (23:58).

As happens in dreams, a voice says: "Notice this, this is it!" . . .
Как это бывает во сне, какой-то голос говорит: «Заметь это, это оно!» и я гляжу всё дальше и дальше в бесконечность вверху и чувствую, что я успокаиваюсь. . . (23:58).

And then, as happens in dreams, I imagine the mechanism . . .

И тут, как это бывает во сне, мне представляется тот механизм, посредством которого я держусь, очень естественным, понятным и несомненным, несмотря на то, что наяву этот механизм не имеет никакого смысла. Я во сне даже удивляюсь, как я не понимал этого раньше. Оказывается, что в головах у меня стоит столб [. . .] Потом от столба проведена петля как-то очень хитро и вместе просто [. . .] даже и вопроса не может быть о падении (23:59).

And it seems as if someone says to me . . .

И как будто кто-то мне говорит: смотри же, запомни. И я проснулся (23:59).

"This dream expressed in condensed form . . ."

Сон этот выразил для меня в сжатом образе всё то, что я пережил и описал, и потому думаю, что и для тех, которые поняли меня, описание этого сна освежит, уяснит и соберёт в одно всё то, что так длинно рассказано на этих страницах (23:57).

"I indeed saw this, I did not make this up."

Это я действительно видел, это я не выдумал.

"answers to the question, what am I, what is God"

То, что отвечает на мой вопрос о том, что такое я, что такое Бог (24:17).

"presenting Christ's teaching as something new after 1,800 years of Christianity."

после 1800 лет исповедания Христова закона [. . .] теперь мне пришлось, как что-то новое, открывать закон Христа (23:335).

"The reading of Tolstoy's religious writings . . ."

Чтение религиозных сочинений Толстого, прежде всего «Исповеди» и «В чем моя вера», сразу захватило меня и поставило жизнь мою на новые рельсы. Вместе с тем эти единственные в своем роде сочинения перекинули мост через бездну, перед которой я стоял в душевном трепете, и дали мне возможность продолжать путь жизни . . .

"If this were not a contradiction . . ."

Если не б[ыло] противоречием бы написать о необходимости молчания, но написать бы теперь: *Могу молчать. Не могу молчать.* Только бы жить перед Богом. . . (57:6).

Chapter 4

"turned out splendidly"
Биография [. . .] вышла превосходная для меня, и для меня только.

"It is interesting for me to reconstruct my life in memory . . ."
Мне интересно восстановить в памяти свою жизнь. И если Бог
даст жизни и я когда-нибудь вздумаю писать свою историю, то это
будет для меня канва чудесная; но для публики это немыслимо. Мы
выберем на днях по вашим вопросам факты и пришлем вам.

"November 27–28, 1878. Yasnaya Polyana."
27–28 ноября 1878 г. Ясная Поляна

"Count Lev Nikolaevich Tolstoy was born on August 28, 1828 . . ."
Граф Лев Николаевич Толстой родился в 1828 году, 28 августа,
Тульской губернии, Крапивенского уезда, в сельце Ясная Поляна,
родовом имении его матери, княжны Волхонской.

"In 1851 he went with brother Nikolai to the Caucasus . . ."
В 1851 граф Л. Н. Толстой поехал с [. . .] братом Николаем на Кавказ.
[. . .] он поступил на службу [. . .] в 4-батарейную батарею 20-ой
артиллерийской бригады, стоявшую в станице Старогладовской, на
Тереке. На Кавказе граф Л.Н. Толстой в первый раз начал писать
в романической форме. Им задуман был большой роман, из начала
которого составились Детство, Отрочество и Юность . . .

In 1862 Count L. N. Tolstoy married in Moscow Sofia Andreevna Bers . . .
В 1862 году Л.Н. Толстой женился в Москве на Софье Андреевна
Берс.[. . .] С той поры он безвыездно живет в именьи своем, Ясная
Поляна, занимаясь воспитанием шестерых детей своих. В эти 16
лет написаны были *Война и мир, Азбука* и *Книга для чтения* и *Анна
Каренина.*

"I was born in Yasnaya Polyana in the Krapivenskii district . . ."
Я родился в Ясной Поляне, Тульской губернии Крапивенского уезда,
1828 года 28 августа. (23:469)

"This is the first and the last comment I make . . ."
Это первое и последнее замечание, которое я делаю о своей жизни
не из своих воспоминаний (23:469).

I am bound; I wish to free my arms . . .

Я связан, мне хочется выпростать руки, и я не могу этого сделать. Я кричу и плачу, и мне самому неприятен мой крик, но я не могу остановиться. Надо мной стоят нагнувшись кто-то, я не помню кто, и все это в полутьме, но я помню, что двое и крик мой действует на них: они тревожатся от моего крика, но не развязывают меня, чего я хочу, и я кричу еще громче. Им кажется, что это нужно (т.е. то, чтобы я был связан), тогда как я знаю, что это ненужно, и хочу доказать им это, и я заливаюсь криком противным для меня самого, но неудержимым. . . (23:470).

I do not know and will never know what it was . . .

Я не знаю и никогда не узнаю, что такое это было: пеленали ли меня, когда я был грудной, и я выдирал руки, или это пеленали меня, уже когда мне было больше года, чтобы я не расчесывал лишаи, собрал ли я в одно это воспоминание, как то бывает во сне, много впечатлений, но верно то, что это было первое и самое сильное мое впечатление жизни. И памятно мне не крик мой, не страданье, но сложность, противуречивость впечатления. Мне хочется свободы, она никому не мешает, и меня мучают. Им меня жалко, и они завязывают меня, и я, кому всё нужно, я слаб, а они сильны (23:470).

"When did I begin? When did I begin to live? . . ."

Когда же я начался? Когда начал жить? И почему мне радостно представлять себя тогда, а бывало страшно; как и теперь страшно многим, представлять себя тогда, когда я опять вступлю в то состояние смерти, от которого не будет воспоминаний, выразимых словами (23:470).

"I wake up, and my brothers' beds . . ."

Я просыпаюсь, и постели братьев, самые братья, вставшие или встающие, Федор Иванович в халате, Николай (наш дядька), комната, солнечный свет, истопник, рукомойники, вода, то, что я говорю и слышу, — всё только перемена сновидения (23:473).

"to avoid the Charybdis of self-praise . . ."

избежать Харибды самовосхваления (посредством умолчания всего дурного) и Сциллы цинической откровенности о всей мерзости своей жизни (73:279).

"To describe all my odiousness, stupidity, viciousness, vileness . . ."

Написать всю свою гадость, глупость, порочность, подлость — совсем правдиво — правдивее даже, чем Руссо, — это будет соблазнительная книга или статья. Люди скажут: вот человек, которого многие высоко ставят, а он вон какой был негодяй, так уж нам-то, простым людям, и Бог велел (73:279).

"than all that artistic prattle . . ."
чем вся та художественная болтовня, которой наполнены мои 12 томов сочинений и которым люди нашего времени приписывают незаслуженное ими значение (34:348).

"6 January 1903. I am now suffering the torments of hell . . ."
6 янв. 1903 г.
Я теперь испытываю муки ада. вспоминаю всю мерзость своей прежней жизни, и воспоминания эти не оставляют меня и отравляют жизнь. Обыкновенно жалеют о том, что личность не удерживает воспоминания после смерти. Какое счастье, что этого нет! Какое бы было мучение, если бы я в этой жизни помнил все дурное, мучительное для совести, что я совершил в предшествующей жизни. А если помнить хорошее, то надо помнить и все дурное. Какое счастье, что воспоминание исчезает со смертью, и остается одно сознание, — сознание, которое как бы представляет общий вывод из хорошего и дурного... [...] Да, великое счастье уничтожение воспоминания, с ним нельзя бы жить радостно. Теперь же, с уничтожением воспоминания, мы вступаем в жизнь с чистой, белой страницей, на которой можно писать вновь и хорошее и дурное (34:346).

"I was born and spent my childhood in the village Yasnaya Polyana."
Родился я и провел первое детство в деревне Ясной Поляне (34:351).

"The further I proceed in my 'Reminiscences' . . ."
Чем дальше я подвигаюсь в своих воспоминаниях, тем перешительнее я становлюсь о том, как писать их. Связно описывать события и свои душевные состояния я не могу, потому что я не помню этой связи и последовательности душевных состояний... (34:372).

"I will write at random, and without making corrections."
буду писать, как придется, без поправок (34:372).

"How clear it is to me now . . ."
Как мне ясно теперь, что смерть Митеньки не уничтожила его, что он был прежде, чем я узнал его, прежде, чем родился, и есть теперь, после того, как умер. ~~Как, где — я не знаю~~ (34:383).

"I have abandoned the chronological form of narrating."
бросил хронологический способ изложения (34:385).

"Yes, the Fanfaron Hill . . ."
Да, Фанфаронова гора. Это одно из самых далеких и милых и важных воспоминаний (34:385).

He announced to us that he possessed a secret . . .
он [. . .] объявил нам, что у него есть тайна, посредством которой, когда она откроется, все люди сделаются счастливыми, не будет ни болезней, никаких неприятностей, никто ни на кого не будет сердиться и все будут любить друг друга, все сделаются муравейными братьями. (Вероятно, это были Моравские братья, о которых он слышал или читал, но на нашем языке это были муравейные братья.) [. . .] Мы даже устроили игру в муравейные братья, которая состояла в том, что садились под стулья, загораживали их ящиками, завешивали платками и сидели там в темноте, прижимаясь друг к другу. Я, помню, испытывал особенное чувство любви и умиления и очень любил эту игру. [. . .]
[. . .] эта тайна была, как он нам говорил, написана им на зеленой палочке, и палочка эта зарыта у дороги, на краю оврага старого Заказа, в том месте, в котором я, так как надо же где-нибудь зарыть мой труп, просил в память Николеньки закопать меня. Кроме этой палочки, была еще какая-то Фанфаронова гора, на которую, он говорил, что может ввести нас, если только мы исполним все положенные для того условия. . . (34:386).

"the first experience of love . . ."
это состояние было первым опытом любви, не любви к кому-нибудь, а любви к любви, любви к Богу (34:391).

"The ideal of ant brothers lovingly cleaving to each other . . ."
Идеал муравейных братьев, льнущих любовно друг к другу, только не под двумя креслами, завешанными платками, а под всем небесным сводом всех людей мира, остался для меня тот же. И как я тогда верил, что есть та зеленая палочка, на которой написано то, что должно уничтожить все зло в людях и дать им великое благо, так я верю и теперь, что есть эта истина и что будет она открыта людям и даст им то, что она обещает (34:386).

"Today I sat down to work . . ."
Нынче сел за работу: хотел продолжать воспоминания, но не мог: не берет (54:177).

"Life, the true life, lies only in the present . . ."
Жизнь, истинная жизнь только в настоящем, т.е. вне времени. [. . .] Всегда в каждый момент жизни можно вспомнить это, перенести свою жизнь в настоящий момент, т. е. в сознание Бога. И как только

сделаешь это, так отпадает все, что может тревожить, воспоминания прошедшего, раскаянье, ожидание или страх будущего. . . (55:48).

"I started Who am I . . ."
Начал *Кто я* (55:104). [. . .] ~~Кто я? Где я? Зачем я? Кто я?~~ . . [. . .] Начал изложение веры. (55:104). [. . .] Остановился в изложении веры. (55:104). [. . .] Писал «Кто я?» Ни хорошо, ни дурно (55:128). [. . .] Вчера попробовал «Зеленую палочку». Не пошло. Все не то. . . (55:133).

If I ask when did I begin, the real I . . .
Если я спрошу, когда начался я, настоящий я, то я получу еще менее удовлетворительный ответ. Мне говорят, что я появился несколько лет тому назад из утробы моей матери. Но то, что появилось из утробы моей матери, есть мое тело, — то тело, которое очень много времени не знало и не знает о своем существовании и которое очень скоро, может быть, завтра, будет зарыто в землю и станет землею. То, что я сознаю своим я, появилось не одновременно с моим телом. Это мое я началось не в утробе матери и не по выходе из нее, когда отрезали пуповину, и не тогда, когда отняли от груди, и не тогда, когда я начал говорить. [. . .] я всегда был и есть и только забыл свою прежнюю жизнь (36:407–408).

"I decisively cannot say what I am . . ."
Так что я решительно не могу сказать, что я такое. Знаю только, что я и мое тело не одно и то же (36:408).

"The procession extended toward the grave . . ."
Потянулась процессия к могиле, вырытой у головы оврага, в лесу, в одной версте от дома, именно там, где, по преданию, была зарыта братом Николаем «Зеленая палочка», чудесный талисман, тайна возрождения человечества. [. . .] Любовь и Разум, (озарявшие эту великую жизнь, освободились от оболочки личности. И наступила новая эпоха распространения великих идей.

ᶜ*"Someone wrote or told me that Nietzsche has read my works . . ."*
Кто-то писал или говорил мне, что Ницше читал мои сочинения. Некоторые выражения прямо как будто у меня взяты 42:622).

Chapter 5

"I had spent my whole life away from the city . . ."
Я всю жизнь прожил не в городе. Когда я в 1881 году переехал на житье в Москву, меня удивила городская бедность. Я знаю деревенскую

бедность; но городская была для меня нова и непонятна. В Москве нельзя пройти улицы, чтобы не встретить нищих, и особенных нищих, не похожих на деревенских (25:182).

"'Why go to look at the sufferings of people . . .'"

Зачем я пойду смотреть на страдания людей, которым я не могу помочь?» — говорил один голос. «Нет, если ты живешь здесь и видишь все прелести городской жизни, поди, посмотри и на это», — говорил другой голос (25:186).

"And the people asked him . . ."

И спрашивал его народ, что же нам делать? И он сказал в ответ: у кого есть две одежды, тот отдай неимущему; и у кого есть пища, делай то же (Лука 3:10–11).

"Why have you, a man from a different world, stopped near us? Who are you?"

зачем ты — человек из другого мира — остановился тут подле нас? Кто ты?

"'Who are you? A self-satisfied rich man . . .'"

Самодовольный ли богач, который хочет порадоваться на нашу нужду, развлечься от своей скуки и еще помучать нас, или ты то, что не бывает и не может быть, — человек, который жалеет нас? На всех лицах был этот вопрос (25:188).

"Widely as life had separated us, after our glances had met twice or thrice . . ."

Как ни разделила нас жизнь, после двух, трех встреч взглядов мы почувствовали, что мы оба люди, и перестали бояться друг друга. Ближе всех ко мне стоял мужик с опухшим лицом и рыжей бородой, в прорванном кафтане и стоптанных калошах на босу ногу. А было 8 градусов мороза. В третий или четвертый раз я встретился с ним глазами и почувствовал такую близость с ним, что уж не то что совестно было заговорить с ним, но совестно было не сказать чего-нибудь. Я спросил, откуда он. Он охотно ответил и заговорил; другие приблизились. . . (25:188).

"I approved this sin, by my presence . . ."

я не умом, не сердцем, а всем существом моим понял . . . Я своим присутствием и невмешательством одобрил этот грех и принял участие в нем (25:190).

"Here, I could have given not only . . ."

Здесь же я мог дать не только [. . .] те ничтожные деньги, которые были со мной, но я мог отдать и пальто с себя и все, что у меня есть дома. А я не сделал этого и потому чувствовал, и чувствую, и не перестану чувствовать себя участником постоянно совершающегося преступления до тех пор, пока у меня будет излишняя пища, а у другого совсем не будет, у меня будут две одежды, а у кого-нибудь не будет ни одной (25:190).

"The majority of the unfortunates I saw were unfortunate . . ."
Большинство несчастных, которых я увидал, были несчастные только потому, что они потеряли способность, охоту и привычку зарабатывать свой хлеб, т.е. их несчастие было в том, что они были такие же, как и я (25:224).

"In them, as in a looking-glass, I saw myself."
я в них, как в зеркале, видел самого себя (25:207).

"I then felt that my life was bad . . ."
Я чувствовал тогда, что моя жизнь дурна и что так жить нельзя. Но из того, что моя жизнь дурна и так нельзя жить, я не вывел тот самый простой и ясный вывод, что надо улучшить свою жизнь и жить лучше, а сделал тот странный вывод, что для того, чтобы мне было жить хорошо, надо исправить жизнь других; и я стал исправлять жизнь других (25:227).

"Who am I who wishes to help people?"
Кто такой я, тот, который хочет помогать людям? (25:245).

I spend my whole life in this way . . .
Я всю свою жизнь провожу так: ем, говорю и слушаю; ем, пишу или читаю, т.е. опять говорю и слушаю; ем, играю, ем, опять говорю и слушаю, ем и опять ложусь спать, и так каждый день, и другого ничего не могу и не умею делать. [. . .] И для того, чтобы я мог это делать, нужно, чтобы с утра до вечера работали дворник, мужик, кухарка, повар, лакей, кучер, прачка; не говорю уже о тех работах людей, которые нужны для того, чтобы эти кучера, повара, лакеи и прочие имели те орудия и предметы, которыми и над которыми они для меня работают: топоры, бочки, щетки, посуду, мебель, стекла, воск, ваксу, керосин, сено, дрова, говядину (25:246).

"And all these people work hard . . ."
И все эти люди тяжело работают целый день и каждый день для того, чтобы я мог говорить, есть и спать (25:246).

"alienation of the land and the implements of labor . . ."
отчуждение земли и орудий труда у тех, которые обрабатывают землю и работают орудиями (25:254).

"[I]n order not to produce suffering and depravity . . ."

для того, чтобы не производить разврата и страданий людей, я должен как можно меньше пользоваться работой других и как можно больше самому работать (25:295).

"For him who sincerely suffers from the sufferings of those about him . . ."

Для того, кто точно искренно страдает страданиями окружающих его людей, есть самое ясное, простое и легкое средство [. . .] то самое, которое дал Иоанн Креститель на вопрос его: что делать, и которое подтвердил Христос: не иметь больше одной одежды и не иметь денег, т.е. не пользоваться трудами других людей. А чтобы не пользоваться трудами других — делать своими руками все, что можем делать (25:295).

b*"Got up at 9, joyfully cleaned the room . . ."*

b Встал в 9, весело убрал комнату с маленькими. Стыдно делать то, что должно — выносить горшок. [. . .] Шил долго и приятно сапоги (49:64).

There lived a washerwoman of about thirty years old . . .

В той ночлежной квартире [. . .] ночевала и прачка, женщина лет 30-ти, белокурая, тихая и благообразная, но болезненная. [. . .] она задолжала за квартиру и чувствовала себя виноватой, и потому ей надо было быть тихой. Она все реже и реже могла ходить на работу — сил не хватало, и потому не могла выплачивать хозяйке. Последнюю неделю она вовсе не ходила на работу и только отравляла всем. . . [. . .] хозяйка отказала прачке и сказала, чтобы она выходила из квартиры, коли не отдаст денег [. . .] Городовой с саблей и пистолетом на красном шнурке пришел в квартиру и, учтиво приговаривая приличные слова, вывел прачку на улицу.

Был ясный, солнечный, неморозный мартовский день. Ручьи текли, дворники кололи лед. Сани извозчиков подпрыгивали по обледеневшему снегу и визжали по камням. Прачка пошла в гору по солнечной стороне, дошла до церкви и села, тоже на солнечной стороне, на паперти церкви. Но когда солнце стало заходить за дома, лужи стали затягиваться стеклышком мороза, прачке стало холодно и жутко. Она поднялась и потащилась . . . Куда? Домой, в тот единственный дом, в котором она жила последнее время. Пока она дошла, отдыхая, стало смеркаться. Она подошла к воротам, завернула в них, поскользнулась, ахнула и упала.

Прошел один, прошел другой человек. «Должно, пьяная». Прошел еще человек и споткнулся на прачку и сказал дворнику: «Какая-то у вас пьяная в воротах валяется, чуть голову себе не проломил через нее; уберите вы ее, что ли!»

Дворник пошел. Прачка умерла (25:299–300).

"her face clean and pale, with prominent closed eyes . . ."

чистое бледное лицо с закрытыми выпуклыми глазами, с ввалившимися щеками и русыми мягкими волосами над высоким лбом. . . (25:301).

"What, then, must we do? . . ."

Но что же делать? Ведь не мы сделали это? Не мы, так кто же? (25:307).

"What came to me from the first at the sight . . ."

То, что с первого раза сказалось мне при виде голодных и холодных у Ляпинского дома, именно то, что я виноват в этом и что так жить, как я жил, нельзя, нельзя и нельзя, — это одно была правда (25:243).

"I like cleanliness, and give my money . . ."

Я люблю чистоту и даю деньги только под тем условием, чтобы прачка вымыла ту рубашку, которую я сменяю два раза в день, и эта рубашка надорвала последние силы прачки, и она умерла (25:306).

If things are so arranged . . .

если это уж раз заведено [. . .] Уж начали, попортили, так отчего же и мне не попользоваться? Ну, что же будет, если я буду носить грязную рубашку . . .? Разве кому-нибудь будет легче? — спрашивают люди, которым хочется оправдать себя. [. . .] Какая разница будет, если я буду носить рубашку неделю, а не день. . .? (25:306).

"consider such a life the most natural and reasonable?"

считает такую жизнь самою естественною и разумною? (25:316).

"Hegel's theory that so long prevailed . . ."

в особенности столь долго царствующая теория Гегеля с его положением разумности существующего и того, что государство есть необходимая форма совершенствования личности. . . (25:317).

"one monstrous deception, or humbug . . ."

один чудовищный обман — humbug, как говорят англичане, скрывающий от людей их неправду (25:326).

"all that exists is reasonable, that there is no evil and no good . . ."

все, что существует, то разумно, что нет ни зла, ни добра, что бороться со злом человеку не нужно, а нужно проявлять только дух: кому на военной службе, кому в суде, кому на скрипке. [. . .] Выводы эти сводились к тому, что все разумно, все хорошо, ни в чем никто не виноват. . . (25:331–32).

"'Thou, or rather you' (for it always takes many to feed one) . . ."
Ты, или скорее вы (потому что всегда многим надо кормить одного), вы меня кормите, одевайте, делайте для меня всю ту грубую работу, которую я потребую [. . .] а я буду делать для вас ту умственную работу . . . Вы давайте мне телесную, а я буду давать духовную пищу (25:349.)

"[B]efore I serve you with bodily food . . ."
прежде чем мне служить вам телесной пищей, мне нужна духовная пища, и, не получив ее, я не могу работать. . . (25:350).

"What will happen if the laborer says that? . . ."
Что, если рабочий скажет это? И если он скажет это, ведь это будет не шутка, а только самая простая справедливость (25:350).

"What shall we, mental workers, reply . . ."
Что же ответим мы, люди умственного труда, если нам предъявят такие простые и законные требования? Чем удовлетворим мы их? (25:350).

"How shall we satisfy a laborer's demands?
Чем удовлетворим мы их? Катехизисом Филарета [. . .] и листками разных лавр и Исакиевского собора—для удовлетворения его религиозных требований; сводом законов и кассационными решениями разных департаментов и разными уставами комитетов и комиссий—для удовлетворения требований порядка; спектральным анализом, измерениями млечных путей, воображаемой геометрией, микроскопическими исследованиями, спорами спиритизма и медиумизма, деятельностью академий наук—для удовлетворения требований знания . . . ? (25:350).

"With Pushkin, Dostoevsky, Turgenev, L. Tolstoy . . ."
Пушкиным, Достоевским, Тургеневым, Л. Толстым, картинами французского салона и наших художников, изображающих голых баб, атлас, бархат, пейзажи и жанры, музыкой Вагнера или новейших музыкантов? Ничто это не годится и не может годиться. . . (25:350).

"I have finished . . ."
Я кончил, сказав все то, что касалось меня [. . .] но не могу удержаться от желания сказать еще то, что касается всех (25:392).

"'Lord, heavenly Father!' he muttered . . ."
«Батюшка, отец небесный!»—проговорил он, и сознание того, что он не один, а кто-то слышит его и не оставит, успокоило его (29:37).

"Is he better or worse off . . ."

Лучше или хуже ему там, где он, после этой настоящей смерти, проснулся? разочаровался ли он или нашел там то самое, что ожидал?—мы все скоро узнаем (29:46).

"March 2, 1889 . . . I dreamt that the purpose . . ."

2 М. 89. [. . .] Во сне видел: цель жизни всякого человека улучшение мира, людей: себя и других. Так я видел во сне, но это неправильно. Цель моей жиз[ни], как и всякой: улучшение жизни; средство для этого одно: улучшение себя. (Не могу разобраться в этом—после.) А очень важно. (50:44).

"I thought about this as I took a walk . . ."

думал об этом, гуляя, и пришел к тому, что удовлетворило меня, что действительно надо быть совершенным, как Отец. Надо быть, как Отец. [. . .] Я и Отец одно. [. . .] Так думал на прогулке. Да, выразить это так: ты посланец от Отца, делать Его дело. . . (50:44).

"I got up at 10. Felt much better . . ."

10 С[снтябр]. 89. Я. П. Встал в 10.—Гораздо лучше. С особенной ясностью думал: Хозяин (это Бог) поручил свое именье рабам (это люди). . . [. . .] Хозяин поручил виноградни к. . . Сделка с должниками [. . .] (двойная аналогия). . . (50: 139).

"One laborer cannot understand the whole business . . ."

14 С. Я. П. 89. [. . .] один частный работник не может понять всего дела предпринимателя. Как ни жалко, мелко это сравнение воли Б[ога], т. е. всего, с волей предпринимателя, но оно именно этой несоразмерностью тем более показывает невозможность человеку понять всю волю Б[ога]. . . [. . .] Лошадь верно знает, что она идет по воле хозяина, когда и возжи не дергают ее, но она не знает воли хозяина и горе ей, если она вообразит, что знает эту волю. . . (50:142–43).

"Without a doubt, the purpose of life . . ."

несомненно то, что жизнь только в том, чтобы исполнять волю пославшего

"They say that the actual is reasonable . . ."

Говорят, существующее разумно; напротив, всё, что есть, всегда неразумно (52:80–81).

"In the morning, in bed, after a bad night . . ."

6 сентября [1894] [. . .] Утром в постели, после дурной ночи, продумал очень живой художественный рассказ о хозяине и работнике. . . (52:137).

"To the question: What am I? What shall I do? . . ."

На вопрос: что я, что мне делать? [. . .]—мне отвечают: исполняй предписание властей и верь церкви. Но отчего же так дурно мы живем в этом мире?—спрашивает отчаянный голос; зачем все это зло, неужели нельзя мне своей жизнью не участвовать в этом зле? неужели нельзя облегчить это зло? Отвечают: нельзя (23:412).

"Christ says, 'You have been taught to consider it right' . . ."

Христос говорит: вам внушено, вы привыкли считать хорошим и разумным то, чтобы силой отстаиваться ото зла и вырывать глаз за глаз, учреждать уголовные суды, полицию, войско, отстаиваться от врагов, а я говорю: не делайте насилия, не участвуйте в насилии, не делайте зла никому, даже тем, кого вы называете врагами (23:328).

"For me, therefore, the destitution of the people . . ."

Для меня, стало быть, и нищета народа, лишенного первого, самого естественного права человеческого—пользования той землей, на которой он родился; для меня эти полмиллиона оторванных от доброй жизни мужиков, одетых в мундиры и обучаемых убийству, для меня это лживое так называемое духовенство, на главной обязанности которого лежит извращение и скрывание истинного христианства. [. . .] Для меня все эти сотни тысяч голодных, блуждающих по России рабочих. Для меня закапывание десятков, сотен расстреливаемых, для меня эта ужасная работа [. . .] людей-палачей . . .

"As strange as it seems to say . . ."

И как ни странно утверждение о том, что все это делается для меня, и что я участник этих страшных дел, я все-таки не могу не чувствовать, что есть несомненная зависимость между моей просторной комнатой, моим обедом, моей одеждой, моим досугом и теми страшными преступлениями. . . (37:95).

"And being conscious of this, I can no longer endure this . . ."

А сознавая это, я не могу долее переносить этого, не могу и должен освободиться от этого мучительного положения. Нельзя так жить. Я по крайней мере не могу так жить, не могу и не буду (37:95).

That is why I write this and will circulate it . . .

Затем я и пишу это и буду всеми силами распространять то, что пишу, и в России и вне ее, чтобы одно из двух: или кончились эти нечеловеческие дела, или уничтожилась бы моя связь с этими делами, чтобы или посадили меня в тюрьму, где бы я ясно сознавал, что не для меня уже делаются все эти ужасы, или же, что было бы лучше всего (так хорошо, что я и не смею мечтать о таком счастье), надели на меня, так же как на тех двадцать или двенадцать крестьян, саван, колпак и так же столкнули с скамейки, чтобы я своей тяжестью затянул на своем старом горле намыленную петлю (37:95).

Endnotes

"In the 1870s, Leo Tolstoy made three attempts . . ."

«В 70-е гг. Лев Толстой трижды садился, чтобы прочесть "Бастия, Милля, Прудона, Маркса", и каждый раз бросал книги, приходя к выводу, что "все, что написано в этих книгах, есть величайший вздор". [. . .] "Я внимательно прочел "Капитал" и готов сдать по нему экзамен"».

Chapter 6

"write with the idea of not showing his writings, including this diary, within one's life-time . . ."

Да, подумал, надо писать с тем, чтобы не показывать своего писания, как и дневник этот, при жизни. И, о ужас! Я задумался—писать ли? Станет ли сил писать для Бога? . . . (50:39).

25 Feb. 1897. N[ikolskoe]. E.b.zh. . . .

25 Февр. Н[икольское]. 1897. Е. б. ж.

25 февраля 1897]. Жив. Писал не много, но не так легко, как вчера. Гости разъехались. Ходил два раза гулять. Читаю Аристотеля. Нынче получил письма с Сережей, который приехал сюда. Неприятное письмо от Сони. Или скорее я не в духе. Вчера, гуляя, молился и испытал удивительное чувство. Вероятно, подобное тому, которое возбуждают в себе мистики духовным деланием: почувствовал себя одного духовного, свободного, связанного иллюзией тела.
26 Ф. II. 97. Е. б. ж. (53:141).

[a]*"Now listen, you who say, 'Today or tomorrow' . . ."*

Теперь послушайте вы, говорящие: «сегодня или завтра отправимся в такой-то город, и проживем там один год, и будем торговать и получать прибыль»; вы, которые не знаете, что случится завтра: ибо что такое жизнь ваша? пар, являющийся на малое время, а потом исчезающий. Вместо того, чтобы вам говорить: «если угодно будет Господу и живы будем, то сделаем то или другое» (Иакова 4:13–17).

"I feel sad because it seems as though . . ."

И мне грустно, точно как будто я и умирая буду писать и после смерти тоже (52:105).

"In one's old age, one can and even should do this . . ."

В старости это уже совсем можно и даже должно, но возможно и в молодости, а именно то, чтобы быть в состоянии не только приговоренного к смертной казни, но в состоянии везомого на место казни (57:4).

"he crossed out the word death from the title . . ."

Слова о *смерти* выкинул. Когда он кончил статью, он решил, что *смерти нет* (26:767).

"I have lived 59 years, and for all this time . . ."

Я жил 59 лет, и во все это время я сознавал себя собою в своем теле, и это-то сознание себя собою, мне кажется, и была моя жизнь (26:402).

"Every day, during deep sleep, consciousness completely ceases . . ."

Каждые сутки, во время полного сна, сознание обрывается совершенно и потом опять возобновляется. [. . .] мы [. . .] сознание теряем всякий день, когда засыпаем (26:404).

"all remembered states of consciousness . . ."

все памятные мне сознания и сознания, предшествующие памятной мне жизни (как это говорит Платон и как мы все это в себе чувствуем) (26:407).

"a continuous ecstasy over Schopenhauer . . ."

Непрестающий восторг перед Шопенгауэром и ряд духовных наслаждений, которых я никогда не испытывал (62:219).

31 October 89. Y[asnaya] P[olyana]. . .

31 О. Я. П. 89.

Апатия, грусть, уныние. Но не дурно мне. Впереди смерть, т. е. жизнь, как же не радоваться? —(50:170).

23 January 90. If I live. . .

23 Я. Я. П. 90. Если буду жив.

И так, нынче *27-е*. Встал поздно. Поговорил с Чертковым очень хорошо об искусстве и смерти и пошел гулять. [. . .] О смерти то, что не надо никогда забывать, что жизнь есть постоянное умирание. И сказать, что я постоянно умираю, всё равно, что сказать—я живу.— (51:15).

"29 June 1894. Y[asnaya] P[olyana]. Morning . . ."

29 Июня 1894. Я. П.

— Потерял странно часы. Всё чаще и чаще и живее думаю о смерти, смерти только плотской. Той, которая ужасала меня прежде, уж не вижу теперь. [. . .] Лучше в этом отношении только готовность. Читаю Шопенгауера Parerga. . . (52:124).

"liberate one's soul."
освобождать свою душу (56:88).

"not death, but liberation from the body . . ."
не смерть, а освобождение от тела.

"Is this new state of mind a step towards liberation?"
Неужели это новое душевное состояние — шаг вперед к освобождению? . . (56:89).

"I want to live in God, not in my bodily self, Lev T[olstoy] . . ."
Я хочу жить Богом, а не своим телесным я, Львом Т[олстым]. Что это значит? То, что я хочу сознание Льва Т[олстого] заменить сознанием всего человечества . . .

"took up this notebook to record . . ."
Нынче взял тетрадь именно для того, чтобы записать то, что утром и ночью в первый раз [. . .] почувствовал свое равнодушие полное ко всему телесному и не перестающий интерес к своему духовному росту, т. е. своей духовной жизни (56:150).

"I haven't written anything all month . . ."
Ровно месяц не писал. [. . .] Работа же внутренняя, слава Богу, идет не переставая и все лучше и лучше. Хочу написать то, что делается во мне и как делается; то, чего я никому не рассказывал и чего никто не знает (56:109).

This is how I live: I get up, my head is clear . . .
Живу я вот как: Встаю, голова свежа и приходят хорошие мысли, и, сидя на горшке, записываю их. Одеваюсь, с усилием и удовольствием выношу нечистоты. Иду гулять. Гуляя, жду почту, которая мне не нужна, но по старой привычке. Часто задаю себе загадку: сколько будет шагов до какого нибудь места, и считаю, разделяя каждую единицу на 4, 6, 8 придыханий: раз, и *а*, и *а*, и *а*; и *два*, и *а*, и *а*, и *а* . . . Иногда по старой привычке хочется загадать, что если будет столько шагов, сколько предполагаю, то . . . все будет хорошо. Но сейчас же спрашиваю себя: что хорошо? и знаю, что и так все очень хорошо, и нечего загадывать. Потом, встречаясь с людьми, вспоминаю, а большей частью забываю то, что хотел помнить, что Он и я одно. Особенно трудно бывает помнить при разговоре. Потом лает собака Белка, мешает думать, и я сержусь и упрекаю себя за то, что сержусь. Упрекаю себя за то, что сержусь на палку, на которую спотыкаюсь (56:109–10).

"Yes, I, the body, is such a disgusting chamber pot . . ."

Да, я—тело—это такой отвратительный нужник—только сними, приоткрой крышку духовности, и смрад и мерзость. Постараюсь нынче жить для души (56:173).

"I remember how in childhood I was surprised . . ."

Помню, как я в детстве почти удивился проявлению в себе этого свойства, которое еще не умело находить для себя матерьял. Помню, меня удивляло то, что я мог, сознавая себя, сознавать сознающего себя, и опять спрашивая, сознавал, что я сознаю себя сознающим сознающего себя. И потом: сознаю себя, сознающего себя, сознающего себя и т.д. до бесконечности (56:128).

"What is consciousness? I will ask myself . . ."

Что такое сознание? То, что я опрошу себя: кто, что я?—И отвечу: я—я. Но я спрошу себя: кто же этот второй «я»?—И ответ только один: опять я, и сколько ни спрашивай; все я—я. Явно, что я есть что то внепространственное, вневременное. . . (58:42).

August 6 [1892] . . . I remember: I am sitting in the bathhouse . . .

Только и помню теперь, что я сижу в бане, и мальчик пастух вошел в сени. Я спросил: Кто там?—Я.—Кто я?—Да я.—Кто ты?—Да я же. [. . .] И так всякий. . . 7 А. Я. П. 92. Если буду жив (52:69).

"I haven't read Fichte . . ."

Я не читал Фихте, но слышал, что у него я человеческое, а у Шеллинга—абсолютное. . .

"About a week ago I got ill . . ."

С неделю тому назад я заболел. Со мной сделался обморок. И мне было очень хорошо. Но окружающие делают из этого fuss (56:109).

"Today, on May 13, upon awakening . . ."

Сегодня, 13 мая, проснувшись, испытываю странное душевное состояние: как будто все забыл [. . .] не могу вспомнить: какое число? что я пишу?—А между тем не столько представления, сколько чувства нынешних сновидений представляются особенно ярко (56:35).

"I now more and more [begin] to forget . . ."

Я нынче все больше и больше [начинаю] забывать. Нынче много спал и, проснувшись, почувствовал совершенно новое освобождение от личности: так удивительно хорошо! Только бы совсем освободиться. Пробуждение от сна, сновидения, это—образец такого освобождения (56:98).

"I can regret, and do regret..."

Я потерял память. И—удивительное дело—ни разу не пожалел об этом. Могу пожалеть о том, что теряю волосы, и жалею, но не о памяти... (56:161).

"I have lost the memory of everything..."

Я потерял память всего, почти всего прошедшего, всех моих писаний, всего того, что привело меня к тому сознанию, в каком живу теперь. [. . .] Как же не радоваться потере памяти? Все, что я в прошедшем выработал (хотя бы моя внутренняя работа в писаниях), всем этим я живу, пользуюсь, но самую работу не помню. Удивительно. А между тем думаю, что эта радостная перемена у всех стариков: жизнь вся сосредотачивается в настоящем. Как хорошо! (58: 121–22).

"a timeless life in the present."

безвременной жизнью в настоящем (58:122).

"22, 23, 24 Feb. [1910.] I poorly remember..."

22, 23, 24 фев. [1910 г.] [. . .] Плохо помню, что было в эти два дня (58:19).

"Dreams [snovideniia] are a complete analogy of life."

Сновидения совершенное подобие жизни (57:91).

"Sleeping-and-dreaming [son] is a complete analogy of death"

Сон   совершенное подобие смерти (56:84).

"I told myself that death is like dreaming..."

Я говорил себе, что смерть похожа на сон, на засыпание: устал и засыпаешь,—и это правда, что похоже, но смерть еще более похожа на пробуждение... (55:89).

"Today is February 5, 1892. Begichevka..."

Сегодня 5 Ф. 92. Бегичевка. Только что встал. В постели думал: От сна пробуждаешься в то, что мы называем жизнью ... Но и эта жизнь не есть ли сон? А от нее смертью не пробуждаемся ли в то, что мы называем будущей жизнью, в то, что предшествовало и следует за сновидением этой жизни? (52:62; 205).

I saw in a dream that a door in my dark room suddenly opened...

Я видел во сне, что в моей темной комнате вдруг страшно отворилась дверь и потом снова неслышно закрылась. Мне было страшно, но я старался верить, что это ветер. Кто-то сказал мне: поди, притвори, я пошел и хотел отворить сначала, кто-то упорно держал сзади. Я хотел бежать, но ноги не шли, и меня обуял неописанный ужас. Я проснулся, я был счастлив пробуждением. Чем же я был счастлив? Я получил сознание и потерял то, которое было во сне. Не может ли также быть счастлив человек, умирая? Он теряет сознание я, говорят. Но разве я не теряю его засыпая, а все-таки живу. Теряет личность, индивидуальное. . . (48:75).

"a nightmare and a philosophical theory of unconsciousness."
кошмар и философская теория бессознательности (52:12).

"I died—I woke up. Yes, death is an awakening!"
Я умер—я проснулся. Да, смерть—пробуждение!

"I dreamt that my wife loves me . . ."
Во сне видел, что жена меня любит. Как мне легко, ясно всё стало! Ничего похожего наяву (49:90).

"This night I saw in my dream . . ."
Ночью видел во сне, что я отчасти пишу, сочиняю, отчасти переживаю драму Христа. Я—и Христос и воин. Помню, как надевал меч. Очень ярко (56:158).

"Everything that I have written down I have . . ."
Всё то, что я записал, я точно видел, слышал во сне. Правда, я часто и много думаю наяву о земельном вопросе, но то, что] я слышал во сне, я не думал сам наяву, а услышал только во сне (57:264).

Had a dream. I am talking with Grot . . .
Видел сон. Я разговариваю с Гротом и знаю, что он умер, и все-таки спокойно, не удивляясь, разговариваю. И в разговоре хочу вспомнить чье-то суждение о Спенсере или самого Спенсера, что тоже не представляет во сне различия. И это рассуждение я знаю и говорил уже прежде. Так что рассуждение это было и прежде и после.—

The conversation with Grot, despite the fact that he had died . . .
То, что я разговариваю с Гротом, несмотря на то, что он умер, и то, что рассуждение о Спенсере было и прежде и после и принадлежало и Спенсеру и другому кому-то—все это не менее справедливо, чем то, что было в действительности, распределенное во времени.
8 марта 1904. Я. П. Е. б. (55:19–20).

"I had a dream that explained a lot . . ."
Я видел сон, который уяснил многое, именно то, что сон соединяет в одно то, что в действительности разбивается по времени, пространству, причинности. . . (55:19–20).

"Life within a dream takes place outside of time and space . . ."

Жизнь в сновидении происходит вне времени, пространства, вне отдельных личностей: имеешь дело во сне с умершими как с живыми, хотя знаешь, что они умершие. Также и место—и в Москве и в деревне, и время—и давнее и настоящее (55:64).

I went for a swim. My horse, tied up . . .

21 июля [1870] Я купаюсь. Лошадь привязана и глядит на меня, когда я выплыл из купальни. Знает ли она, что это я,—тот я, который приехал на ней?

Кант говорит, что пространство, время—суть формы *нашего* мышления. Но, кроме пространства и времени, есть форма нашего мышления—*индивидуальность*. Для меня лошадь, я, козявка, суть индивидуумы, потому что я сам вижу себя индивидуумом, но так ли лошадь? (48:126)

"I have read Kant, Schopenhauer . . ."

я читал Канта, Шопенгауэра и это им обязан взглядам на пространство и время как формы восприятия. Но, знаете, мысль становится близка тогда, когда в душе уже сознаешь ее, когда при чтении кажется, что она уже была у тебя, что все это ты знал, когда ты точно только вспоминаешь ее.

"[one] cannot help thinking about falling asleep . . ."

Нельзя не думать о засыпании и пробуждении, как о подобии смерти и рождения (56:114).

The main analogy was with respect to time . . .

Главное подобие в отношении ко времени: в том, что как во сне, так и наяву времени нет, но мы только воображаем, не можем не воображать его. Я вспоминаю длинный, связный сон, который кончается выстрелом, и я просыпаюсь. Звук выстрела—это был стук ветром прихлопнутого окна. Время в воспоминании о сновидении мне нужно, необходимо было для того, чтобы в бдящем состоянии расположить все впечатления сна. Так же и в воспоминаниях о событиях бдения: вся моя жизнь в настоящем, но не могу в воспоминании о ней, скорее в сознании ее—не располагать ее во времени. Я ребенок, и муж, и старик—все одно, все настоящее. Я только не могу сознавать этого вне времени (56: 114).

"Just as, awakened by the knock of a window slamming shut . . ."

Как, просыпаясь от стука захлопнувшегося окна, я знаю, что сновидение было иллюзия, так я при смерти узнаю это обо всех, кажущихся мне столь реальными событиях мира (56:115).

I come to see my brother and find him . . .

Все знают и все замечали те странные сны, которые кончаются пробуждением от какого-нибудь внешнего воздействия на сонного: или стук, шум, или прикосновение, или падение,— при чем этот в действительности случившийся шум, толчок или еще что получает во сне характер заключительного впечатления после многих, как будто подготавливавших к нему. Так что сон я вспоминаю, например, так: я приезжаю к брату и встречаю его на крыльце с ружьем и собакой. Он зовет меня итти с собой на охоту, я говорю, что у меня ружья нет. Он говорит, что можно вместо ружья взять, почему-то, кларнет. Я не удивляюсь и иду с ним по знакомым местам на охоту, но по знакомым местам этим мы приходим к морю (я тоже не удивляюсь). По морю плывут корабли, они же и лебеди. Брат говорит: стреляй. Я исполняю его желание, беру кларнет в рот, но никак не могу дуть. Тогда он говорит: ну, так я,— и стреляет. [. . .] я просыпаюсь. . . (57:139–40).

"there is no time, and we imagine things . . ."

времени нет, а что нам представляется всё во времени только потому, что таково свойство нашего ума (57:140).

"At night, I thought: what is time?"

Ночью думал: что такое время? (55:10).

"The same illusion takes place in what we call real life . . ."

Точно тот же обман происходит и в том, что мы называем действительной жизнью. Только с той разницей, что от того сновидения мы проснулись, а от жизни проснемся только при смерти. Только тогда мы узнаем и убедимся, что реально было в этой жизни то, что спало и что проснулось при смерти.—(57:140).

I would like to say that life before birth was perhaps just the same . . .

Хотелось бы сказать, что жизнь до рождения, может быть, была такая же, что тот характер, который я вношу в жизнь, есть плод прежних пробуждений, и что такая же будет будущая жизнь, хотелось бы сказать это, но не имею права, потому что я вне времени не могу мыслить. Для истинной же жизни времени нет, она только представляется мне во времени. Одно могу сказать—то, что она есть, и смерть не только не уничтожает, но только больше раскрывает ее. Сказать же, что *было* до жизни, и *будет* после смерти, значило бы прием мысли, свойственный только в этой жизни, употреблять для объяснения других, неизвестных мне форм жизни (курсив Толстого; 57:142).

Today I had several thought-feelings . . .

Нынче было несколько мыслей-чувств. Одна из них о том, что нынче во сне испытал толчок сердца, который разбудил меня, и, проснувшись, вспомнил длинный сон, как я шел под гору, держался за ветки и все-таки поскользнулся и упал,—т.е. проснулся. Все сновидение, казавшееся прошедшим, возникло мгновенно, так одна мысль о том, что в минуту смерти будет этот, подобный толчку сердца в сонном состоянии, момент вневременный, и вся жизнь будет этим ретроспективным сновидением. Теперь же ты в самом разгаре этого ретроспективного сновидения.—Иногда мне это кажется верным, а иногда кажется чепухой (89:230).

g*"Had a dream. Grushenka, a novel . . ."*

Видел сон, Грушенька, роман будто бы Н. Н. Страхова. Чудный сюжет (58:123).

I thought: life, not my life, but the life of the whole world . . .

Думал: жизнь, не моя, но жизнь мира с тем renouveau христианства со всех сторон выступающая, как весна, и в деревьях, и в траве, и в воде, становится до невозможности интересна. В этом одном весь интерес и моей жизни; а вместе с тем моя жизнь земная кончилась. Точно читал, читал книгу, которая становилась всё интереснее и интереснее, и вдруг на самом интересном месте кончилась книга и оказывается, что это только первый том неизвестно сколь многотомного сочинения и достать продолжения здесь нельзя. Только за границей на иностранном языке можно будет прочесть его. А наверно прочтешь.—(50:4).

"There is no time. There is my life . . ."

Времени нет. Есть моя жизнь. А она только написана на времени. Есть сочинение, а нет строк, букв. Оно написано только посредством строк и букв. И то, что хорошее сочинение написано строками и буквами, никак не доказывает того, что дальнейшие строки и буквы книги будут продолжать сочинение или составят подобное же сочинение (57:19).

"In my dreams, I keep thinking about The Circle of Reading . . ."

Я во сне все думаю о «Круге чтения». Сегодня вижу во сне, как на бумажке написано: «У тебя есть душа, но ты должен образовывать в себе другую, культурную душу». И подписано: Кант. Я думаю: «Кант, надо обратить внимание».

though Pascal had died two hundred years ago . . .

Вот Паскаль умер двести лет тому назад, а я живу с ним одной душой—что может быть таинственнее этого? Вот эта мысль [. . .] которая меня переворачивает сегодня, мне так близка, точно моя! . . Я чувствую, как я в ней сливаюсь душой с Паскалем. Чувствую, что Паскаль жив, не умер, вот он! Так же как Христос . . .

"the soul, with its ability for knowledge and memory . . ."

душа с своей способностью знания, воспоминания о прежней жизни] не может умереть вместе с телом; как идеи [. . .] не подлежат смерти, то также не подлежит смерти наша душа (42: 67).

"They say: do not think of death, and there will be no death . . ."

Говорят: не думай о смерти—и не будет смерти. Как раз наоборот: не переставая помни о смерти—и будет жизнь, для которой нет смерти.

Why are the Xanthippes so malicious? . . .

Отчего Ксантипы бывают особенно злы? А от того, что жене всегда приятно, почти нужно осуждать своего мужа. А когда муж Сократ или приближается к нему, то жена, не находя в нем явно дурного, осуждает в нем то, что хорошо. А осуждая хорошее, теряет la notion du bien et du mal—и становится всё ксантипистее и ксантипистее. Софья Андреевна готовится к Стокгольму и как только заговорит о нем, приходит в отчаяние. На мои предложения не ехать не обращается никакого внимания. Одно спасение: жизнь в настоящем и молчание (57:111).

" 'The Circle of Reading,' he wrote, 'is Tolstoy's silence.' "

«Круг чтения» есть молчание самого Толстого.

"One could view life as a dream and death as an awakening . . ."

Можно смотреть на жизнь как на сон, а на смерть как на пробуждение. [. . .] Мы можем только гадать о том, что будет после смерти, будущее скрыто от нас. Оно не только скрыто, но оно не существует, так как будущее говорит о времени, а умирая, мы уходим из времени.

"The candle, by the light of which she had been reading . . ."

В минуту смерти человека свеча, при которой он читал исполненную обманов, горя и зла книгу, вспыхивает более ярким, чем когда-либо, светом, освещает ему все то что прежде было во мраке, трещит, меркнет и навсегда потухает (44:384).

Notes

Introduction

1 Throughout this book, references to Tolstoy's work are to *Polnoe sobranie sochinenii v 90 tomakh* (Moscow-Leningrad, 1928–58), with volume and page number indicated in the text. The quote is from "A History of Yesterday" (*Istoriia vcherashnego dnia*), cited here and further in George L. Kline's translation, from *Tolstoy's Short Fiction*, ed. Michael R. Katz (New York: Norton, 1991), 279–93 (translation adjusted).

2 Andrei Belyi, "Lev Tolstoi i kul'tura" [1912], in *Lev Tolstoi. Pro et Contra* (St. Petersburg: RKhGI, 2000), 583.

3 Tolstoy's diaries, in the original Russian, can be found in volumes 46–58 of the 90-volume edition (issued between 1934 and 1953), the letters in volumes 59–89. Excerpts from the diaries had appeared earlier in the compendiums of biographical documents. For detailed bibliographic information, see commentaries to volumes 46–58 of the 90-volume edition. For publications of selected diaries and letters in English, see *Tolstoy's Diaries*, 2 vols., edited and translated by R. F. Christian (London: Athlone Press, 1985); *Tolstoy's Letters*, 2 vols., selected, edited, and translated by R. F. Christian (London: Athlone Press, 1978).

4 The story is known from Ivan Bunin's memoir *Osvobozhdenie Tolstogo* (Paris: Sovremennye zapiski, 1937), 103–4; English translation *The Liberation of Tolstoy: A Tale of Two Writers*, trans. Thomas Gaiton Marullo (Evanston, IL: Northwestern University Press, 2001), 58 (translation adjusted). Bunin's memoir, published in 1937 in an émigré journal in Paris, may be the first work that makes extensive and insightful use of Tolstoy's fragmented memoirs, excerpts from his diaries, and his essays to speak about Tolstoy's efforts to achieve "liberation" from his self.

5 Suffice it to mention Charles Taylor, *Sources of the Self: The Making of the Modern Identity* (Cambridge, MA: Harvard University Press, 1989); Jerrold Seigel, *The Idea of the Self: Thought and Experience in Western Europe since the Seventeenth Century* (Cambridge, U.K.: Cambridge University Press, 2005); Richard Sorabji, *Self: Ancient and Modern Insights about Individuality, Life, and Death* (Chicago: University of Chicago Press, 2006); Paul Ricouer, *Time and Narrative*, trans. Kathleen McLaughlin and David Pellauer, 3 vols. (Chicago: University of Chicago Press, 1984, 1985, 1988) and *Oneself as Another*, trans. Kathleen Blamey (Chicago: University of Chicago Press, 1992); Peter Brooks, *Psychoanalysis and Storytelling* (Cambridge, MA: Blackwell, 1994) and *Enigmas of Identity* (Princeton, NJ: Princeton University Press, 2011); Paul John Eakin, *How Our Lives Become Stories:*

Making Selves (Ithaca, NY: Cornell University Press, 1999) and *Living Autobiographically: How We Create Identity in Narrative* (Ithaca, NY: Cornell University Press, 2008).

6 Richard Gustafson, in his *Leo Tolstoy, Resident and Stranger: A Study in Fiction and Theology* (Princeton, NJ: Princeton University Press, 1986), emphasizes the role of Eastern Christian thought in Tolstoy. In my view, Eastern Orthodox Christianity was only one of many and varied sources of Tolstoy's views on the self.

7 Tolstoy's involvement with Eastern (Indian and Chinese) thought will largely remain outside the purview of this book because these sources lie outside my expertise. I will offer some factual and bibliographic information. Beginning in the 1870s (when he was debating issues of faith with Nikolai Strakhov), Tolstoy became interested in non-Western religious thought. He was obviously attracted by the emphasis on limitations of self in Hindu and Buddhist religion. It is likely that his interest was inspired by Schopenhauer. Tolstoy first mentions the Chinese thinkers Confucius and Lao-Tzu (along with Hindu and Buddhist sources) in 1877, in his correspondence with Strakhov. In 1884, he intensely read Confucius and Lao-Tzu as he first thought about compiling the *Circle of Reading*, his own almanac of spiritual readings (49:68). There is a collection of excerpts from Tolstoy's personal writings concerned with Eastern religions, issued by his disciple and biographer Paul Birjukoff [Biriukov], *Tolstoi und der Orient: Briefe und sonstige Zeugnisse über Tolstois Beziehungen zu den Vertretern orientalischer Religionen* (Zurich and Leipzig: Rotapfel Verlag, 1925). A catalogue of the books on India in Tolstoy's library was compiled by his last secretary, Valentin Bulgakov, "Knigi ob Indii v biblioteke L. N. Tolstogo," *Kratkie soobshcheniia Instituta vostokovedeniia* 31 (1959): 45–56. Fuller information on Tolstoy's sources on Indian and Chinese thought can be found in the recent catalogue of Tolstoy's library, *Biblioteka L'va Nikolaevicha Tolstogo v Iasnoi Poliane*, vol. 3 (Tula: Iasnaia Poliana, 1999). A recent edition presents Tolstoy's correspondence on India from his archives: T. N. Zagorodnikova, ed., *L. N. Tolstoi i Indiia: Perepiska* (Moscow: Vostochnaia literatura, 2013). Scholarship on Tolstoy and the East (which remains insufficient) includes: Derk Bodde, with the cooperation of Galia Speshneff Bodde, *Tolstoy and China* (Princeton, NJ: Princeton University Press, 1950); A. F. Shifman, *Lev Tolstoi i vostok* (Moscow: Nauka, 1971); Radha Balasubramanian, *The Influence of India on Leo Tolstoy and Tolstoy's Influence on India: A Study of Reciprocal Receptions* (Lewiston, NY: Mellen Press, 2013).

8 Here I echo George Steiner's 1959 study *Tolstoy or Dostoevsky*. Steiner spoke of the "cyclical pattern of Tolstoy's evolution" and located the "coincidence between imagined and experienced reality" in "the recurrence of a small number of decisive motifs and emblematic actions" in the early diaries and the major novels. George Steiner, *Tolstoy or Dostoevsky: An Essay in the Old Criticism*, 2nd ed. (New Haven: Yale University Press, 1996), 242–43. Richard Gustafson, in his *Leo Tolstoy, Resident and Stranger* (Princeton, NJ: Princeton University Press, 1986), advanced a similar approach, speaking of Tolstoy's "emblematic realism"—a way of expressing a theological vision in images. Gustafson looks for such "verbal icons" (images and actions) in both the diaries and the novels before and after the conversion.

9 Vladimir Nabokov, *Lectures on Russian Literature*, ed. Fredson Bowers (New York: Harcourt Brace Jovanovich, 1981), 140. For this quotation, I am indebted to Eric Naiman.

10 Many have made this argument. Here I cite René Girard, *Deceit, Desire, and the Novel: Self and Other in Literary Structure*, trans. Yvonne Freccero (Baltimore: John Hopkins University Press, 1965), 260.

11 See Mikhail Bakhtin's unfinished essay "Author and Hero in Aesthetic Activity," published in English in *Art and Answerability: Early Philosophical Essays by M. M. Bakhtin*, ed. Michael Holquist and Vadim Liapunov (Austin: University of Texas Press, 1990).

12 Here I echo Ann Banfield's comments on the representation of consciousness in "Where Epistemology, Style, and Grammar Meet Literary History: The Development of Represented Speech and Thought," *New Literary History* 9, no. 3 (Spring 1978): 415–54.

Chapter 1

1 Historians of private life have connected the practice of diary writing with anxieties about death. A companion to the account book, the diary was a means to stem the expenditure of life. See Alain

Corbin, "Backstage," in *A History of Private Life*, vol. 4, ed. Michelle Perrot (Cambridge, MA: Harvard University Press, 1990), 498–502.

2   My concept of "yesterday's tomorrow" is inspired by Reinhart Koselleck's *Vergangene Zukunft*; in English, *Futures Past: On the Semantics of Historical Time*, trans. Keith Tribe (Cambridge, MA: MIT Press, 1985).

3   In formulating Augustine's views, in a modern interpretation, I have used Henry Chadwick's translation (the Oxford University Press edition of 1991) and Paul Ricoeur, *Time and Narrative*, 1:7–9, 231n3.

4   This is how Rousseau sets his task at the beginning of the "First Promenade." He does not refer to Augustine (whom he briefly mentions, in another context, in the "Second Promenade"). Jean Starobinski, *Jean-Jacques Rousseau: Transparency and Obstruction* (Chicago: University of Chicago Press, 1988), 180–200.

5   Boris Eikhenbaum was the first to note parallels between Tolstoy's early diaries and Rousseau's *Confessions*, in his *Molodoi Tolstoi* (Peterburg-Berlin, 1922). This book provides the first treatment of Tolstoy's diaries and his "History of Yesterday." Here and elsewhere, Eikhenbaum is cited from: B. M. Eikhenbaum, *Lev Tolstoi. Issledovaniia. Stat'i* (St. Petersburg, 2009); on the diaries, see 75–100; on Rousseau's presence in the diaries, 87–89.

6   Here I rely on the remarkable, little-known work of Alla Polosina; in her work on Tolstoy and Rousseau, she notes the Augustinian echo in the meditations on time in Rousseau's *Les Rêveries du promeneur solitaire*. A. N. Polosina, "Russoism L. N. Tolstogo," *Literaturovedcheskii zhurnal* 28 (2011): 74–75. Tolstoy and Augustine will be also discussed later in the book.

7   On its first publication, in the 90-volume edition, the commentator (A. E. Gruzinskii) treated "A History of Yesterday" as an outgrowth of the diary (1:342), but some have disagreed. Viktor Shklovsky, challenging Gruzinskii, claims that "A History of Yesterday" was Tolstoy's first work of fiction, albeit an experimental one. See Viktor Shklovskii, "'Istoriia vcherashnego dnia' v obshchem khode trudovykh dnei pisatelia Tolstogo" [1959], in *Povesti o proze* (Moscow. Khudozhestvennaia literatura, 1966), 273 and *Lev Tolstoi* (Moscow: Molodaia gvardiia, 1967), 75.

8   The metaphor of the "book of life" is of enormous importance in European culture. It has theological origins: The Old Testament features the "Book of Life" written by God; the names of the righteous are inscribed in it. The New Testament also contains a large stock of book metaphors. Before Christianity, a purely literary form of the metaphor, in which life itself is compared to a book, was widely used in Greek and Roman texts. There are also metaphors derived from the images of "the book of nature" and "the book of the world." As Curtius has noted in his classic study of tropes ("topoi"), the religious and the literary metaphorics, as well as the two meanings of the "book of life," intersect as this image becomes commonplace. Images of the book of the heart, the book of the mind, the book of memory, and the book of experience abound in sources ranging from medieval Latin texts to Dante to Rousseau and beyond. See Ernst Robert Curtius, *European Literature and the Latin Middle Ages*, trans. Willard R. Trask (Princeton, NJ: Princeton University Press, 1990), 302–47 ("The Book as Symbol"); Hans Blumenberg, *Die Lesbarkeit der Welt* (Frankfurt am Main: Suhrkamp, 1981). I return to Tolstoy's uses of this metaphor in chapter 6.

9   From "Vstupleniia, predisloviia i varianty nachal 'Voiny i mira'" (undated) (13:53–55). Eikhenbaum describes and interprets these aspects of the history of *War and Peace* in his *Lev Tolstoi: shestidesiatye gody*; see Eikhenbaum, *Lev Tolstoi. Issledovaniia. Stat'i*, 460–61.

10   Shklovskii, "O zhanre" and "'Istoriia vcherashnego dnia'," in *Povesti o proze*, 270, 271.

11   Immanuel Kant, *Critique of Pure Reason*, trans. Norman Kemp Smith (New York, 1965), 218–23; *Kritik der reinen Vernunft*, II.3.B. (*Zweite Analogie*).

12   Shklovsky comments: "Time is pulled apart, broadened, lengthened, as it were." V. Shklovskii, *Lev Tolstoi*, 78.

13   Sterne's influence has been noted and discussed by Eikhenbaum, *Lev Tolstoi. Issledovaniia. Stat'i*, 89–90, 173; A. E. Gruzinskii's commentaries to the 90-volume edition (1:301, 343); Shklovskii, "O kharaktere kak ob osnove novoi russkoi prozy," "'Istoriia vcherashnego dnia'," and "Siuzhet i analiz," in *Povesti o proze*, 270, 273, 274; and Peter Rudy, "Lev Tolstoj's Apprenticeship to Laurence Sterne," *Slavic and East European Journal* 15, no. 1 (1971): 1–21.

14   I paraphrase Paragraphs 2 and 3 of Chapter XIV, Book II of John Locke's *Essay concerning Human Understanding*.

15 Sterne's connection to Locke has been discussed in Ian Watt, *The Rise of the Novel* (Berkeley: University of California Press, 1957). I use Locke's formulations from Book II, Chapter XIV, paragraphs 2–4 as well as Watt's formulations on 290–95.

16 Here I follow Erich Kahler, *The Inward Turn of Narrative*, trans. Richard and Clara Winston (Princeton, NJ: Princeton University Press, 1973), 189–96.

17 Tolstoy did not make explicit references to Kant until 1862. His reading of Kant's *Critique of Pure Reason* in 1869 has been discussed, among others, in Gary R. Jahn, "Tolstoy and Kant," in *New Perspectives on Nineteenth-Century Russian Prose*, ed. George J. Gutsche and Lauren G. Leighton (Columbus, OH: Slavica, 1982) and, most recently, A. N. Kruglov, "Lev Nikolaevic Tolstoj als Leser Kants," *Kant Studien* 99 (2008): 361–86 and "L. N. Tolstoi–chitatel' I. Kanta," in *Lev Tolstoi i mirovaia literatura. Materialy V Mezhdunarodnoi nauchnoi konferentsii* (Yasnaya Polyana, 2008).

18 Both connections have been noted by Shklovsky in his *Lev Tolstoi*, 79.

19 Henri Ellenberger, *The Discovery of the Unconscious: The History and Evolution of Dynamic Psychiatry* (New York: Basic Books, 1970), 205.

20 Shklovsky saw Tolstoy's engagement with the dream as another indication of his interest in what he called the "subconscious"; Shklovsky does not seem to distinguish between the "subconscious" and the "unconscious." *Lev Tolstoi*, 79.

21 Ellenberger, in *Discovery of the Unconscious*, connects Carus, via the mediation of Eduard von Hartmann and Schopenhauer, to Freud (207–10). He also briefly describes some of the nineteenth-century studies of dreams (303–11). James L. Rice explores the literary uses of Carus and his interest in dreams in his *Dostoevsky and the Healing Art: An Essay in Literary and Medical History* (Ann Arbor, MI: Ardis, 1985), 137–42, 152.

22 Well-known examples of dream studies include L.-F. Alfred Maury, *Le sommeil et les rêves* (Paris, 1861) (excerpts appeared in the medical journal *Annales médico-psychologiques* in 1848 and 1853); A. Garnier, *Traité des facultés de l'âme, contenant l'histoire des principales théories psychologiques* (Paris, 1852); Anonymous [Marquis d'Hervey de Saint-Denis], *Les rêves et les moyens de les diriger* (Paris, 1867); F. W. Hildebrandt, *Der Traum und seine Verwertung für's Leben* (Leipzig, 1875); J. Volkelt, *Die Traumphantasie* (Stuttgart, 1875). Carl Du Prel offered a metaphysical interpretation of retrospective dreams (as an opening into the transcendental) in *Die Philosophie der Mystik* (Leipzig, 1885)—to be discussed in chapter 6. Freud in *The Interpretation of Dreams* (1900) surveyed such studies, including the discussions of retrospective dreams, in the chapter "Scientific Literature Dealing with the Problem of Dreams," before proceeding to his own theory. He mentions Maury's "Guillotine" dream and Garnier's dream of the "Crossing of Tagliamento" more than once.

23 Quotes taken from "Neskol'ko slov po povody knigi 'Voina i mir,'" first published in 1868.

24 Shklovskii, *Lev Tolstoi*, 292.

25 Varieties of false historical narrative in *War and Peace* have been analyzed in Gary Saul Morson, *Hidden in Plain View: Narrative and Creative Potentials in "War and Peace"* (Stanford, CA: Stanford University Press, 1987).

26 The original source of this often-cited assertion is a French visitor who related his conversation with Tolstoy in 1901: Paul Boyer, "Le Temps," August 28, 1901, cited in Paul Boyer, *Chez Tolstoi*, introduction by André Mazon et al. (Paris, 1950), 40. Tolstoy's reading of Rousseau is discussed in minute detail by Alla Polosina in her dissertation, *Frantsuzskie knigi XVIII veka iasnopolianskoi biblioteki kak istochniki tvorchestva L. N. Tolstogo* (Moscow: Institut mirovoi literatury im. A. M. Gor'kogo, 2008), 83–169.

27 Scholars believe that Tolstoy may have learned of the Franklin method from a Russian novel, D. N. Begichev's *The Kholmsky Family* (*Semeistvo Kholmskikh. Nekotorye cherty nravov i obraza zhizni, semeinoi i odinokoi, russkikh dvorian, chast' chetvertaia*; 1832), the young hero of which uses Franklin's method, described in great detail, and achieves remarkable results (chapter 12). Years later, in 1891, Tolstoy named this popular novel (along with Rousseau's *Confessions* and Sterne's *Sentimental Journey*) among the books that had produced a strong impression on him between the ages of 14 and 20 (66:67). Curiously, in Tolstoy's diary, the name "Begichev" appears several times on the same page as a reference to his Franklin journal (46:48–49). According to Tolstoy's recent biographers, this is Tolstoy's young friend, the nephew of the author of *The Kholmsky Family*. See Aleksei Zverev and Vladimir Tunimanov, *Lev Tolstoi* (Moscow: Molodaia gvardiia, 2006), 58.

Tolstoy's use of Franklin and Begichev was noted in Boris Eikhenbaum, *Molodoi Tolstoi*, in *Lev Tolstoi. Issledovaniia. Stat'i*, 83; and Shklovsky, *Lev Tolstoi*, 73. For more on Tolstoy and Franklin, see G. V. Alekseeva, *Amerikanskie dialogi L'va Tolstogo* (Tula, 2010), 27–32.

28   In speaking of Rousseau, Franklin, and the Puritans, I follow Karl Joachim Weintraub, *The Value of the Individual: Self and Circumstance in Autobiography* (Chicago: University of Chicago Press, 1978), 230–31, 251–56, 299–301, 320–21. Weintraub calls Benjamin Franklin "the Puritan personality without the Puritan motivation and the Puritan objective" (251) and articulates Augustine's move to establish "the right relation between his soul and the infinity of God," which was secularized in Rousseau's *Confessions* (300). Weintraub has also emphasized Franklin's use of "method," a term predominant throughout his text (256).

29   John Mason, *A Treatise on Self-Knowledge* (London: R. Reynolds and C. Baldwyn and Co., 1818). This book bears the mark of use, but it remains unclear who marked it (no. 2184 in the catalogue of Tolstoy's personal library). *Biblioteka L'va Nikolaevicha Tolstogo v Iasnoi Poliane*, vol. 3 (Tula, 1999).

30   In his diaries from 1804–06, Vasily Zhukovsky (born in 1783), too, asked "What am I? What is good in me? What is bad? . . . What should be corrected and how?"; he, too, made schedules of daily occupations to be reexamined in the evening. I would note that the similarities stop here: Tolstoy's experiments with self, narrative, and temporality are his own. The similarities have been discussed by Lidiia Ginzburg, who largely attributed it to a common source in John Mason's *Self-Knowledge*. Ginzburg, *O psikhologicheskoi proze* (Leningrad, 1977), 39–45. Ia. S. Ianushkevich also names John Mason and emphasizes Franklin's influence in his "Dnevniki V. A. Zhukovskogo kak literaturnyi pamiatnik," in *Polnoe sobranie sochinenii i pisem V. A. Zhukovskogo v 20 tomakh*. Tom 13 (Moscow, 1999). Ianushkevich documents the penetration of both John Mason and Benjamin Franklin into Russia via the Freemasons at the end of the eighteenth century and the start of the nineteenth century. Several scholars claim that John Mason's *Self-Knowledge* in itself was a Masonic source, but I have found no evidence to substantiate this.

31   Scholars, beginning with Eikhenbaum (in *Molodoi Tolstoi*), have noted that Tolstoy embraced the eighteenth century, including Sentimentalism, and rejected his immediate predecessors (the Romantics) as well as his contemporaries. (It may be that the composition of the Yasnaya Polyana library, rich in eighteenth-century editions procured by Tolstoy's grandparents and parents, prompted his choices.) The theologian Georges Florovsky notably claims that Sentimentalism was important for Tolstoy as a literary trend with both psychological and religious underpinnings, naming Edward Young's *Night Thoughts* and the Pietist movement, which had also influenced Goethe and Rousseau. Florovsky calls Rousseau "a secularized pietist." Florovsky, unlike other scholars, points to the religious dimension that thus opened to the young Tolstoy, in sources far removed from his own age: "This was the awakening of the heart, the discovery of the inner world, the discovery of the inner depth in daily, home, family life. The books of the sentimental authors thus received the significance of a religious revelation." G. V. Florovskii, "U istokov" [1936], in *Lev Tolstoi. Pro et Contra* (St. Petersburg: RKhGI, 2000), 678.

32   John Mason, *Treatise on Self-Knowledge*, 4–7, 200–201.

33   This view is forcefully expressed by Boris Eikhenbaum in his *Molodoi Tolstoi* (1922); Eikhenbaum, *Lev Tolstoi. Issledovaniia. Stat'i* (St. Petersburg, 2009), 75–100; citations are from 85, 96, 99. Shklovsky, when he wrote about Tolstoy's diary, took a similar approach, even in his biography of Tolstoy, first published in 1963. Shklovsky saw "A History of Yesterday" as an experimental piece of fiction and, as such, a "draft" of Tolstoy's later fiction; see Shklovskii, "O zhanre," "'Istoriia vcherashnego dnia' v obshchem khode trudovykh dnei pisatelia Tolstogo" and "Siuzhet i analiz," in *Povesti o proze*, 266–78, and *Lev Tolstoi*, 73–84. This view was clearly formed from within the formalist approach to literature. Yet even in Eikhenbaum's later *Lev Tolstoi: piatidesiatye gody* (1928), with its declared "biographical bent," a tendency to emphasize the "method" and "devices" in the diaries and "A History of Yesterday" prevails. *Lev Tolstoi. Issledovaniia. Stat'i*, 166. Much indebted to Eikhenbaum and Shklovsky in their pioneering analysis of the diary and "A History of Yesterday," I have chosen—in accordance with the spirit of my own time and my own field—to take a different view on the meaning and function of these texts.

34   Paraphrasing Eikhenbaum, in *Molodoi Tolstoi*, in *Lev Tolstoi. Issledovaniia. Stat'i*, 95–96. The "dialectics of the soul" (*dialektika dushi*) is Nikolai Chernyshevsky's famous formula, from his

1856 review of Tolstoy's early prose. "*Detstvo i Otrochestvo. Voennye rasskazy grafa L. N. Tolstogo.*" Eikhenbaum describes it on pp. 112–13.

35   Among the (not very numerous) works on Tolstoy's diaries, the unpublished doctoral dissertation of Robert E. Gurley, "The Diaries of Leo Tolstoy: Their Literariness and Their Relations to his Literature" (University of Pennsylvania, 1979), deserves special mention. I am indebted to Gary Saul Morson for attracting my attention to this (almost unknown) source.

36   I echo Paul Ricoeur's observation on the narrative structure of psychoanalytic interviews: "a history that would remain inconsistent, incoherent, or incomplete would clearly resemble what we know of the course of life in ordinary experience." "The Question of Proof in Freud's Psychoanalytic Writings," *Journal of the American Psychoanalytic Association* 25, no. 4 (1977): 862.

Interlude

1   Of Tolstoy's many biographies in English, I recommend the following: Victor Shklovsky, *Lev Tolstoi,* trans. from Russian (Moscow: Progress, 1978); and Ernest J. Simmons, *Leo Tolstoy* (first published in 1946, with many subsequent editions).

2   The idea of Tolstoy's "transition" (*perekhod*) from diary-writing to fiction was advanced by Boris Eikhenbaum, both in his early book, *Molodoi Tolstoi* (1922), and in the later *Lev Tolstoi. Kniga pervaia. Piatidesiatye gody* (1928). Eikhenbaum, *Lev Tolstoi. Issledovaniia. Stat'i* (St. Petersburg, 2009), 102–13, 167–76, 189–200. Eikhenbaum's comprehensive, three-volume study of Tolstoy's work follows Tolstoy's evolution as a writer in the cultural context of his time. This study has largely informed the work of later Tolstoy scholars as well as of his biographers. Viktor Shklovsky, in his famous biography *Lev Tolstoi* (1963), mostly follows Eikhenbaum's scenario. I cite from the second edition, *Lev Tolstoi* (Moscow: Molodaia gvardiia, 1967), 73–122, 136–44. More recently, Andrew Baruch Wachtel has interpreted the implications of this transition for the genre of *Childhood* in his *The Battle for Childhood: Creation of a Russian Myth* (Stanford, CA: Stanford University Press, 1990), 7–57. See also his "History and Autobiography in Tolstoy," in *The Cambridge Companion to Tolstoy,* ed. Donna Tussing Orwin (Cambridge, U.K.: Cambridge University Press, 2002), 176–90.

3   Letter to T. A. Ergol'skaia, November 12, 1851 (original in French).

4   Eikhenbaum, *Lev Tolstoi. Piatidesiatye gody,* in *Lev Tolstoi. Issledovaniia. Stat'i,* 166–67.

5   Letter to N. A. Nekrasov (who published Tolstoy's *Childhood* in the journal *The Contemporary*), November 27, 1852.

6   Letter to N. A. Nekrasov, September 15, 1852.

7   Tolstoy's diary, November 30, 1852.

8   The Russian titles of the projected novel of the four epochs of life are *Detstvo, Otrochestvo, Iunost',* and *Molodost'.*

9   I follow Andrew Wachtel's analysis of *Childhood* in his *Battle for Childhood,* 20–21.

10   John Bayley, *Tolstoy and the Novel* (Chicago: University of Chicago Press, 1988), 86.

11   Wachtel, in *The Battle for Childhood,* speaks of "a kind of compromise," suggesting that *Childhood* is best seen as a boundary work, designed to be ambiguous, "a threshold genre" (the concept is Gary Saul Morson's).

12   From Andrew Wachtel, "History and Autobiography in Tolstoy," 176.

13   The idea of recurrent crises as a pattern in Tolstoy's life and work is shared by most (if not all) of Tolstoy's interpreters. It was defined by Boris Eikhenbaum in the article "O krizisakh Tolstogo" (1920), first published in his *Skvoz' literaturu* (Leningrad, 1924, 67–72). As his starting point, Eikhenbaum takes a popular idea (articulated already in Tolstoy's own lifetime) that Tolstoy experienced a major crisis in the late 1870s, documented in his *Confession,* a crisis that split him into two, Tolstoy the artist and Tolstoy the moralist and religious thinker. By contrast, Eikhenbaum claims that crises accompany Tolstoy throughout his life. He points out that, judging by his diary, already in 1855, Tolstoy had conceived the idea of founding "a new religion" befitting the contemporary stage in the "development of humankind" (47:37) and that the first crisis of his commitment to literature as a vocation dates to the late 1850s and the early 1860s, when Tolstoy abandoned literature to dedicate himself to popular education. It should be noted that in "O krizisakh Tolstogo"

Eikhenbaum insists on viewing Tolstoy's crises not as existential experiences but as stages in the search for literary form. *Lev Tolstoi. Issledovaniia. Stat'i,* 69–70. Such an interpretation is part and parcel of the formalist approach to literature, which, at the time, Eikhenbaum followed as a conscious agenda. In his later studies (especially in the third volume, published in 1960), Eikhenbaum speaks about the crises in biographical, if not existential, terms as an act that had "personal," "moral," and "emotional" significance (374); nevertheless, he continues to discuss Tolstoy's literary evolution as a search for "literary form" (599). Richard Gustafson has commented that this interpretation is "at best backward": "The crises were moral and religious, and they led to reevaluations of literary form." Gustafson, *Leo Tolstoy, Resident and Stranger: A Study in Fiction and Theology* (Princeton, NJ: Princeton University Press, 1986), 4n1.

14 This letter is written in late April or early May, 1859. For both sides of the correspondence, see *L. N. Tolstoi i A. A. Tolstaia. Perepiska (1857–1903)* (Moscow: Nauka, 2011).

15 From the diary for September 1853 (46:176). Noted by Alla Polosina in *Frantsuzskie knigi XVIII veka iusnopolianskoi biblioteki kak istochniki tvorchestva L. N. Tolstogo* (Moscow: Institut mirovoi literatury im. A.M. Gor'kogo, 2008), 121–22.

16 When he finished the manuscript of "Family Happiness," Tolstoy wrote in his diary: "Finished Anna, but it's not good" (April 9, 1859; 48:20).

17 A. B. Gol'denveizer, *Vblizi Tolstogo* (Moscow: Khudozhestvennaia literatura, 1959), 81. (This episode dates to 1901.)

18 Tolstoy's letter to the critic A. V. Druzhinin, October 9, 1859.

19 Tolstoy's letters to Boris Chicherin, October–November, 1859 (60:316), and March 1, 1860 (60:327). Similar statements abound in Tolstoy's letters to Afanasy Fet. Noted by Eikhenbaum, *Lev Tolstoi. Issledovaniia. Stat'i,* 337–38, 370, and 373.

20 Tolstoy's letter to the critic Vasily Botkin. Noted by Eikhenbaum, *Lev Tolstoi. Issledovaniia. Stat'i,* 356, 362, 367.

21 This piece, "Dream" (Son), was first published after Tolstoy's death; see 7.117–19, 361–63, 60.247, 250.

22 On the "personality of the author" and the transition from *Childhood* to *War and Peace,* I follow Bayley, *Tolstoy and the Novel,* 86–87. (Quotation marks indicate Bayley's phrases.)

23 Eikhenbaum describes Tolstoy's "new" attempt to "renounce literature" and his "new flight from literature" (*novyi ukhod iz literatury*) in the third volume of his study, devoted to Tolstoy in the 1870s, *Lev Tolstoi. Semidesiatye gody* (1960), in *Lev Tolstoi. Issledovaniia. Stat'i,* 575–78, 600–601. This crisis is also highlighted in Aleksei Zverev and Vladimir Tunimanov, *Lev Tolstoi* (Moscow: Molodaia gvardiia, 2006), 269–73.

24 *L. N. Tolstoi i N. N. Strakhov: Polnoe sobranie perepiski,* 2 vols., edited and introduction by Andrew Donskov, compiled by L. D. Gromova and T. G. Nikiforova (Ottawa and Moscow: Slavic Research Group at the University of Ottawa and the State L. N. Tolstoy Museum, 2003), 1:164.

25 Eikhenbaum discussed *What Is Art?* in the context of Tolstoy's recurrent crises in his "O krizisakh Tolstogo."

26 On *What Is Art?* and its contradictions, see Caryl Emerson, "Tolstoy's Aesthetics," *Anniversary Essays on Tolstoy,* ed. Donna Tussing Orwin (Cambridge, U.K.: Cambridge University Press, 2010), 237–50. Justin Weir has offered an approach to Tolstoy's contradictory "model of authorship" in his *Leo Tolstoy and the Alibi of Narrative* (New Haven: Yale University Press, 2011).

Chapter 2

1 See Donna Tussing Orwin, "Strakhov's *World as a Whole*: A Missing Link between Dostoevsky and Tolstoy," in *Poetics. Self. Place. Essays in Honor of Anna Lisa Crone,* ed. Catherine O'Neil et al. (Bloomington, IN: Slavica, 2007), 473–93.

2 The Tolstoy-Strakhov correspondence is cited throughout the chapter (indicating the volume and page number in the text) from: *L. N. Tolstoi i N. N. Strakhov: Polnoe sobranie perepiski,* 2 vols., edited and introduction by Andrew Donskov, compiled by L. D. Gromova and T. G. Nikiforova (Ottawa, Moscow: Slavic Research Group at the University of Ottawa and the State L. N. Tolstoy

Museum, 2003). Tolstoy's other texts are cited from *Polnoe sobranie sochinenii v 90 tomakh*; cited in the text of this chapter as PSS, with volume and page.

3   Inessa Medzhibovskaya offered a different analysis of Tolstoy's essay "O dushe" and of his November 30 letter. Medzhibovskaya, *Tolstoy and the Religious Culture of His Time: A Biography of a Long Conversion, 1845–1887* (Lanham, MD: Lexington Books, 2008), 162–63, 166–67.

4   *Émile*, in Jean-Jacques Rousseau, *Oeuvres Complètes*, vol. 4 (Paris: Pléiade, 1959), 570.

5   On Tolstoy's reactions to Strakhov's *Mir kak tseloe*, see Donna Tussing Orwin, "Strakhov's *World as a Whole*," 166–70.

6   Commentators to *L. N. Tolstoi i N. N. Strakhov: Polnoe sobranie perepiski* note that Strakhov's letter relating his understanding of the novel is unknown to us. I would add that there may or may not have been a specific letter: Strakhov consistently offered Tolstoy his "judgments" (*suzhdeniia*) about the novel (July 23, 1874, 1:171–72; November 8, 1876, 1:186; January 1, 1875, 1:190), and he had earlier reproached Tolstoy for his failure to respond (January 1, 1875, 1:190).

7   I use the Maude translation.

8   The complex story of the serial publication of the novel has been described in William Mills Todd, "Reading *Anna* in Parts," *Tolstoy Studies Journal* 8 (1995–96): 12–28, and "The Responsibilities of (Co-)Authorship: Notes on Revising the Serialized Version of *Anna Karenina*," in *Freedom and Responsibility in Russian Literature: Essays in Honor of Robert Louis Jackson*, ed. Elizabeth Cheresh Allen and Gary Saul Morson (New Haven: Yale University Press, 1995), 162–69.

9   On *starchestvo* and Tolstoy, see Pål Kolstø, "Lev Tolstoi and the Orthodox *Starets* Tradition," *Kritika: Explorations in Russian and Eurasian History* 9, no. 3 (Summer 2008): 533–54.

10   The visit to Optina was discussed in the correspondence, 1:355, 349. For a detailed description of this visit, see N. N. Gusev, *Lev Nikolaevich Tolstoi: Materialy k biografii s 1870 po 1881 god* (Moscow: Izdatel'stvo Akademii Nauk SSSR, 1963), 440–41.

11   As Grigorii Gukovskii recalls, B. M. Eikhenbaum once wrote: "Levin in *Anna Karenina* is not, after all, Tolstoy: there is one difference between them—only one, but what a difference! Levin does and thinks exactly the same things that Tolstoy did and thought, except one: he had not written *War and Peace*." Grigorii Gukovskii, *Izuchenie literaturnogo proizvedeniia v shkole* (Moscow-Leningrad, 1965, 62–63). Lidiia Ginzburg mentioned this in her notebook in 1928. Lidiia Ginzburg, *Zapisnye knizhki. Vospominaniia. Esse* (St. Petersburg: Iskusstvo, 2002), 43. This witticism seems to have been shared by the Formalists, who were intent on drawing a distinction between author and hero.

12   Medzhibovskaya interprets Tolstoy's coinage "religiia-vera" differently. *Tolstoy and the Religious Culture of His Time*, 173.

13   For commentary on the prototypes (some of them Tolstoy's acquaintances), see PSS 17:735–36. Later Tolstoy used the name he gave to himself in his celebrated story "Death of Ivan Il'ich" ["Ivan Ilyich"] written in 1884–86. However, Tolstoy's story is believed to be based on a real-life person, Ivan Il'ich Mechnikov (brother of the famous biologist Il'ia Il'ich Mechnikov, who tried to prolong life by medical means), who died in 1881.

14   Strakhov's treatise was first published in the *Zhurnal ministerstva narodnogo prosveshcheniia* in May–June 1878, then as a separate edition in 1886. The "cogito" is discussed in section VI of chapter 1, subtitled "Dusha."

15   In the strict sense, Strakhov takes liberties here: Descartes called his true self a thinking thing, deliberately opting to describe it as an abstract entity. (For expert advice on Descartes, I am indebted to Carlos Montemayor.) But, as contemporary scholars point out, Descartes was anticipated in his "cogito" by Augustine, who postulated the "I" as "the soul." Gareth B. Matthews, *Thought's Ego in Augustine and Descartes* (Ithaca, NY: Cornell University Press, 1992), 29; Jerrold Seigel, *The Idea of the Self: Thought and Experience in Western Europe since the Seventeenth Century* (Cambridge, U.K.: Cambridge University Press, 2005), 57.

16   Much has been written about the links between Tolstoy's religious views and Rousseau's. I have been particularly inspired by Hugh McLean's "Rousseau's God and Tolstoy's God," in his *In Quest of Tolstoy* (Boston: Academic Studies Press, 2008), 143–58. Tolstoy's involvement with "Profession de foi du vicaire Savoyard," which he read and reread many times, is discussed in Galina Galagan, *L. N. Tolstoi: khudozhestvenno-eticheskie iskaniia* (Leningrad: Nauka, 1981), 55–58; Donna Tussing Orwin, *Tolstoy's Art and Thought, 1847–1880* (Princeton, NJ: Princeton University Press,

1993), 39–49; and Alla Polosina, who surveyed Tolstoy's marginal notes on the text of Rousseau's "Profession" in *Frantsuzskie knigi XVIII veka iasnopolianskoi biblioteki kak istochniki tvorchestva L. N. Tolstogo*, 120–30; see also her "Leo Tolstoy and the *Encyclopédistes*," *Tolstoy Studies Journal* 20 (2008): 56.

17   "Profession de foi du vicaire Savoyard," cited from *Émile* in Jean-Jacques Rousseau, *Oeuvres Complètes*, vol. 4 (Paris: Pléiade, 1959), 554, 570.

18   From Tolstoy's letter to Bernard Bouvier, president of the Société Jean-Jacques Rousseau, March 20, 1905 (75:234; original in French).

19   Here and further, for the interpretation of Rousseau's "Profession de foi du vicaire Savoyard," I follow Dorothea von Mücke's reading, in her "Profession/Confession," *New Literary History* 34, no. 2 (Spring 2003): 257–74. I am indebted to Dorothea von Mücke also for advice offered in a personal letter.

20   Von Mücke, "Profession/Confession," 267.

21   I follow von Mücke's argument and her formulations, 270–72; the quotation is from 271. In this article, von Mücke views the confession of sins and the profession of belief as "traditionally very separate types of speech" (269) made exchangeable in Rousseau's "Profession de foi du vicaire Savoyard." Other scholars have argued that they overlap. For one thing, as has been pointed out, Augustine in his *Confessions* uses the terms *confession* and *profession* interchangeably. For a recent comment on the subject, see Chloë Taylor, *The Culture of Confession from Augustine to Foucault: A Genealogy of the "Confessing Animal"* (New York: Routledge, 2008), 44–45; Taylor follows (among other sources) Robert Bernasconi, "The Infinite Task of Confession: A Contribution to the History of Ethics," *Acta Institutionis Philosophiae et Aestheticae* 6 (1988): 80.

22   Tolstoy's role as a "heterodox *starets*" was noted in Kolstø, "Lev Tolstoi and the Orthodox *Starets* Tradition," 545–49.

23   Strakhov's letter to I. S. Aksakov, December 12, 1884, in *I. S. Aksakov–N. N. Strakhov. Perepiska*, ed. Marina Shcherbakova (Ottawa, 2007), 120.

24   I echo von Mücke on the "soteriological promise" in Rousseau's interaction with his readers. "Confession/Profession," 272.

Chapter 3

1   In the question of dating, I rely on the commentaries to the 90-volume edition. The commentators believe that this work was written mostly at the end of 1879, revised in July 1881, and then amended and revised in April 1882 (23:516–20). Tolstoy scholars usually echo these conclusions. It should be noted that these reconstructions presume that a work with which Tolstoy was occupied beginning in 1879 was an early variant of the text released for publication in April 1882, the text that was eventually known under the title *Ispoved'*, which may or may not be the case.

2   For the history of publication, I follow N. N. Gusev's commentaries to the 90-volume edition (23:520–22). Iur'ev's letter is cited by Gusev (23:520).

3   The word *confession* appears in Tolstoy's wife's diary, for January 31, 1881; in the correspondence between members of the *Russkaia mysl'* editorial board in April 1882; in Strakhov's correspondence in September 1883; and in a critical essay by the journalist I. E. Obolenskii in the journal *Russkoe bogatstvo* in 1883 (see commentaries, 23:523). Tolstoy used the word in letters to L. D. Urusov (May 1, 1885) and to his own wife (December 15–18, 1885). See the commentaries in 23:524.

4   While it has become rare, at least among scholars, to call the *Confession* an "autobiography" or "fiction," Tolstoy scholars differ in their opinions on the genre and meaning of the *Confession* and on the nature of Tolstoy's conversion experience. I would highlight recent views. Inessa Medzhibovskaya sees it as a complex structure (not easy to classify in terms of genre), which refuses to adhere to the available forms of conversion narratives. As regards Tolstoy's religious experience itself, Medzhibovskaya treats Tolstoy's conversion as a long process that dates back to his youth; see her *Tolstoy and the Religious Culture of His Time: A Biography of a Long Conversion, 1845–1887* (Lanham, MD: Lexington Books, 2008), 234–51. Jeff Love treats the *Confession* as "Tolstoy's attempt to

fashion a new rhetoric adequate to the task of promoting a Christian doctrine" and a "return to an essentially theocratic vision of the world." *Tolstoy: A Guide for the Perplexed* (London: Continuum, 2008), 119, 124. G. M. Hamburg sees Tolstoy's conversion as both an event, described in the *Confession*—which he treats as a conversion narrative—and an ensuing process, the very essence of his life after 1879. G. M. Hamburg, "Tolstoy's Spirituality," *Anniversary Essays on Tolstoy*, ed. Donna Tussing Orwin (Cambridge, U.K.: Cambridge University Press, 2010), 138–58. Valuable commentaries on the *Confession* have been provided, in a post-Soviet edition, by Galina Galagan; see L. N. Tolstoi, *Ispoved'. V chem moia vera?* (Leningrad: Khudozhestvennaia literatura, 1991).

5   Hadot, "Conversio," in *Historisches Wörterbuch der Philosophie* (Darmstadt: Wissenschaftliche Buchgesellschaft, 1971), vol 1, col. 1033–36.

6   Kenneth Burke, *The Rhetoric of Religion* (Boston: Beacon Press, 1961), 104.

7   Here and further, in discussing the structure and rhetoric of the conversion narrative, I draw on Patrick Riley's *Character and Conversion in Autobiography: Augustine, Montaigne, Descartes, Rousseau, and Sartre* (Charlottesville: University of Virginia Press, 2004). I am indebted to Chloë Kitzinger for directing my attention to this source.

8   This argument is common in studies of Augustine. Most recently, J. Lenore Wright has applied it to modern philosophical autobiography in her *The Philosopher's "I": Autobiography and the Search for the Self* (Albany: State University of New York Press, 2006), 8.

9   Riley, *Character and Conversion in Autobiography*, 16. With this argument, Riley extends Paul de Man's idea that the dominant figure of autobiographical discourse is the voice from beyond the grave (a variant of prosopopoeia). Paul de Man, "Autobiography as De-Facement," *The Rhetoric of Romanticism* (New York: Columbia University Press, 1984), 77.

10 I follow Robert Bernasconi, who claims that all three meanings are closely associated in "The Infinite Task of Confession: A Contribution to the History of Ethics," *Acta Institutionis Philosophiae et Aestheticae*, 6 (1988): 80, 90n24. The different meanings of *confession* are discussed in Pierre Courcelle's classic *Recherches sur les "Confessions" de Saint Augustin* (Paris, F. de Boccard, 1968), 13–29. Most recently, Chloë Taylor has discussed this issue in a book that traces "confession" to our days, *The Culture of Confession from Augustine to Foucault: A Genealogy of the "Confessing Animal"* (New York: Routledge, 2008), 44–45.

11 Burke believes that this happens already in the last books of the *Confessions*; as he puts it, "the 'confessions' gradually become more and more like 'professions.'" *Rhetoric of Religion*, 123.

12 Burke has described the specific rhetoric of address to God, the "I-Thou" structure. *Rhetoric of Religion*, 56–57, 71.

13 James O'Donnell's formulation, in his *Augustine: A New Biography* (New York: Harper, 2005), 64.

14 Hannah Arendt, *The Human Condition*, 2nd ed. (Chicago: University of Chicago Press, 1998), 10–11n2.

15 Here I rely on formulations from Karl Joachim Weintraub, *The Value of the Individual: Self and Circumstance in Autobiography* (Chicago: University of Chicago Press, 1978), 40; and Charles Taylor, *Sources of the Self: The Making of the Modern Identity* (Cambridge, MA: Harvard University Press, 1989), 132. These scholars focus on the modern implications of Augustine's inwardness. Here and elsewhere, from the immense scholarship on Augustine, I have mostly relied on recent work accessible to a non-expert like myself, such as Peter Brown, *Augustine of Hippo: A Biography* (Berkeley: University of California Press, 2000); and James O'Donnell, *Augustine: A New Biography*, as well as, on the meanings of Augustine's inwardness, Phillip Cary, *Augustine's Invention of the Inner Self* (Oxford, U.K.: Oxford University Press, 2000), 127, 140–42. I have also consulted the classics, such as Etienne Gilson, *The Christian Philosophy of Saint Augustine* (New York: Random House, 1960); and Pierre Courcelle, *Recherches sur les "Confessions" de Saint Augustin* and *Les Confessions de Saint Augustin dans la tradition littéraire; antécédents et postérité* (Paris: Études augustiniennes, 1968).

16 The disappearance of the speaking subject in the last books of the *Confessions* has been noted by many. I follow Riley, *Character and Conversion in Autobiography*, 26, 52.

17 I follow John Owen Ling III, *The Iron of Melancholy: Structures of Spiritual Conversion in America from the Puritan Conscience to Victorian Neurosis* (Middletown, CT: Wesleyan University Press, 1983), 14–16.

18   Many scholars have compared and contrasted Augustine and Rousseau. Weintraub and Charles Taylor (cited above) use the comparison to posit a trajectory for both the conception of self and the genre of autobiography. Chloë Taylor, who focuses on the confessional mode, has surveyed a variety of such comparisons in her recent *The Culture of Confession from Augustine to Foucault*, 28–30. Ann Hartle has dedicated a whole book to a comparison between the two texts: *The Modern Self in Rousseau's Confessions: A Reply to St. Augustine* (Notre Dame, IN: University of Notre Dame Press, 1983). Patrick Riley, in *Character and Conversion in Autobiography*, revisits the comparison with a critical eye. He reads Rousseau's *Confessions* and his subsequent *Dialogues* and *Reveries* as an "inversion" of the Augustinian conversion paradigm, discussing different implications of this inversion (88–137). Of course, an Augustinian scholar may see the modern link as forced or argue that Rousseau misreads Augustine. For such a reaction, see Paul J. Archambault, "Rousseau's Tactical (Mis)reading of Augustine," *Symposium: A Quarterly Journal in Modern Literatures* 41, no. 1 (Spring 1987): 6–14; this work is discussed in Riley, *Character and Conversion in Autobiography*, 192–93n3.

19   Weintraub, *Value of the Individual*, 299–301. Starobinski sees the situation in the same way as Weintraub: While Rousseau imagines handing his *Confessions* to the Sovereign Judge, yet, Starobinski claims, "he usurps the place of the judge." Jean Starobinski, *Jean-Jacques Rousseau: Transparency and Obstruction*, trans. Arthur Goldhammer (Chicago: University of Chicago Press, 1988), 279.

20   From the "First Walk" in *Rêveries du promeneur solitaire*. The three dialogues *Rousseau juge de Jean-Jacques* are also highly significant in this respect. Weintraub, *Value of the Individual*, 299, 307. The problem of self-knowledge and the meanings of "Who am I?" in Rousseau are discussed in Starobinski, *Jean-Jacques Rousseau*, 180–86.

21   Peter Brooks, *Troubling Confessions: Speaking Guilt in Law and Literature* (Chicago: University of Chicago Press, 2001), 52.

22   In describing this paradoxical situation, which emerges still more strongly in the *Dialogues* and the *Reveries*, I follow Starobinski, *Jean-Jacques Rousseau*, 36–39, 49, 55, 141, 273; Weintraub, *Value of the Individual*, 301–7; and Riley, *Character and Conversion in Autobiography*, 92, 112–15, 175–77.

23   Loosely after Riley, *Character and Conversion in Autobiography*, 175–76.

24   After Starobinski, *Jean-Jacques Rousseau*, 63. This argument has been also made by Lejeune, *On Autobiography*, 145.

25   Loosely after Weintraub, *Value of the Individual*, 299.

26   Commentators to the 90-volume edition, published in Soviet times, downplayed the place of Tolstoy's *Confession* in the paradigm that includes Augustine and Rousseau (23:523). More recently, Galina Galagan, Inessa Medzhibovskaya, and Jeff Love, in the studies listed above, have placed Tolstoy in this context. So has Andrew Wachtel, who believes that in some respects Tolstoy's *Confession* is far more like Augustine's than Rousseau's. Wachtel, "History and Autobiography in Tolstoy," in *The Cambridge Companion to Tolstoy*, ed. Donna Tussing Orwin (Cambridge, U.K.: Cambridge University Press, 2002), 187.

27   I use the English translation of *Confession* by Louise and Aylmer Maude, available at www.online-literature.com/tolstoy/a-confession/, accessed March 24, 2014.

28   There are always two or more kinds of "I" in discourse, as scholars have long shown. This argument starts in classic linguistic studies: Émile Benveniste's "The Nature of Pronouns" (1956) and "Subjectivity in Language" (1958); and Roman Jakobson's "Shifters and Verbal Categories" (1957). Greg Urban has provided a semiotic analysis of different kinds of "I"; see his "The 'I' of Discourse," in *Semiotics, Self, and Society*, ed. Benjamin Lee and Greg Urban (New York: Mouton de Gruyter, 1989), 27–51. Philippe Lejeune discusses the situation of the autobiographical "I" and the role of the author's proper name in *On Autobiography*, ed. Paul John Eakin, trans. Katherina Leary (Minneapolis: University of Minnesota Press, 1989), 8–21. Discussions of the workings of the first person in literature include, most recently, Michael Lucey, *Never Say I: Sexuality and the First Person in Colette, Gide, and Proust* (Durham, NC: Duke University Press, 2006).

29   The Russian religious tradition incorporates the notion of eight deadly sins, systematized by Evagrius and Cassian (available in *Dobrotoliubie* [*Philokalia*], a collection of Eastern Orthodox spiritual readings to which Tolstoy often referred). They included gluttony (*chrevougodie*); lust, or

fornication (*blud*); avarice, or greed (*srebroliubie*); melancholia (*pechal'*); anger (*gnev*); despair, or *acedia* (*unynie*); vainglory (*tshcheslavie*); and pride (*gordost'*). Tolstoy's conception of sin and its sources has been described in Hamburg, "Tolstoy's Spirituality," 151–54.

30 Victoria Frede's treatment of melancholy experienced as the mortal sin of *acedia* by the secular Russians in the 1860s has inspired this comment; see Frede, *Doubt, Atheism, and the Nineteenth-Century Russian Intelligentsia* (Madison: University of Wisconsin Press, 2011), 130, 246n36.

31 Tolstoy's personal library contains the 1875 edition of *Prolog*, which he carefully perused in 1880 (judging by the bookmarks made from newspapers from that year). Tolstoy chose a fable with a distinct "Oriental" flavor; its origin is believed to be the Sanskrit collection *Panchatantra*, and the fable entered the Christian tradition through an Arabic translation. This cross-denominational identity of the fable must have appealed to Tolstoy, who searched for a universal religion. Tolstoy and his readers may have also remembered the fable from its rendition in Vasily Zhukovsky's "Two Tales" (*Dve povesti*). (I rely on Galina Galagan's commentary to the *Confession*, cited above.)

32 Tolstoy's use of Bunyan's *Pilgrim's Progress* and the English Puritan tradition has been discussed in D.D. Blagoi, "Dzhon Ben'ian, Pushkin i Lev Tolstoi," in *Pushkin. Issledovaniia i materialy* 4 (Moscow: Akademiia Nauk, 1962), 50–75. As he notes, in Tolstoy's library, there were two different editions of *The Pilgrim's Progress*. Blagoi believes that Tolstoy's interest in Bunyan may have been reinforced by Pushkin's famous poem "Wanderer" (*Strannik*), which was based on *The Pilgrim's Progress*.

33 Noted in Medzhibovskaya, *Tolstoy and the Religious Culture of His Time*, 246–47.

34 The symbolism of light in the conversion narrative has been discussed in Charles Taylor, *Sources of the Self*, 128–29.

35 Medzhibovskaya highlights this episode in *Tolstoy and the Religious Culture of His Time*, 248.

36 These statements, discussed in chapter 2 of this book, are from Tolstoy's letters to Strakhov of January 27, 1878, and November 30, 1875. *L. N. Tolstoi i N. N. Strakhov: Polnoe sobranie perepiski*, 2 vols., edited and introduction by Andrew Donskov, compiled by L.D. Gromova and T.G. Nikiforova (Ottawa, Moscow: Slavic Research Group at the University of Ottawa and the State L.N. Tolstoy Museum, 2003), 1:399, 234.

37 N.N. Gusev, *Dva goda s L. N. Tolstym* (Moscow: Posrednik, 1912), 86–87 (diary entry for February 15, 1908).

38 See Peter Gay, *The Naked Heart: The Bourgeois Experience, Victoria to Freud*, vol. 4 (London: Fontana Press, 1998), 123–36; and John D. Barbour, *Versions of Deconversion: Autobiography and the Loss of Faith* (Charlottesville: University of Virginia Press, 1994); Barbour mentions Tolstoy's *Confession* in this context (140–42).

39 Tolstoy's own library contains the following editions: L.N. Tolstoi. *Ispoved'. Vstuplenie k sochineniiu "V chem moia vera?"* (Geneva: . Elpidine, 1888); and L.N. Tolstoi, *Vstuplenie k kritike dogmaticheskogo bogosloviia i issledovaniiu khristianskogo ucheniia ("Ispoved'")* (Christchurch: Svobodnoe slovo, 1901) (both published by V. and A. Chertkov). Another edition, *Christ's Christianity, by Count Leo Tolstoy*, translated from the Russian (London, 1885), contains the English translation of the *Confession* and *What I Believe?* and a condensed form of Tolstoy's Gospel, *Kratkoe izlozhenie Evangeliia*, under the title *The Spirit of Christ's Teaching (a commentary of the essence of the Gospel)* (24:1001–1006). In English, this very popular text also became known as *The Gospel in Brief*; in French, *Abrégé de l'Evangile*; in German, *Kurze Darlegung des Evangelium*.

40 N.G. Nikiforova has published the first chapter and described the whole notebook, known under the provisional title "Iskaniia istinnoi very," in *Neizvestnyi Tolstoi v arkhivakh Rossii i SShA* (Moscow: AO-Tekhna-2, 1994), 122–30. I am indebted to N.G. Nikiforova for guidance in examining this archival source in the State L.N. Tolstoy Museum in Moscow (Gosudarstvennyi Muzei L. N. Tolstogo). It should be noted that the division into five parts seems to have been an afterthought on Tolstoy's part: the Roman numerals, I to V, overlay continuous text.

41 G.M. Hamburg's recent "Tolstoy's Spirituality" provides a brief overview of Tolstoy's religious thought as distinct from Christian teachings, while also treating Tolstoy's religious conversion and his *Confession*. Recently, Jeff Love has succinctly summarized Tolstoy's Christian doctrine and its political implications in *Tolstoy: A Guide for the Perplexed*, 126–33. George Steiner's classic study

Tolstoy or Dostoevsky offers a far-reaching interpretation of Tolstoyan theology, related to his life story and to the poetics of his novels (I used the 1996 edition from Yale University Press, 242–300).

42   The topic has been treated in Hugh McLean's essay "Tolstoy and Jesus" in his *In Quest of Tolstoy* (Boston: Academic Studies Press, 2008), 117–42. Ani Kokobobo treats Tolstoy's project for its literary qualities in "Authoring Jesus: Novelistic Echoes in Tolstoy's Harmonization and Translation of the Four Gospels," *Tolstoy Studies Journal* 20 (2008): 1–13.

43   From Biriukov's unpublished memoirs, as cited in the commentaries to the 90-volume edition of Tolstoy's works (63:229–30).

44   Here and elsewhere, in describing Wittgenstein's encounter with Tolstoy's religious writings, I have followed and cited Ray Monk's biography, *Ludwig Wittgenstein: The Duty of Genius* (New York: Macmillan, 1990), 115–17. His evidence comes from Wittgenstein's letters and from Bertrand Russell's recollections of Wittgenstein. Monk mentions Wittgenstein's reading of *Varieties of Religious Experience* on page 112. (I bear the responsibility for the guess that this work may have first exposed Wittgenstein to Tolstoy's religious writings.) On Wittgenstein teaching the rural poor in the footsteps of Tolstoy, see page 192.

45   In discussing parallels between Tolstoy's *Confession* and Wittgenstein's *Tractatus*, I follow Caleb Thompson, "Wittgenstein, Tolstoy, and the Meaning of Life," *Philosophical Investigations* 20, no. 2 (1997): 97–116. Thompson's article attracted my attention to the fact that "Tolstoy concludes his work with a dream rather than with argument" (110); he elucidated the Wittgensteinian implications of this move (116). Other scholars have compared Tolstoy and Wittgenstein, arguing for affinity and possible influence, including Anthony Flew, "Tolstoi and the Meaning of Life," *Ethics* 73 (1963); and Emyr Thomas, "Wittgenstein and Tolstoy: The Authentic Orientation," *Religious Studies* 33 (1997): 363–77. Ilse Somavilla has identified "traces" of Tolstoy in Wittgenstein's notebooks from 1914–16, in her "Spuren Tolstois in Wittgensteins Tagebüchern von 1914–1916," *Austrian Ludwig Wittgenstein Society Symposium Proceedings* (2002): 237–40. Nikolay Milkov argues that the later Wittgenstein shows an affinity with Tolstoy; see "Tolstoi und Wittgenstein: Einfluss und Ähnlichkeiten," *Prima Philosophia* 16 (2003): 187–206. There is also an early statement by E. B. Greenwood, who noted that Tolstoy and Wittgenstein have a common source in Schopenhauer. Greenwood, "Tolstoy, Wittgenstein, Schopenhauer," *Encounter* (April 1971), 60–71.

Chapter 4

1   Published in volume 9 of *Russkaia biblioteka*, ed. A. M. Stasiulevich (St. Petersburg, 1879).

2   *L. N. Tolstoi i N. N. Strakhov: Polnoe sobranie perepiski*, 2 vols., edited and introduction by Andrew Donskov, compiled by L. D. Gromova and T. G. Nikiforova (Ottawa, Moscow: Slavic Research Group at the University of Ottawa and the State L. N. Tolstoy Museum, 2003), 1:480.

3   All quotations are from *L. N. Tolstoi i N. N. Strakhov*, 1:482–84.

4   *L. N. Tolstoi i N. N. Strakhov*, 1:429.

5   Translations of "My Life" are from the English-language edition of Pavel Biriukov's biography, in which Tolstoy's autobiographical texts are cited in long excerpts: *Leo Tolstoy. His Life and Work. Autobiographical Memoirs, Letters, and Biographical Material. Compiled by Paul Birukoff, and Revised by Leo Tolstoy*, translated from the Russian, vol. 1 (New York: Charles Scribner's Sons, 1906), 35–36. Translations are adjusted.

6   Philippe Lejeune has commented on the difference between the narrative models of biography and autobiography and on the paradox of "I was born. . . . I died. . . ." *On Autobiography*, ed. Paul John Eakin, trans. Katherine Leary (Minneapolis: University of Minnesota Press, 1989), 235.

7   Sigmund Freud, "Screen Memories" [1899], *The Standard Edition of the Complete Psychological Works of Sigmund Freud*, trans. James Strachey with Anna Freud, 24 vols. (London: Hogarth Press, 1953–74), 3:309, 315–16, 321.

8   Noted by Sara Pankenier, "The Birth of Memory and the Memory of Birth: Daniil Kharms and Lev Tolstoy on Infantile Amnesia," *Slavic Review* 68, no. 4 (Winter 2009): 810–11.

9   In recent years, the psychoanalyst Néstor A. Braunstein noticed Tolstoy's first recollection, commenting on how this retroactive memory reflects Tolstoy's life-long quest for liberty. See

Braunstein, *Memory and Dread or the Memory of Childhood*, trans. Peter Kahn (New York: Jorge Pinto Books, 2010), 178—80.

10 Remarkably, the philosopher Richard Sorabji, in his study of conceptions of the self, cites taking a hot bath as a quintessential activity evoking a sense of the body. Richard Sorabji, *Self: Ancient and Modern Insights about Individuality, Life, and Death* (Chicago: University of Chicago Press, 2006), 13.

11 Freud, "Three Essays on the Theory of Sexuality" [1905], *Standard Edition* 7:174. Noted by Pankenier, "The Birth of Memory," 804.

12 The commentators of the 90-volume edition believe that work on this manuscript was limited to one day. The manuscript contains five pages, covered on both sides (23:561). Tolstoy published part of this manuscript under the title "First memories. From the unpublished autobiographical notes of L. N. Tolstoy" (*Pervye vospominaniia. Iz neizdannykh avtobiograficheskikh zametok L. N. Tolstogo*) in an anthology of reading for mothers, *Russkim materiam*, ed. I. Gorbunov-Posadov (Moscow, 1892); reprinted in 1897 in volume 10 of *Polnoe sobranie sochinenii*.

13 The word *avtobiografiia* appears in the draft of "Vvedenie" (archival document); the State L. N. Tolstoy Museum in Moscow (Gosudarstvennyi Muzei L. N. Tolstogo), folder 105, no. 90/3, 2.

14 Biriukov's biography appeared, in four volumes, between 1906 and 1923; later, the earlier volumes were reissued in revised form: P. I. Biriukov, *Biografiia L'va Nikolaevicha Tolstogo*, vol. 1 (Moscow: Posrednik, 1906; 2nd ed., Moscow: Posrednik, 1911; 3rd ed., Berlin: Ladyzhnikov, 1921; 4th ed., Moscow: Gosizdat, 1923); vol. 2 (Moscow: Posrednik, 1908; 2nd ed., Moscow: Posrednik, 1913; 3rd ed., Berlin: Ladyzhnikov, 1921; 4th ed., Moscow: Gosizdat, 1923); vol. 3 (Berlin: Ladyzhnikov, 1921; 2nd ed., Moscow: Gosizdat, 1922); vol. 4 (Moscow: Gosizdat, 1923). English, French, and German translations appeared beginning in 1906 (the author's name is also spelled Birukoff, Birukov, and Birukof).

15 Translations of "Reminiscences" are from *Leo Tolstoy: His Life and Work*, xxiii–xxiv. I have adjusted the translation of the poem.

16 This comment appears in a draft (archival document from February 1903 in the State L. N. Tolstoy Museum in Moscow (Gosudarstvennyi Muzei L. N. Tolstogo), folder 105, 90/3, 13.

17 This work appeared, in 1911, in the twelfth volume of Tolstoy's collected works, under the title *Vospominaniia detstva*.

18 See December 2 and 19, 1903 (54:199, 200); June 4 and 5, 1904 (55:44–45); and December 9 and 16, 1905 (55:172).

19 Diary entries for June 11, 1904 (55:49); and June 13, 1904 (55:52).

20 Noted in the diary entry for June 13, 1904 (55:50).

21 Tolstoy is believed to have stopped working on "The Green Stick" in December 1905. It was first published soon after his death, in 1911 (36:737–41).

22 Cited *de visu* from the archives of the State L. N. Tolstoy Museum, folder 105, no. 90/9, 2.

23 Biriukov, *Biografiia L'va Nikolaevicha Tolstogo*, 4:257.

24 *U Tolstogo 1904–1910. "Iasnopolianskie zapiski" D. Makovitskogo* (Moscow: Nauka, 1979), 2:228–29, 287; see also Tolstoy 34:600.

25 Jean Starobinski commented that Rousseau intends to trace the determinants of his present to a source in the past: *Jean-Jacques Rousseau: Transparency and Obstruction*, trans. Arthur Goldhammer (Chicago: University of Chicago Press, 1988), 192–93.

26 Rousseau, *The Confessions*, trans. J. M. Cohen (London: Penguin Books, 1953), 262; and Jean-Jacques Rousseau, *Oeuvres Complètes*, vol. I (Paris: Pléiade, 1959), 278.

27 English translation of Stendhal, *The Life of Henry Brulard*, trans. and introduction John Sturrock (New York: NYRB, 2002). The standard French edition is from Pléiade, 1982.

28 In a conversation with a French visitor, Paul Boyer, in 1901, Tolstoy paired Rousseau and Stendhal as the two most important influences in his life, but he added that he would speak of Stendhal "only as the author of *Chârtreuse de Parme* and *Le Rouge et le noir*." This Stendhal had taught him to understand war. Paul Boyer, *Chez Tolstoi*, introduction by André Mazon (Paris, 1950), 40.

29 See Peter Gay, *The Naked Heart: The Bourgeois Experience: Victoria to Freud*, vol. 4 (London: Fontana Press, 1998), 107–8.

30 Ivan Bunin, *Osvobozhdenie Tolstogo* (Paris: YMCA Press, 1937), 63–66. Writing in the mid-1930s in France, Bunin claimed that he was the first to notice the unique qualities of Tolstoy's first memories.

31 Hannah Arendt, *The Human Condition*, 2nd ed. (Chicago: University of Chicago Press, 1998), 10–11n2; and Paul Ricoeur, *Time and Narrative*, vol. 3 (Chicago: University of Chicago Press, 1988), 246. Ricoeur, commenting on Arendt's reflections, calls the answer to the question "Who am I?" "narrative identity."

32 Here and further, in discussing Augustine's turn to the self in his *Confessions*, I rely on established interpretations. (See chapter 3 for references.)

33 Paul Ricoeur, relying on the Augustine scholar Jean Guitton, comments on this quotation. Ricoeur, *Time and Narrative*, 1:231n3.

34 The Chadwick translation, "It is I who remember, I who am mind" (10.16.25), is adjusted here. I make the same adjustment in the next paragraph, 10.17.26, translating *animus* as "soul" rather than "mind." The standard Russian translation uses "soul": "вот я, помнящий себя, я, душа" (10.16.25).

35 Here and elsewhere I have used the World Classics Paperback edition of Augustine's *Confessions*, translated with an introduction and notes by Henry Chadwick (Oxford: Oxford University Press, 1992).

36 It should be noted that scholars differ in their opinions on Platonic sources of Augustine's conception of memory. I follow Charles Taylor, who allows for a Platonic notion of memory in Augustine, albeit one cut off from its roots in the theory of prenatal existence, which would be incompatible with the orthodox Christian view. *Sources of the Self*, 135.

37 Carl G. Vaught, *The Journey toward God in Augustine's Confessions, Books I–VI* (Albany: State University of New York Press, 2003), 28–33.

38 Alla Polosina, "L. N. Tolstoi i Avrelii Avgustin o pamiati, vremeni i prostranstve," in *Lev Tolstoi i mirovaia literatura*, ed. Galina Alekseeva (Tula: Yasnaya Polyana, 2005), 65–76. Here and further, I follow Polosina. She has noted a number of striking parallels between Tolstoy's and Augustine's reflections on memory and the timeless being of the true self, especially (but not exclusively) in "On Life" (*O zhizni*; 1886–87) and in Tolstoy's last philosophical essay, "The Path of Life" (*Put' zhizni*; 1910). Polosina, who has carefully documented Tolstoy's perusal of Augustine's *Confessions* from his own copy in the Yasnaya Polyana library, dates his reading to 1884.

39 The d'Andilly translation, prepared in Convent Port-Royal, the theological center of the Jansenist movement, is part of the long process of the modern recovery of Augustine that continues to this day. (It was this translation that inspired Pascal.) Such recent studies as James O'Donnell's modernizing biography *Augustine, A New Biography* (New York: Harper, 2005) provide strong evidence of the viability of this trend.

40 Cited *de visu* from the copy in Tolstoy's library in Yasnaya Polyana: *Les Confessions de Saint Augustin / Traduction française d'Arnauld d'Andilly très soigneusement revue et adaptée pour la première fois au texte latin; avec une introduction par M. Charpentier*. Bibliothèque latine-française (Réimpression des classiques latins de la Collection Panckoucke). Paris, Garnier Frères, 375. The edition has no year, but the catalogue of Tolstoy's library identifies the year as 1861. The book bears an inscription in pencil, "Notes by L. N. Tolstoy" (*Otmetki L. N.*), identified in the catalogue as belonging to Tolstoy's secretary, Valentin Bulgakov.

41 On May 24, 1884, Tolstoy noted in his diary: "Read Augustine. There are good things. Chercher la vie dans la région de la mort." Tolstoy's copy of Augustine's *Confessions* has a mark at the words "Vous cherchez une vie heureuse dans la région de la mort: vous ne l'y trouverez pas" (4.12.18). This is the part in which Augustine, following the death of his close friend, confronts his own mortality and notes that he has become "a vast problem to myself." But Augustine's name is briefly mentioned in Tolstoy's earlier writings, too, in the drafts for the epilogue to *War and Peace* from the late 1860s (15:225; 243) and in the diary from December 15, 1877 (48:348).

42 Polosina makes this argument. See "L. N. Tolstoy and Avrelii Avgustin," 65.

43 I follow Karol Berger, "Interlude: Jean-Jacques contra Augustinum: A Little Treatise on Moral-Political Theology," in *Bach's Cycle, Mozart's Arrow: An Essay on the Origins of Musical Modernity* (Berkeley: University of California Press, 2007), 171–72. Berger revisits the contrast between

Augustine and Rousseau to draw conclusions on temporality in music (he contrasts the temporality of Bach and Mozart). In this context, he emphasizes the fact that the secularization, or autonomy, of the modern self ("a modern answer to the question, Who am I?"; 158) altered the relationship to time ("temporal biography and history replace God's eternity"; 167). Karol Berger's interpretations and his formulations have helped me to locate Tolstoy in this intellectual context.

44 In his attempts at "re-sacralization" of self Tolstoy was not alone. Laura Engelstein described the case of Ivan and Natal'ia Kirevskii from the 1840s–50s. She argues that some educated nineteenth-century Russians did not follow the progression "in which patterns established in religious life are transmuted into secular structures," but took "the opposite route, attempting to recapture a religious dimension with which they had lost contact." Engelstein mentions Leo Tolstoy and Vladimir Solov'ev. As she notes, such desire to "re-enchant" the world is itself "a symptom of modern life." (The term "re-sacralization" is hers.) Engelstein, "Orthodox Self-Reflection in a Modernizing Age: The Case of Ivan and Natal'ia Kireevskii," in her *Slavophile Empire: Imperial Russia's Illiberal Path* (Ithaca, N.Y.: Cornell University Press, 2009), 126.

45 Peter Brooks linked the nineteenth-century reliance on the plot with the broad context of intellectual history, including evolutionary biology and positivistic sociology. Peter Brooks, *Reading for the Plot: Design and Intention in Narrative* (Cambridge, MA: Harvard University Press, 1984). I have used Brooks's formulations.

Chapter 5

1   I use, with adjustments, Aylmer Maude's translation, entitled "What Then Must We Do?" which is available at http://vidyaonline.org/dl/whatthenmustwedo.pdf, accessed March 25, 2014.

2   In the brief overview of the master-and-slave dialectic that follows, I use Hegel's concepts as translated in G. W. F. Hegel, *Phenomenology of Spirit*, trans. A. V. Miller (Oxford, U.K.: Clarendon Press, 1977). Throughout this chapter, I also use some formulations from Charles Taylor, *Hegel* (Cambridge, U.K.: Cambridge University Press, 1975), 153–57.

3   Paragraphs 179, 182, 184; Miller's translation.

4   The phrase is from Judith Shklar, *Freedom and Independence: A Study of the Political Ideas of Hegel's Phenomenology of Mind* (New York: Cambridge University Press, 1976), 61.

5   The role of mediation has been stressed by Jean Hyppolite in *Genesis and Structure of Hegel's Phenomenology of Spirit*, trans. Samuel Cherniak and John Heckman (Evanston, IL: Northwestern University Press, 1974), 173.

6   Rousseau's link to the master-and-slave dialectic has been noted in Hyppolite, *Genesis and Structure*, 172; and Shklar, *Freedom and Independence*, 59–70.

7   Hans-Georg Gadamer, *Hegel's Dialectic: Five Hermeneutic Studies*, trans. P. Christopher Smith (New Haven: Yale University Press, 1976), 67, 73.

8   Hyppolite, *Genesis and Structure*, 172. Hyppolite argues that "if the master genuinely existed he would be God" (174n6).

9   Alexandre Kojève, *Introduction to the Reading of Hegel*, trans. James H. Nichols Jr. (Ithaca, NY: Cornell University Press, 1980), 42–43.

10 After Shklar, *Freedom and Independence*, 60–61.

11 Consider the following testimony from a contemporary: "In the 1870s, Leo Tolstoy made three attempts to read Bastille, Mill, Proudhon, Marx, and every time he dropped the book, concluding that 'everything written in these books is the greatest nonsense' [25: 634]. But it turned out that he could not make do without this 'nonsense.' In 1895, Tolstoy announced: 'I have carefully read *Das Kapital* and feel ready to pass an exam on this book.'" *L. N. Tolstoy v vospominaniiakh sovremennikov* (Moscow, 1960), 2:50–51.

12 These biographical circumstances have been described in detail by Ernest J. Simmons in his *Leo Tolstoy* (first published in 1946).

13 Shklar, *Freedom and Independence*, 65, 207.

14 Hegel's notorious slogan appears in the introduction to his *Philosophy of Right* (*Grundlinien der Philosophie des Rechts*), cited here in T. M. Knox's translation (Oxford, U.K.: Oxford University

Press, 1942). It has been a subject of many misunderstandings; see Taylor, *Hegel*, 422. Misunderstanding of Hegel's formula figures prominently in Russian intellectual history, and this notorious episode from the 1840s has received various interpretations from historians. According to Dmitry Chizhevskii, Hegel's proposition was transformed by Vissarion Belinsky, who took his cue from Mikhail Bakunin, into a statement: "all that exists is rational" (*vsyo sushchestvuiushchee razumno*). Rephrasing Hegel's philosophical formula in colloquial language, this operation reduced the philosophical category of *Wirklichkeit* (translated into Russian as *deistvitel'nost'*) to a simple reference to the existing order of things: "what exists" (*sushchestvuiushchee*). D. I. Chizhevskii, *Gegel' v Rossii* (Paris: Sovremennye zapiski, 1939), 134. A similar interpretation appears in M. M. Karpovich, *Lektsii po intellektual'noi istorii Rossii (XVIII—nachalo XIX veka)* [1955] (Moscow, 2012), 122–23. A different interpretation appears in Gustaf Shpet, "K voprosu o gegel'ianstve Belinskogo" [1923], *Voprosy filosofii*, no. 9 (1991): 115–76. The many meanings and uses of the phrase in Russia have been recently discussed in Nikolaj Plotnikov, "'Vsyo deistvitel'noe razumno': diskurs personal'nosti v russkoi individual'noi istorii," in *Issledovaniia po istorii russkoi mysli. Ezhegodnik za 2007–2008 god* (Moscow: Modest Kollerov, 2009), 191–210. I have benefited from discussing this issue with Ilya Kliger and Nikolaj Plotnikov at the "Hegel to Russia and Back" conference at NYU's Jordan Center for the Advanced Study of Russia in April 2013.

15 Not every scholar has believed Tolstoy; see, for example, a sober comment in Donna Orwin, *Tolstoy's Art and Thought, 1847–1880* (Princeton, NJ: Princeton University Press, 1993), 15, 221n1, 221n2.

16 Nikolai Ogarev, cited by Chizhevskii, *Gegel' v Rossii*, 66.

17 It has been noted that such reflections prefigure Tolstoy's *What Is Art?* (completed in 1897) and that Tolstoy's aesthetic views, from their first articulations in the pedagogical essays of the early 1860s to "What Should We Do Then?" to *What Is Art?*, draw on the language and argumentation of Rousseau's *First Discourse* and *Discourse on Inequality*. See Thomas Barran, "Rousseau's Political Vision and Tolstoy's *What Is Art?*" *Tolstoy Studies Journal* 5 (1992): 1–12.

18 Jeffrey Brooks, *When Russia Learned to Read: Literacy and Popular Literature, 1861–1917* (Princeton, NJ: Princeton University Press, 1985), 337.

19 I have used, with adjustments, the Louise and Aylmer Maude translation, available at www.gutenberg.org/files/986/986-h/986-h.htm, accessed March 25, 2014.

20 Information from the commentary to the 90-volume edition, 29:375.

21 Alexandre Kojève, "The Idea of Death in the Philosophy of Hegel," *Interpretation: A Journal of Political Philosophy* 3/2, no. 3 (Winter 1973): 154.

22 Biriukov, who calls this Tolstoy's "doctrine of mission" (*uchenie o poslannichestve*), describes it at length in chapter 3 of volume 3 of his biography.

23 For Tolstoy's letter to Alexander III, see 63:44–56. Tolstoy's dream was described in his letter to his biographer Pavel Biriukov, written on the anniversary of these events, on March 3, 1906, as well as in the memoirs of V. I. Alekseev, his children's tutor, who was then living in the Tolstoy household (cited here from 63:54–55).

24 A complex picture of Tolstoy's public status as a moral authority is provided in an on-line installation created by William Nickell (the phrase "moral celebrity" is his), available at http://humweb.ucsc.edu/bnickell/tolstoy/celebrity.html, accessed March 25, 2014.

Chapter 6

1 Tolstoy kept a regular diary until 1858. In the years 1858–65 Tolstoy made only occasional notes; several entries were made in the years 1873 and 1878. Attempts to restart the diary were made in April–May 1878 (48:69–70) and in 1881. In 1881, he also tried a different autobiographical genre, "Notes of a Christian" (*Zapiski khristianina*), a documentary account of the life and deeds of a new Christian. The project was soon abandoned. Inessa Medzhibovskaya suggested that this work "was intended to replace Tolstoy's regular diary and signal a change in his spiritual calendar": his acquisition of faith. Medzhibovskaya, *Tolstoy and the Religious Culture of His Time: A Biography of a Long Conversion, 1845–1887* (Lanham, MD: Lexington Books, 2008), 232–33. Another text

of this period that deals with conversion and uses autobiographical material, "Notes of a Madman" (*Zapiski sumasshedshego*), an unfinished text from 1884, is fiction that uses autobiographical material. On this text as fiction, treated in the context of Tolstoy's preoccupation with death, see Kathleen Parthé, "Tolstoy and the Geometry of Fear," *Modern Language Studies* 15, no. 4 (Autumn 1985), 80–94.

2   Rousseau (as he famously described on the first page of his *Confessions*) pictured himself coming forward, "with my work in hand, before my Sovereign Judge" when "the last trumpet sounds." Jean Starobinski comments that Rousseau nevertheless "usurps the place of the judge": "Having examined the depth of his own heart, Jean-Jacques wants [himself] to pronounce judgment." Starobinski, *Jean-Jacques Rousseau: Transparency and Obstruction*, trans. Arthur Goldhammer (Chicago: University of Chicago Press, 1988), 279–80.

3   Tolstoy's late diaries have been an object of a religious-philosophical study by the Russian philosopher V. V. Bibikhin (1938–2004), in his course of lectures (2000–2001), published posthumously, V. V. Bibikhin, *Dnevniki L'va Tolstogo* (St. Petersburg: Izdatel'stvo Ivana Limbakha, 2012).

4   The "secret diary" was kept from late July to the end of October 1910 (that is, almost until the end of Tolstoy's life). On October 13, the tiny book of "The Diary for Myself Alone" (*Dnevnik dlia odnogo sebia*), which Tolstoy kept in the high leg of his riding boot, was discovered by Sofia Andreevna when she helped to undress her husband after he had fainted. The episode is described in the diary of Tolstoy's disciple and live-in physician. Dushan Makovitskii, *U Tolstogo 1904–1910. Iasnopolianskie zapiski" D P. Makovitskogo, Literaturnoe nasledstvo* 90, no. 4 (1979): 379.

5   V. F. Bulgakov, *Kak prozhita zhizn'. Vospominaniia poslednego sekretaria L. N. Tolstogo* (Moscow: Kuchkovo pole, 2012), 244–48.

6   Tolstoy's philosophical preoccupation with death has been noted by several Russian thinkers, beginning in the early twentieth century, Dmitry Merezhkovsky in *L. Tolstoy and Dostoevsky* (*Lev Tolstoi i Dostoevskii. Zhizn' i tvorchestvo*; 1909); P. M. Bitsilli, "Problema zhizni i smerti v tvorchestve Tolstogo" (1928); Ivan Bunin, *The Liberation of Tolstoy* (*Osvobozhdenie Tolstogo*; 1937) and others. A number of scholars have focused on the representation of death in Tolstoy's fiction, most recently Aage Hansen-Löve, "Am Ende des Tunnels ... Tolstojs Tode," *Akzente*, no. 6 (2010): 514–37 and "V kontse tunnelia ... smerti L'va Tolstogo," *Novoe literaturnoe obozrenie* 109 (2011). Richard Gustafson, who views Tolstoy's fiction and nonfiction as one process of the articulation of identity, notes that "only in death" did Tolstoy hope to find his "true and complete self" and proceeds to argue that "the process of articulation of death provides the key to reading Tolstoy." Gustafson saw Tolstoy's diaries as the most important vehicle for the articulation of his metaphysics. *Leo Tolstoy, Resident and Stranger: A Study in Fiction and Theology* (Princeton, NJ: Princeton University Press, 1986), 6, 88–89.

7   I have spotted the first use of this time scheme on April 4, 1889, and the last on October 30, 1910, six days before Tolstoy's death.

8   Tolstoy evoked the Jesus prayer, in commenting on the limits of verbal representation, already in *Childhood* (*Detstvo*, 1852): the "holy fool" Grisha, who has a special, authentic relationship to language, prays in this way. See Liza Knapp, "Language and Death in Tolstoy's *Childhood* and *Boyhood*: Rousseau and the Holy Fool," *Tolstoy Studies Journal* 10 (1998): 50–62. Richard Gustafson has emphasized the importance of the Jesus prayer for Tolstoy. Gustafson connects Tolstoy's attempts at "silence" and liberation from self to Eastern Christianity. Gustafson, *Leo Tolstoy, Resident and Stranger*, 10–11, 326–37, 416–17.

9   The use of this metaphor by Dostoevsky has been discussed in A. L. Bem, "Pered litsom smerti" [1936], *O Dostojevském: sborník statí a materiálu* (Prague, 1972), 168–69; Liza Knapp, *The Annihilation of Inertia: Dostoevsky and Metaphysics* (Evanston, IL: Northwestern University Press, 1996), 67–75, 84–96; and Irina Paperno, *Suicide as a Cultural Institution in Dostoevsky's Russia* (Ithaca, NY: Cornell University Press, 1997), 128–31.

10   In *Being and Time* (1927), Heidegger refers to Tolstoy's *Death of Ivan Ilyich*. Walter Kaufmann has commented that Heidegger in his discussion of death owes much to Tolstoy; Jeff Love thinks that the situation is more complex. Kaufmann, ed., *Existentialism, Religion, and Death* (New York: Signet, 1976), 22; Love, *Tolstoy: A Guide for the Perplexed* (London: Continuum, 2008), 151.

11   Maury's dream and Tolstoy's dream account in "A History of Yesterday" are discussed in chapter 1 of this book.

12 Mikhail Bakhtin, "Towards a Reworking of the Dostoevsky Book" [1961], in his *Problems of Dostoevsky's Poetics*, trans. Caryl Emerson (Minneapolis: University of Minnesota, 1984). 289–90. On this issue, see Caryl Emerson and Inessa Medzhibovskaya, "Dostoevsky, Tolstoy, Bakhtin on Art and Immortality," in *Critical Theory in Russia and the West*, ed. Alaistair Renfrew and Galin Tihanov (London: Routledge, 2010), 26–43.

13 James P. Scanlan called Tolstoy's "On Life" the most theoretical of his principal philosophical writings; he connects this work to Tolstoy's philosophical correspondence with Strakhov in the 1870s and his philosophical readings done at the time. Scanlan, "Tolstoy among the Philosophers: His Book *On Life* and its Critical Reception," *Tolstoy Studies Journal* 18 (2006): 52–69.

14 Medzhibovskaya, *Tolstoy and the Religious Culture of His Time*, 333. Medzhibovskaya and Michael Denner are working on an English-language annotated critical edition of Tolstoy's "On Life."

15 Sigrid McLaughlin, who makes this claim, has provided the most thorough documentation and discussion of Tolstoy's involvement with Schopenhauer (first noted by Eikhenbaum) in "Some Aspects of Tolstoy's Intellectual Development: Tolstoy and Schopenhauer," *California Slavic Studies* 5 (1970): 187–248. I have echoed McLaughlin's remark that Tolstoy could have said that he wrote many of Schopenhauer's pages himself (195). I follow and extend McLaughlin's conclusions (225–30) on Schopenhauer's presence in "On Life."

16 Arthur Schopenhauer, *The World as Will and Representation*, trans. E. F. J. Payne, 2 vols. (New York, 1969), 466–67 (vol. 2, ch. 41). Tolstoy's involvement with Kant has been most thoroughly explored in A. N. Kruglov, "Lev Nikolaevic Tolstoj als Leser Kants," *Kant Studien* 99 (2008): 361–86; see also his "L. N. Tolstoi–chitatel' I. Kanta," in *Lev Tolstoi i mirovaia literatura. Materialy V Mezhdunarodnoi nauchnoi konferentsii* (Tula, 2008), 197–207. Kruglov points out that Tolstoy came to appreciate Kant's theory of time and space only after he had read Schopenhauer (in 1869).

17 Schopenhauer, *World as Will and Representation*, vol. 1, no. 54, and Chapter 41 of vol. 2.

18 To support my argument on the historical topicality of Tolstoy's view of death, it suffices to recall Georg Simmel's essay "The Metaphysics of Death," published in 1910 (the year of Tolstoy's death). Writing, as Tolstoy did, in the shadow of Schopenhauer, Simmel also spoke of death as inextricably tied to life: "Indeed, in every single moment of life we are those who must die. Each of life's moments is revealed only through a temporal approximation to death: life is shaped by death as a real element of life." Simmel concluded that, in contemporary culture, immortality was more appropriately understood as a separation of the self (the "I") from the contingency of the contents of an individual life. Simmel, "The Metaphysics of Death," in *Theory, Culture, and Society* 24, nos. 7–8 (2007): 72–77. I have used Thomas Harrison's reading of Simmel, in his *1910: The Emancipation of Dissonance* (Berkeley: University of California Press, 1996), 97.

19 In describing "spiritual exercises," I follow Pierre Hadot, *Philosophy as a Way of Life: Spiritual Exercises from Socrates to Foucault* (Malden, MA: Blackwell, 1995) and *What Is Ancient Philosophy?* (Cambridge, MA: Belknap Press of Harvard University Press, 2002). In a book of conversations, Hadot extends the notion of "spiritual exercises" from ancient philosophy to modern times and suggests that many non-Western religions, such as Buddhism and Taoism, "impose a mode of life on their adepts that includes spiritual exercises." Hadot, *The Present Alone is Our Happiness: Conversations with Jeannie Carlier and Arnold I. Davidson*, trans. Marc Djaballah (Stanford, CA: Stanford University Press, 2009), 37. It was frequent complaints of the type "Saint Augustine writes poorly" (Hadot comments) that led him to the idea that such works "were not written as the exposition of a system but in order to produce an effect of formation" (59).

20 It should be noted that repetition has been claimed as a major principle in Tolstoy's fiction. See Natasha Sankovich, *Creating and Recovering Experience: Repetition in Tolstoy* (Stanford, CA: Stanford University Press, 1998).

21 J. G. Fichte, *Introductions to the Wissenschaftslehre and Other Writings*, trans. and ed. Daniel Breazeale (Cambridge, U.K.: Cambridge University Press, 1994), 86. This is from *Versuch einer neuen Darstellung der Wissenschaftslehre*, in Johann Gottlieb Fichte, *Sämmtliche Werke*, ed. I. H. Fichte, 8 vols. (Berlin: Veit, 1845–46), 1:500.

22 Here and elsewhere, in my attempts to understand Fichte, I have relied on Breazeale's commentary.

23 Fichte, *Introductions to the Wissenschaftslehre and Other Writings*, 89 (*Sämmtliche Werke* 1:504).

24 The connection between Tolstoy and Fichte has been only sparsely discussed by scholars. Eikhenbaum notes that Tolstoy's familiarity with Fichte's concept of the "I" clearly reveals itself in

Tolstoy's philosophical reflections recorded in his student years in Kazan (1:226), which sound like paraphrases from Fichte. Eikhenbaum, "Tolstoy—student (1844–47)," in *Lev Tolstoi. Issledovaniia. Stat'i* (St. Petersburg, 2009), 762–63. Patricia Carden finds Pierre's reflections on the sense of the "I" very close to Fichte's. Carden, "The Expressive Self in *War and Peace*," *Canadian-American Slavic Studies* 12, no. 4 (Winter 1978): 530. I would add that the diary notes cited above also sound like paraphrases from Fichte. My interpretation of these diary notes, as derived from Fichte, differs from Richard Gustafson's, who, drawing on these and other statements, connects Tolstoy's notion of the second, spiritual consciousness with the theological concept "God within you," derived from Eastern Orthodox thought. Gustafson, *Leo Tolstoy, Resident and Stranger*, 266–69.

25   Stankevich's letter to Ia. M. Neverov of November 10, 1835, in P.V. Annenkov, *Nikolai Vladimirovich Stankevich. Perepiska ego i biografiia* (Moscow, 1857), 154. It is known that Tolstoy read, and greatly admired, this collection of letters.

26   Stankevich's letter to Mikhail Bakunin of November 12, 1835, in *Perepiska Nikolaia Vladimirovicha Stankevicha 1830–1840*, ed. Aleksei Stankevich (Moscow, 1914), 584. This letter, as far as I know, was first published in 1914.

27   Noted in Boris Eikhenbaum, "Nasledie Belinskogo i Lev Tolstoi" [1961], in Eikhenbaum, *Lev Tolstoi. Issledovaniia. Stat'i*, 852–56; Orwin, *Tolstoy's Art and Thought*, 64–68; and Medzhibovskaya, *Tolstoy and the Religious Culture of His Time*, 23, 44–46, 64, 199–207.

28   The fainting spell was described in the diary of Tolstoy's secretary. N.N. Gusev, *Dva goda s L.N. Tolstym* (Moscow: Posrednik, 1912), 101–2.

29   These episodes were recorded in Gusev, *Dva goda*, 101–2, 125–26, and in the diary of a family friend, B. Goldenweizer, *Vblizi Tolstogo* (Moscow, 1959), 1:207.

30   Stephen Lovell has compared Tolstoy's and Mechnikov's attitudes to physical decline and death as an aspect of the period's intellectual climate, defined by the conflict of religious and secular. Lovell, "Finitude at the Fin de Siècle.: Il'ia Mechnikov and Lev Tolstoy on Death and Life," *Russian Review* 63 (April 2004): 296–316.

31   From the diary of Tolstoy's secretary, Gusev, for June 5, 1909; *Dva goda s L.N. Tolstym*, 288. The article appeared in *Russkoe slovo*.

32   The use of Tolstoy's own dream in *War and Peace* has been noted by Gustafson, who analyzes this scene in his *Leo Tolstoy, Resident and Stranger*, 322–35.

33   Many students of dreams have addressed this issue. Maurice Blanchot confronted it directly in "Sleep, Night." Blanchot, *The Space of Literature*, trans. Ann Smock (Lincoln: University of Nebraska Press, 1982). Michel Foucault suggested that the subject of the dream might not be the personage who says "I" but the whole dream in the entirety of its content; see "Dream, Imagination and Existence," in Michel Foucault and Ludwig Binswanger, *Dream and Existence: A Special Issue from the Review of Existential Psychology and Psychiatry*, ed. Keith Hoeller (Seattle, 1986), 43. This idea has been developed by Bert O. States, *Dreaming and Storytelling* (Ithaca, NY: Cornell University Press, 1993), 61 and passim. I have used these and other ideas about dreams in my own earlier work, where a more detailed discussion and bibliography may be found. Irina Paperno, *Stories of the Soviet Experience: Memoirs, Diaries, Dreams* (Ithaca, NY: Cornell University Press, 2009), 162–63.

34   Sigmund Freud, *The Interpretation of Dreams, The Standard Edition of the Complete Psychological Works of Sigmund Freud*, trans. and ed. James Strachey (London: Hogarth Press, 1967), 4:112.

35   Jürgen Habermas, *Knowledge and Human Interest*, trans. Jeremy L. Shapiro (Boston: Beacon Press, 1971), 219–20.

36   His first attempt to publish a work based on an actual dream (that of his brother Nikolai), "Dream" (*Son*), dates to 1858; see 7:117–19, 361–63 and 60:247, 250 (this dream is briefly mentioned in the present book in the "Interlude").

37   From the 1910 diary of Tolstoy's secretary, Valentin Bulgakov, *L. N. Tolstoi v poslednii god ego zhizni* (Moscow, 1989), 160.

38   Several scholars have cited the quotation from the 1870 notebook as evidence of Tolstoy's involvement with Kantian epistemology—but they ignore the horse. The horse is important. After all, Tolstoy wrote an entire story of a horse's life in the first person, from the horse's perspective ("Kholstomer"; 1863, 1885). Turgenev told several people that once, as they walked in the

countryside, Tolstoy stopped by an old horse and, petting the animal, told Turgenev what the horse "felt and thought," "what went on in this horse's consciousness." See N. N. Apostolov, *Zhivoi Tolstoi. Zhizn' L'va Nikolaevicha Tolstogo v vospominaniiakh i perepiske* [1928] (St. Petersburg: Lenizdat, 1995), 252, 255. Throughout his life, Tolstoy was intensely interested in other types of consciousness.

39 See, for example, 54:172, 55:23.

40 For references to this literature, see the discussion of retrospective dreams in chapter 1of this book.

41 Carl Du Prel, *Die Philosophie der Mystik* (Leipzig, 1885), 44–94; the Luther quotation is on p. 89. Du Prel was well known in his time; in Germany, Eduard von Hartmann discussed him at great length in his *Moderne Probleme* (1886). As for retrospective dreams, the topic continued to attract attention. There was a debate in *Revue philosophique* in which reports and interpretations of such dreams were challenged by scientists. Jacques Le Lorrain, "De la durée du temps dans les rêves," in vol. 38 (1894); Victor Egger, "La durée apparente des rêves" and Le Lorrain, "Le rêve," in vol. 40 (1895). The subject became a dissertation topic: J. Tobowolska, *Étude sur les illusions de temps dans les rêves du sommeil normal* (1900). Freud, in his *Interpretation of Dreams* (1900), briefly discussed such dreams as specific distortions of thought processes. *The Standard Edition of the Complete Psychological Works of Sigmund Freud*, 4:26–29. Among philosophers who struggled with the linearity of time, Bergson wrote about retrospective dreams in *Le rêve* (1901) and, in Russia, Pavel Florensky in *Ikonostas* (1922). For Florensky, a twentieth-century scientist-mystic, dream time was an instance of relativity, testifying to the real presence of the transcendental in human life. See Pavel Florenskii, *Sobranie sochinenii*, vol. 1 (Paris, 1985), 194–202. (Florensky mentions Du Prel but does not acknowledge Du Prel's importance for his own ideas.) For a present-day discussion of dream time, see B. A. Uspenskii, "Istoriia i semiotika (Vospriiatie vremeni kak semioticheskaia problema)," *Trudy po znakovym sistemam* 22 (Tartu, 1988).

42 V. G. Chertkov, *O poslednikh dniakh L. N. Tolstogo* (Moscow, 1911), 28–29.

43 The quotation is from "A History of Yesterday" (1851). This story is told in detail in chapter 1 of this book.

44 On this metaphor, see Ernst Robert Curtius, *European Literature and the Latin Middle Ages*, trans. Willard R. Trask (Princeton, NJ: Princeton University Press, 1990), 302–47; and Hans Blumenberg, *Die Lesbarkeit der Welt* (Frankfurt am Main: Suhrkamp, 1981).

45 From the commentaries to "Mysli mudrykh liudei na kazhdyi den'," 40:479.

46 The complex design of the almanacs has been described by Tolstoy's secretary, Valentin Bulgakov, who assisted Tolstoy in this work. V. F. Bulgakov, *Kak prozhita zhizn'*, 146–50.

47 N. N. Gusev, *Dva goda s L.N. Tolstym* (Moscow: Posrednik, 1912), 193 (September 7, 1908).

48 Bulgakov, *Tolstoi v poslednii god ego zhizni*, 303.

49 As far as reading is concerned, in 1891 Tolstoy listed *Phaedo*, as well as *Symposium* (in Victor Cousin's French translation), among the books that had had the strongest impact on him in his youth (66:68). His personal library also contains an edition (1866–71) in the original Greek; at least one volume contains traces of Tolstoy's reading. See *Biblioteka L'va Nikolaevicha Tolstogo v Iasnoi Poliane*, vol. 3 (Tula, 1999), no. 2589; the French edition is described under no. 2588.

50 *Grecheskii uchitel' Sokrat* by Kalmykova and Tolstoy was published by *Posrednik* in 1886 (25:459–61). It included "Smert' Sokrata" (chapter 13). This project, with its autobiographical echoes, has been described in Shklovsky, *Lev Tolstoi* (Moscow: Molodaia gvardiia, 1967), 585–86. *Posrednik* also issued Plato's *Phaedo*, translated into Russian by Dmitry Lebedev, in 1896 (see PSS 42:65–72).

51 Chertkov, *O poslednikh dniakh L. N. Tolstogo*, 22.

52 From Andrei Belyi, "Lev Tolstoi i kul'tura," published in 1912 in *O religii L'va Tolstogo*; cited from the recent publication, in *Lev Tolstoi. Pro et Contra* (St. Petersburg: RKhGI, 2000), 583.

53 "Zamechatel'noe sovpadenie," *Rech'*, November 8, 1910. A similar report appeared in a penny-press organ, *Gazeta-kopeika* ("7-oe noiabria v 'Krugu Chteniia,'" November 8, 1910). For this information, and other advice, I am indebted to William Nickell, the author of *The Death of Tolstoy: Russia on the Eve, Astapovo Station, 1910* (Ithaca, NY: Cornell University Press, 2010).

54 The Maude translation.

Index

Note: References to other scholars' work in endnotes are not indexed

"Address to the Russian People: to the Gov
ernment, to the Revolutionists, and to the
People" (Tolstoy, *Obrashchenie k russkim
liudiam. K pravitel'stvu, revoliutsioneram, i
narodu*), 126
Aksakov, Ivan Sergeevich, 57
Alexander II, 125
Alexander III, 126
almanacs, Tolstoy's, 4, 152–56
Amiel, Henri, 135, 153
Anna Karenina (Tolstoy): death in, 45 46;
Tolstoy forgot the content of, 140; and
Tolstoy's death, 157; Tolstoy the author of, 4,
7, 47, 67, 82, 101; writing of, 37, 40, 42–47, 49,
57, 67. *See also* Levin
Arendt, Hannah, 62, 100
Aristotle, 108
arts, role in society, 38, 65–67, 77, 113–17;
sacralization of, 65–66, 115. *See also*
literature
Augustine, 4–6, 19, 27, 77, 86, 102, 208n15;
Confessions, 4, 13–14, 61–64, 69n, 70, 73–74,
98–102, 209n21; read or followed by Tolstoy,
64, 86, 100–101, 215n38, 215n40–215n41;
and Rousseau, 13–14, 27, 63–64, 73–79,
98–101, 203n6, 211n18, 215–16n23; Tolstoy,
Augustine and Rousseau compared, 64,
73–74, 77, 98–102
author and hero, 7–8, 31–33, 36, 46–47, 61, 67,
131, 142, 157, 208n11

autobiographical writings, Tolstoy's, 3, 6, 31, 36,
41, 52–53, 74, 101, 209n4. *See also* "My Life";
"Reminiscences"
autobiography: limitations of, 95; modern,
73–74; tradition of, 95–102
awakening, 22, 61, 63, 77, 85–86, 139 43,
146–50; death as, 118, 120, 141–42, 146–47,
153, 156. *See also* dreams; sleep
Azbuka (Tolstoy), 37

Bakhtin, Mikhail, 8, 131
Bakunin, Mikhail, 216–17n14
Baxter, Richard, 27
Begichev, D. N., *The Kholmsky Family*, 204–5n27
Belinsky, Vissarion, 216–17n14
Bely, Andrey, 4, 156
biography of Tolstoy, 81–82, 87, 92n, 93, 95
Biriukov, Pavel Ivanovich, 78, 87, 90, 92n, 93, 95,
119, 121, 214n14
body: deterioration/shedding, 4, 78–79, 91, 94,
136–37; separation from the mind/head/soul,
14, 23, 66, 71, 94, 129, 131, 132, 135, 137–39,
154; writing on, 95
book of life, metaphor of, 2, 4–5, 28, 128,
151–52, 156–57; first appearance in Tolstoy,
14; origins of, 203n8
Botkin, Vasily, 33–34
Boyhood (Tolstoy, *Otrochestvo*), 31–33, 82, 88, 137n
Buddhism, 6, 48, 68–69, 133, 202n7, 219n19; and
Schopenhauer, 202n7

Bulgakov, Valentin, 128, 153–54, 221n46
Bunin, Ivan, 98; *Osvobozhdenie Tolstogo,* 201n4, 215n30, 218n6
Bunyan, John, *Pilgrim's Progress,* 68, 212n32

Carus, Carl Gustav, *Psyche,* 22, 204n21
Catherine the Great, *Instruction,* 9–10
causality, 18, 21, 24, 69, 96, 133, 145–46, 149–50
Chernyshevsky, Nikolai, 205n34
Chertkov, Vladimir, 112, 120, 128, 134, 150–51, 155–56
Childhood (Tolstoy, *Detstvo*), 30–32, 36, 82, 86, 88, 206n11, 218n8
"Christian Catechism" (Tolstoy, *Khristianskii katikhizis*), 47
Christianity, doctrine as revised by Tolstoy, 3, 26, 57, 71, 74–77, 98, 115, 120, 123–24, 151. *See also* Orthodox Christianity
Circle of Reading, The (Tolstoy, *Krug chteniia*), 4, 98n, 152–56, 202n7
Cogito, ergo sum, 42, 51, 208n15
Comte, Auguste, 114
confession: and conversion, 55, 73; followed by "professions," 77; meaning of, 61, 210n10; at Optina Pustyn, 46; in Rousseau, 54–55, 96–97; secularization of, 63–64, 73; of sins, 53, 55, 61, 65, 67, 73, 209n21; in Tolstoy's correspondence, 33, 39, 49–50, 52–53, 57–59; in Tolstoy's writing, 93. *See also* Augustine: *Confessions; Confession* (Tolstoy); *profession de foi;* Rousseau: *Confessions*
Confession (Tolstoy, *Ispoved'*), 3–4, 6–7, 41, 56, 59, 109; analysis of text, 64–73; as conversion narrative, 61, 99; death in, 66, 68, 70; dreams in, 71–73, 78–80, 150; guillotine episode in, 105; influence of, 78–80; metaphor of journey of life, 68, 150; publication of, 60, 75; related to Rousseau and Augustine, 73–74; religious conversion in, 3, 65–66, 69–70, 72–74, 77, 83, 98–99; revision of Christian doctrine, 74–77; on sacralization of art, 115–16; title of, 60; writing of, 82
Confucius, 6, 202n7
consciousness: and dreams, 144–45; of horses, 36–37, 118–19, 121, 146, 220–21n38; liberation from, 4, 6, 132–33, 135–42, 146–48, 152–53, 156; and narrative, 17–23, 27, 29, 31, 131, 156. *See also* self-consciousness; stream of consciousness; unconscious
conversion, 3, 59, 61–63, 69, 73, 77, 117; in Augustine, 61–62, 64, 73–74, 211n18; and confession, 55, 73; definition of, 61, 69; Levin's, 46; in Rousseau, 21, 63–64, 73; Strakhov's, 56, 78; Tolstoy's, 2–3, 74, 77, 117, 119, 122–23, 202n8, 209–10n4; in Tolstoy's *Confession,* 3, 65–66, 69–70, 72–74, 77, 83, 98–99; under Tolstoy's influence, 56, 78–79

conversion narrative, 3, 64, 68, 72–74, 77, 99, 209–10n4; roots of, 61–62. *See also* conversion
Cossacks, The (Tolstoy, *Kazaki*), 36
Crimean War, 32
Critique of Dogmatic Theology (Tolstoy, *Kritika dogmaticheskogo bogosloviia*), 75

D'Andilly, Arnauld, 100
Darwin, Charles, 114–15
death: after death, 130, 141, 148, 150, 152, 156; in Augustine, 62; and autobiography, 83, 94–95, 99, 102; as awakening, 118, 120, 141–42, 146–47, 153, 156; and the body, 132, 135; condemned to death, 22–23, 32, 66, 124–26, 130–31 (*see also* execution); and consciousness, 131, 133; and conversion narrative, 61; depiction of in fiction, 131; and dreams, 14, 20, 118, 141–51, 156; in early diaries, 28; and faith, 7, 46, 74, 119; as falling asleep, 141–42, 146–47, 153; to give an account of one's own death, 20, 131, 156–57; in Hegel, 107, 109; in Heidegger, 130; the joy of, 143; in late diaries, 4, 129–30, 134; as liberation, 4–6, 135; and life cycle, 4, 40–41, 70; and master-and-slave dialectic, 107, 109, 113, 118–19, 124; and materialism, 133; and meaning of life, 35, 38, 41, 44, 68; in Mechnikov, 139; and memory, 4, 85–86, 89, 99–100, 139; and philosophy, 41, 44, 131–32, 134–35, 145, 147–48; in Plato, 133, 145, 154–55; and progress, 66; in Schopenhauer, 6, 132–34; and self, 131–32, 134; in Simmel, 134; Socrates' death, 154–55; suicide, 45, 61, 63, 67–69; "there is no death," 91, 131, 133, 153–54; and time, 24, 101, 130, 133, 147–50, 152, 156–57; in Tolstoy's *Anna Karenina,* 45–46; of Tolstoy's brothers, 35, 45–46, 66, 90–91, 139; in Tolstoy's *Confession,* 66, 68, 70; and Tolstoy's crises, 35; Tolstoy's death, 155–56; in Tolstoy's *War and Peace,* 142; in Wittgenstein, 78–79; and writing, 13, 89, 130–31, 155, 202n1. *See also* finitude
"Death of Ivan Ilyich" (Tolstoy, *Smert' Ivana Il'icha*), 111, 208n13, 218n10
"Death of Socrates" (Tolstoy, *Smert' Sokrata*), 154–55
Decembrists, 15–16
"Definition of religion-faith, A" (Tolstoy, *Opredelenie religii-very*), 47–48
Descartes, René, 5–6, 19, 41–43, 107, 133, 137, 139, 141, 208n15; *Cogito, ergo sum,* 51, 208n15; *Discourse on Method,* 62
diaries. *See* Tolstoy's diaries
"Diary for Myself Alone, The" (Tolstoy, *Dnevnik dlia odnogo sebia*), 218n4
division of labor, 115–17
Dobroliubov, Nikolai, 109n

Dostoevsky, Fyodor, 39, 131; *The Brothers Karamazov*, 151n; *The Idiot*, 130; *Notes from Underground*, 97
"Dream" (Tolstoy, *Son*, 1858), 34, 220n36
"Dream" (Tolstoy, *Son*, 1911), 144
dreams: and consciousness, 19–22, 141, 146–48; daytime, 86; and death, 14, 20, 118, 141–51, 156; dream narratives, 19–24, 72–73, 144–51; in early diaries and "History of Yesterday," 19–24, 90, 118–19, 147; of execution, 22–23, 32, 125–26, 131, 149, 204n22; and the inexpressible, 79–80; in late diaries, 141–51; life as a dream, metaphor of, 141, 149–51, 156; Maury's dream, 22–23, 131, 149, 204n22; and memory, 83–84, 86–87, 90, 140; philosophical conceptions made on the basis of dreams, 71–73, 120, 140–49, 153; retrospective, 22–24, 147, 149–50, 221n41; and self, 143–44; studies of dreams, 22–23, 143–44, 149–50, 204n22, 221n41; and time, 19–24, 144–51; Tolstoy's, 6, 142–44; in Tolstoy's *Confession*, 71–73, 78–80, 150; Tolstoy's dreams, general comment on, 142–44; in Tolstoy's *War and Peace*, 142; written work produced on the basis of, 34, 71–73, 125–26, 144. *See also* awakening; sleep
Du Prel, Carl, *Die Philosophie der Mystik*, 149–50, 204n22
Durkheim, Émile, *The Division of Labor in Society*, 115

Eastern Orthodox Church. *See* Orthodox Christianity
Eikhenbaum, Boris, 28, 203n5, 205n33, 206n2, 206n13, 208n11
Emancipation Act of 1861, 109
Engels, Friedrich, 143
Enlightenment, 10, 27, 76, 102
Epictetus, 27, 153
ethics. *See* morality; nonparticipation in evil
execution, 124–26, 130; dreams of, 22–23, 32, 125–26, 131, 149, 204n22; by guillotine, 23, 32, 66, 105, 131, 149, 204n22; metaphor of, 130–31

fables, 52, 71–72; in *Confession*, 68, 72; "Master and Man," 117–20; in New Testament, 121; washerwoman, 111–13
faith: conversion to, 62–63, 66, 70, 73, 79; and death, 7, 74, 119; falling away from, 33, 61, 63–67, 73–74; false faith, 62, 66; and reason, 71; and telling one's life, 52; Tolstoy's attempts to define, 6, 46–49, 58–59, 71, 73–77, 80, 93; yearning for, 39, 46, 49, 69–70, 73–74, 79. *See also profession de foi*
Family Happiness (Tolstoy, *Semeinoe schast'e*), 33, 37, 207n16

Fet, Afanasy, 35, 37, 48, 132–33
"Few Words about the Book *War and Peace*, A" (Tolstoy, *Neskol'ko slov po povodu knigi "Voina i mir"*), 24
Fichte, Johann Gottlieb, 6, 42, 137–39, 219–20n24
finitude, 2, 24, 101–2, 130. *See also* death
"First Step, The" (Tolstoy, *Pervaia stupen'*), 124, 127
Four Epochs of Life, The (Tolstoy, *Chetyre epokhi zhizni*), 31, 88, 206n8
Four Gospels Harmonized and Translated, The (Tolstoy, *Soedinenie i perevod chetyrekh Evangelii*), 3, 75, 77. *See also* Gospel in Brief
Franklin, Benjamin, 10, 27, 65n, 205n28; and Tolstoy, 27, 204–5n27
French Revolution, 23
Freud, Sigmund, 3, 6, 84–86, 92, 204n21; *Interpretation of Dreams*, 204n22, 221n41
Froude, James Anthony, *The Nemesis of Faith*, 73

Garnier, Adolphe, 149; *Traité des facultés de l'âme*, 23, 204n22
George, Henry, *Progress and Poverty*, 144
Goethe, Johann Wolfgang von, *Dichtung und Wahrheit*, 95
Gospel in Brief, The (Tolstoy, *Kratkoe izlozhenie Evangeliia*), 3, 75, 78, 212n39. *See also Four Gospels*
Gospels, 49–50, 110; Luke, 104; Tolstoy's revision of, 52, 75
"Green Stick, The" (Tolstoy, *Zeleniaia palochka*), 93–95, 214n21
Grot, Nikolai, 131, 145

Hartmann, Eduard von: *Moderne Probleme*, 221n41; *The Philosophy of the Unconscious*, 150
Hegel, Georg Wilhelm Friedrich, 6, 42–43, 66, 110–11, 113, 120–23, 139, 216–17n14; *The Phenomenology of Spirit*, 107–8; *The Philosophy of Right*, 114, 124; repudiated by Tolstoy, 66, 98, 114–15. *See also* master and slave
Heidegger, Martin, 130; *Being and Time*, 218n10
Heine, Heinrich, 97
Hervey de Saint-Denis, 149
Hildebrandt, F. W., 149
Hindu thought, 6, 48, 133, 202n7; and Schopenhauer, 202n7
historiography, 17, 23, 102
"History of Yesterday, A" (Tolstoy, *Istoriia vcherashnego dnia*), 1–2, 14–17, 29–31, 83, 129, 131, 156, 203n7, 205n33; dreams in, 19–24, 90, 118–19, 147
horses, consciousness of, 36–37, 118–19, 121, 146, 220–21n38

Hugo, Victor, *Le dernier jour d'un condamné*, 130–31
Hume, David, 22

"I Cannot Be Silent" (Tolstoy, *Ne mogu molchat'*), 124, 127
"I," kinds of, 2–3, 5, 8, 20, 30–34, 36–37, 42–43, 61, 64–68, 72, 75, 77, 83, 86–87, 94, 101–2, 107–8, 116, 127, 132, 134–35, 137–39, 143–44, 150, 208n15, 211n28. *See also* self; "Who am I?/What am I?"
immortality, 4, 33, 40, 56, 76, 135, 143, 145, 154, 218n18
individualism, 7
individuality, liberation from, 89, 95, 134, 146. *See also* self: effacement/dissolution of/ liberation from
inexpressible, the, 45–47, 73, 79, 157
intelligentsia, 115
"Interlocutors" (Tolstoy, *Sobesedniki*), 48
Introduction to an unpublished work (Tolstoy, *Vstuplenie k nenapechatannomu sochineniiu*), 59–60. *See also Confession*
Iranian religious thought, 48
Islam, 69
Iur'ev, Sergei, 60

James, William, *Varieties of Religious Experience*, 79
Jansenism, 100
Jesus prayer, 129–30, 218n8
John the Baptist, 104, 110
journey of life, metaphor of, 40–41, 68–69, 150

Kalmykova, A. M., *Socrates, a Greek Teacher*, 154
Kant, Immanuel, 3, 5–6, 17–19, 23–24, 48–49, 51, 70, 104, 133, 137, 139, 145–46, 148, 150, 153, 156; *The Critique of Pure Reason*, 17–19, 40; read or followed by Tolstoy, 134, 145–46, 153, 156, 204n17, 219n16; and Schopenhauer, 133, 145–46, 219n16
Katkov, Mikhail, 46
"Kholstomer" (Tolstoy, *Kholstomer*), 36, 220n38
Kingdom of God Inside Us, The (Tolstoy, *Tsarstvo Bozhie vnutri nas*), 123
Kireevskii, Ivan and Natal'ia, 216n44
Kojève, Alexandre, 108
Kovalevsky, Egor, 34–35

laborers, 106–7, 111–13, 116. *See also* peasants
Lao Tzu, 6, 48, 202n7
Levin (character in *Anna Karenina*), and Tolstoy, 46–47, 67, 208n11
Lichtenberg, Georg Christoph, *Sudelbücher*, 153
literature: role in society, 34–35, 37, 44, 65–67, 115–17; Rousseau's renunciation of, 54, 63; Tolstoy's renunciation of, 2, 7, 29, 32–38,

44–46, 66–67, 74, 77, 125; Tolstoy's transition to, 2, 30–32. *See also* arts; writing
Locke, John, 6, 18, 27, 100, 204n15; *Essay*, 22
Luther, Martin, 150

Malthus, Thomas Robert, 114
Marcus Aurelius, 5; *Meditations*, 135
Marx, Karl, 6, 108, 143, 216n11; *Das Kapital*, 110, 115
Mason, John, *Self-Knowledge*, 27–28, 205n30
"Master and Man" (Tolstoy, *Khoziain i rabotnik*), 117–20, 123
master and slave: and *barin i rab*, 109n; in Hegel, 3, 107–9, 113, 121–22; justifications for, 114–17; and man and God, 110, 120–21, 123; and nonparticipation in evil, 123; in Rousseau, 108; in Russia, 109; in Tolstoy, 22–23, 107, 109–13; and Tolstoy's "Master and Man," 117–20
Maury, Alfred, 22–23, 131; guillotine dream, 149–50, 204n22; *Le sommeil et les rêves*, 23
Mechnikov, Il'ia, 140, 208n13, 220n30
memory: *anamnesis*, 100; in Augustine, 13, 62, 74, 99–101; and autobiography or memoir, 81, 83, 86–87, 89, 94–95, 101–2; of childhood, 21, 83–85, 91–92; and dreams, 83–84, 86–87, 90, 140, 149; of life before birth and after death, 85–86, 89; and life in the present, 93; in Locke, 18, 27, 100; as moral reckoning, 88–89, 93; and narrative (ordering in time), 86, 90, 96; in Plato, 100; repressed, 85; in Rousseau, 96, 101; and self, 94, 132; spatial patterns, 90; in Stendhal, 97; and time, 13, 86; Tolstoy's first memories, 83–85, 90, 92, 213–14n9; weakening and loss of, 4, 99, 139–41. *See also* screen memories
modernism and Tolstoy, 97–98, 101–2
Montaigne, Michel de, 135
Montesquieu, *L'Esprit de lois*, 9
morality, 3, 6–7, 9–12, 15, 25–26, 28–29, 32–38, 44, 65–66, 83–85, 87–89, 95–96, 98, 101, 103–7, 113, 117, 126–27, 135, 140, 143, 206n13, 217n24. *See also* nonparticipation in evil
moral missives by Tolstoy, 126
Müller, Max, 48
"My Life" (Tolstoy, *Moia zhizn'*), 3, 6, 83–87, 89–90, 94, 99–100; writing of, 52

Nabokov, Vladimir, 7
Napoleon I, 23
narrative: and consciousness, 17–23, 27, 29, 31, 131, 156; digression in, 15, 18; dream narratives, 19–24, 72–73, 144–51; narrative identity, 215n31; ordering in time and memory, 86, 90, 96; progress in, 15–16, 18, 23–24, 52, 61, 102; and rule of linear succession, 17–19,

21, 23–24; and time, 11–20, 23, 29, 67, 86, 90, 96, 101–2, 129–31, 151–52. *See also* conversion narrative
New Circle of Reading, or For Every Day, The (Tolstoy, *Novyi krug chteniia, ili Na kazhdyi den'*), 152–53, 157. *See also Circle of Reading*
Newman, John Henry, *Apologia Pro Vita Sua,* 73
New Testament, 27, 103–4, 121, 129, 203n8. *See also* Gospels
Nicholas II, 126
Nietzsche, Friedrich, 6, 98; *Also sprach Zarathustra,* 98n; *Der Antichrist,* 98n
nonparticipation in evil, Tolstoy's conception of, 76, 123–27, 143, 153; and master-and-slave dialectic, 123; and Tolstoy's vegetarianism, 124
"Notes of a Christian" (Tolstoy, *Zapiski khristianina*), 217n1
"Notes of a Madman" (Tolstoy, *Zapiski sumasshedshego*), 218n1

Old Testament, 28, 203n8
"On Famine" (Tolstoy, *O golode*), 126–27
"On Life" (Tolstoy, *O zhizni*), 131–34, 145, 154
"On Public Education" (Tolstoy, *O narodnom obrazovanii,* 1862), 35
"On Public Education" (Tolstoy, *O narodnom obrazovanii,* 1874), 37
"On Searching for Faith" (Tolstoy, *Ob iskanii very*), 49
"On the Soul and Its Life Outside of the Life That is Known and Understood by Us" (Tolstoy, *O dushe i zhizni ee vne izvestnoi i poniatnoi nam zhizni*), 42
Optina Pustyn, 39, 46, 48–49, 56, 151n, 155
Orthodox Christianity (Eastern Orthodox Church), 6, 39, 47, 49, 64, 67–68, 70, 75, 130, 202n6, 219–20n24

Pascal, Blaise, 5, 141; *Pensées,* 135
Path of Life, The (Tolstoy, *Put' zhizni*), 152
peasants, 5, 21, 57, 65, 71, 111, 117–19, 144, 153; education for, 3, 34–38, 67, 79, 82; emancipation of, 67; envy for, 71; faith of, 71, 119; poverty of, 103–5, 109, 111, 119; rebellion by, 124–26; Tolstoy's relationship with, 21, 65, 109, 124; writing for, 82, 117–18, 126. *See also* laborers
Pietists, 63, 205n31
Plato, 6, 41, 79, 86, 100, 115, 132–34, 141, 146, 215n36; *Phaedo,* 133, 145, 154–55, 221n49–221n50; Platonic dialogues, 48, 57, 135; *Symposium,* 221n49. *See also* Socrates
Plutarch, 27
political economy, 109–11
Posrednik (The Intermediary), 117, 154

poverty, urban, 103–7, 111–13. *see also* laborers; peasants
present, the, 2, 10, 12–14, 16, 24, 61, 66, 77, 82–84, 96, 101–2, 104, 145, 147, 155–56; depth of, 19; and dreams, 22; and loss of memory, 140–41; in Tolstoy's diaries, 129–30; true life in, 76, 93. *See also* time
profession de foi, 6, 33, 41–42, 47, 49, 53–59, 61, 77, 82, 209n21, 210; as element of Tolstoy's crisis, 35; influence of Rousseau on Tolstoy, 54–55; pedagogical, 37–38. *See also* confession
progress, 7, 26, 34, 48, 63, 66, 109, 115, 117, 144, 216n44; and digression, 15, 18; in narrative, 15–16, 18, 23–24, 52, 61, 102; and retrogression, 7, 74, 84, 98, 101–2
Prolog (Orthodox readings), 68
psychoanalysis, 5, 21, 206n36, 213n9. *See also* Freud; screen memories
Puritans, 27, 63, 205n28
Pushkin, Alexander: *The Captain's Daughter,* 21, 119; "Reminiscence," 88; "Wanderer," 212n32

"religion-faith," 47–48
religious conversion. *See* conversion; conversion narrative
"Reminiscences" (Tolstoy, *Vospominaniia*), 3, 6, 21n, 87–95, 98–100
Renan, Ernest, 48; *Souvenirs d'enfance et de jeunesse,* 74; *Vie de Jésus,* 49
repetition in Tolstoy's work, 135, 219n20
revolutionaries, 124–26
Revolution of 1905, 126
Romantics, 97, 205n31
Rousseau, Jean-Jacques, 1, 4–6, 102, 116, 128; *Confessions,* 6, 55, 58, 63–64, 73–74, 77, 96, 99, 101; *Dialogues,* 63; *Discourse on Inequality,* 217n17; "Discourse on the Origins and the Foundations of Inequality among Men," 108; *Émile, ou de l'éducation,* 54–55, 85, 113; *First Discourse,* 217n17; and Hegel, 108; "Profession de foi du Vicaire Savoyard," 6, 33, 42, 47, 54–55, 58, 209n21; read or followed by Tolstoy, 9, 14, 18, 26–27, 30, 32–33, 36, 54, 58, 65n, 73–74, 85, 87, 95–97, 99, 108–9, 113, 116–17, 128, 203n5, 204n26–204n27, 208–9n16, 209n18, 214n28, 217n17; *Reveries of the Solitary Walker,* 13, 63; self-examination and self-revelation, 4, 14, 26–28, 63, 87, 95–97; "Social Contract," 113; Tolstoy, Rousseau and Augustine compared, 64, 73–74, 77, 98–102

salvation, 27, 47, 55–57, 59, 72, 117, 155; allegory in "Master and Man," 119–20
Schelling, 137–39

Schopenhauer, Arthur, 6, 51, 68–70, 114n, 132–34, 141, 145–46, 150, 156, 202n7; and Kant, 133, 145–46, 219n16; *Parerga and Paralipomena,* 132, 135, 153; read and followed by Tolstoy, 42–43, 48, 68–69, 114n, 132–34, 145–46, 153, 156, 202n7, 219n15–219n16; repudiated by Tolstoy, 51, 133; *The World as Will and Representation,* 132–33, 149n, 153

sciences, 42, 63, 68, 113–17, 126

screen memories, 3, 84–85, 92, 98, 101–2. *See also* memory

secularization, 6–7, 14, 55, 63–65, 74, 77, 101, 120, 215–16n43; and resacralization, 7, 28, 55, 73, 77, 101, 123, 216n44; and sacralization, 7, 28, 55, 74, 77, 101, 115, 120, 123

self: beyond the confines of time, space, biological life, 4, 6, 86, 89, 91, 94–94, 99, 101–2, 129, 132; continuity of, 3, 61, 132; and conversion, 61–63, 66, 68, 77; and death, 131–32, 134; effacement/dissolution of/liberation from, 3–5, 62–63, 74, 77–78, 130, 132, 156–57, 218n8; in fiction and non-fiction, 7–8; the idea of, 5–7; modern, 101; moral and social aspects, 3, 6, 11–12, 25–26, 28; and other, 85, 104–7, 110–11, 113–14, 120, 122–23 (*See also* master and slave); secularization and resacralization of, 28, 99, 101; and speaking subject, 2; and time, 13, 29, 132. *See also* "I," kinds of; "Who am I?/What am I?"

self-consciousness, 29, 107, 130–32. *See also* consciousness

self-improvement, 10, 25, 65, 135

Seneca, 27; *Epistles,* 135

Sentimentalism, 205n31

Sentimentalists, 27

serfdom, 109. *See also* slavery

Shakespeare, William, 141

Shklovsky, Viktor, 24, 28, 203n7, 203n12, 204n20, 205n33, 206n2

silence, 4, 80, 130, 155–57, 218n8

Simmel, Georg, 134; "The Metaphysics of Death," 219n18

sins, 36, 57, 87, 105; confession of, 53, 55, 61, 65, 67, 73, 209n21; eight cardinal, 65–66

slavery, 109–11. *See also* master and slave

"Slavery of Our Time, The" (Tolstoy, *Rabstvo nashego vremeni*), 110

sleep: death as falling asleep, 133, 141–42, 146–47; sleeping mind, 22, 131; Tolstoy's investigation of, 141–42; as transitional space, 19. *See also* awakening; dreams

Smith, Adam, 115

"Snowstorm" (Tolstoy, *Metel'*), 119

social order, 113–17

Socrates, 5, 27–28, 68, 133–35, 145, 153; death of, 154–55; Tolstoy identified with, 154–55. *See also* Plato

Solomon, 68–69

Soloviev, Vladimir, 48, 216n44

soul: in Augustine, 13, 70, 99–101, 208n15, 215n34; "behind the soul," 17, 22, 29; collective soul, 153; concept/doctrine of, 23, 27, 42, 51, 131, 145, 150; "cultural soul," 153; dialectics of, 28, 205n34; immortality of, 40, 145, 154; in Rousseau, 13–14, 55, 63, 96; salvation of, 40, 47, 119; states of, 90; Strakhov's definition of, 51; in Tolstoy, 42, 53–54, 56, 75, 83, 90–91, 101–2, 135–36, 154; in Wittgenstein, 79. *See also* body: separation from the mind/head/soul

Spencer, Herbert, 114, 145

Stankevich, Nikolai, 138–39

state, philosophy of, 108, 114–15

Stendhal: *La Vie de Henry Brulard,* 96–97; ready by Tolstoy, 214n28; and Rousseau, 97; and Tolstoy, 97

Sterne, Laurence, 6, 13, 18–19, 22; and Locke, 18, 22, 27, 204n15; and Tolstoy, 18, 27, 204n27

Stoics, 27, 130

Strakhov, Nikolai Nikolaevich, 39; *On the Fundamental Concepts of Psychology,* 51; religious conversion of, 78; and Tolstoy's biography, 81; *The World as a Whole,* 42

Strakhov's correspondence with Tolstoy, 3, 5, 37–40, 57–59, 73, 79, 88, 104, 151n; on *Anna Karenina,* 44–47; on faith, 47–50, 56–59; philosophical dialogue, 40–44; on telling one's life, 49–54

Strauss, D. F., 48

stream of consciousness, 2, 17. *See also* consciousness

St. Thomas (Tolstoy's tutor), 21

subconscious, 2, 17–18, 204n20

suicide, 45, 61, 63, 67–69

Taoism, 219n19

Thoughts of Wise People for Every Day (Tolstoy, *Mysli mudrykh liudei na kazhdyi den'*), 152

time: in Augustine, 13–14, 101; and death, 24, 101, 130, 133, 147–50, 152, 156–57; and the diary, 4, 10–12, 29, 129–30, 154; and dreams, 19–24, 144–51; in du Prel, 149–50; in early diaries, 11–12, 29; in Kant, 17–19, 146, 148, 150; in late diaries, 129–30; in Locke, 18; and memory, 13, 86; and narrative, 11–20, 23, 29, 67, 86, 90, 96, 101–2, 129–31, 151–52; outside/beyond/apart from time, 4, 6, 10, 19, 22, 62, 69, 77, 93, 102, 138, 141, 145, 147–52, 156–57; in Rousseau, 13–14, 101; in Schopenhauer, 146, 150; and self, 13, 29, 132; in Sterne, 13, 18–19; writing and, 5, 151–52. *See also* present, the

Tolstaya, Alexandra (cousin), 33, 49, 59

Tolstaya, Alexandra (daughter), 155

Tolstaya, Sofia Andreevna, 82, 111, 128, 155, 218n4

Tolstoy, Leo: biographical information on, 30–38, 81–82, 110–11; biographies of, 81–82, 87, 92n, 93, 95; brothers' deaths, 35, 45–46, 66, 90–91, 139; death of, 155–56; family life, 67, 110–11, 128, 143, 155; new program of life, 110–11; personal crises, 2, 32–33, 35, 37–38, 47, 67, 70, 133, 206n13, 207n23; sexuality and venereal diseases, 9–10, 26, 36, 65, 88, 135; vanity, 26, 34, 38, 44, 65, 88, 135–36

Tolstoy's Confession. See Confession

Tolstoy's diaries, 1–5, 201n3, 202n1, 217n1; early, 11–12, 25–26, 28–30; first diary, 9–10; late, 128–29, 134–36, 138–42, 154; secret, 128, 218n4; as spiritual exercise, 134–35; temporal scheme in, 9–12, 129–30; and Tolstoy's work on his memoirs, 83, 89, 92–93; and Tolstoy's work on "What Should We Do Then?" and "Master and Man," 112, 120–22

"To the Tsar and his Assistants" (Tolstoy, *Tsariu i ego pomoshchnikam*), 126

unconscious, 6, 21–23, 29, 84, 142, 150, 204n20
urban poor, 103–7, 111–13. *See also* laborers; peasants

vegetarianism, 124

War and Peace (Tolstoy, *Voina i mir*): death in, 142; dreams in, 142; progress of time in narrative, 15–16, 23–24; writing of, 36–37, 67
What I Believe? (Tolstoy, *V chem moia vera?*), 3, 75, 77, 119, 123
What Is Art? (Tolstoy, *Chto takoe iskusstvo?*), 38, 217n17

"What People Live by?" (Tolstoy, *Chem liudi zhivy*), 52
"What Should We Do Then?" (Tolstoy, *Tak chto zhe nam delat'?*), 3, 6, 103–7, 109, 111, 114, 116, 120, 122–24, 144, 217n17
"Who am I?/What am I?": in Augustine, 13, 61–62, 99; cultural precedents of, 26–28; and fear of death, 131–32; in Hegel, 108; in Mason, 28; and memory, 132; as narrative identity, 215n31; in Rousseau, 13, 42, 54, 63; in Stendhal, 97; as title of *Tolstoy's Confession*, 60; in Tolstoy, 1, 3, 5–6, 25–26, 28, 40, 42, 49–50, 58, 68–69, 77, 93–94, 104–6, 122–23, 138; in Zhukovsky, 205n30
"Who Should Learn to Write from Whom, the Peasant Children from Us or We from the Peasant Children?" (Tolstoy, *Komu u kogo uchit'sia pisat', krest'ianskim rebiatam u nas, ili nam u krest'ianskikh rebiat?*), 35
"Why Do I Write?" (Tolstoy, *Dlia chego ia pishu?*), 41
Wittgenstein, Ludwig, 6, 78–79; *Tractatus Logico-Philosophicus*, 79; and Tolstoy, 78–79, 213n45
writing: and death, 13, 89, 130–31, 155, 202n1; Tolstoy's desire to stop, 4, 128, 130, 151, 157; Tolstoy's difficulty with starting, 1, 10, 29, 151. *See also* literature

Xanthippe, 154–55

Yasnaya Polyana (journal), 35
Young, Edward, *Night Thoughts*, 27, 205n31
Youth (Tolstoy, *Iunost'*), 31–32, 88

Zhukovsky, Vasily, 27, 205n30